Also by J. S. Marcus

The Art of Cartography

THE CAPTAIN'S FIRE

THE CAPTAIN'S FIRE

a novel by J. S. Marcus *THE CAPTAIN'S FIRE* a novel by **J. S. Marcus** *THE CAPTAIN'S FIRE* a novel by J. S. Marcus *THE CAPTAIN'S FIRE* a novel by J. S. Marcus *THE CAPTAIN'S FIRE* a novel by J. S. Marcus

Alfred A. Knopf   New York   1996

This Is a Borzoi Book Published by Alfred A. Knopf, Inc.

Copyright © 1996 by J. S. Marcus

All rights reserved under International and Pan-American Copyright Conventions. Published in the United States by Alfred A. Knopf, Inc., New York, and simultaneously in Canada by Random House of Canada Limited, Toronto. Distributed by Random House, Inc., New York.

The author wishes to thank the Mrs. Giles Whiting Foundation and the Wisconsin Arts Board for their support, and A. C. for her patience and insight. And a special thanks to Lois Wallace.

Owing to limitations of space, acknowledgments for permission to reprint previously published material may be found on page 326.

Library of Congress Cataloging-in-Publication Data
Marcus, J. S.
The captain's fire : a novel / by J. S. Marcus.
p.   cm.
ISBN 0-679-40184-9
I. Title.
PS3563.A6386C37   1996
813'.54—dc20   95-23457   CIP

Manufactured in the United States of America
First Edition

*Die Räuber hatten mich gefesselt und da lag ich nahe
beim Feuer des Hauptmanns.*

The robbers had me tied up, and there I lay close to
the captain's fire.

—Franz Kafka

Contents

PART I

[1]

Herr and Frau Krüger have asked me to leave. I just assume that they had been working for the secret police while the wall was still up, which is how I account for the details of the apartment that I have been subletting from them (choice location, telephone, central heating, toilet in the apartment). Their note, written in the old-fashioned German handwriting that Frau Krüger must have learned in the late 1930s, told me to be out of the apartment in two months, before the first of March. They came over to leave the note at four-thirty in the morning on the Sunday before Christmas, when they assumed I would be sleeping. At the time, in fact, I was wide awake, in my room and listening to the radio (to a repeat broadcast of "It Made Our World" on the BBC World Service; "it" being penicillin, the microchip, etc.), and, while they were there, I continued listening, quietly but fiercely, like in wartime. Occasionally, above the radio, I could hear their voices whispering about where to leave the note, but not that they had taped it on the bedroom door, which opens outward, and I didn't find it until after I had given up searching and gone back to my room to go to sleep. For some time now, they have been showing up at odd hours, when I would seem to be sleeping; they rummage around in the closetlike bedroom they keep locked (I live and sleep in the living room), or silently rearrange the dirty dishes. When I first moved in a fall ago last September, they liked to drop by in the late afternoons: I remember them as jovial and too helpful, always washing the dishes, often washing my clothes, reshelving my books; then, gradually, they became covert, adversarial, re-

arranging the furniture, disappearing with most of the towels, rais-
ing the rent, disconnecting the telephone. I think of their change
as symbolic and inconvenient (East Germans, learning the ropes),
and as premeditated. Both of their professions were suspect, as
these things go; he was a plumber at a hard-currency hotel on
Unter den Linden, and she was a librarian, though now they're
both unemployed, living, presumably, off their two unemployment compensations and off the extra money I pay them, which
is three times the rent they have to pay to the mysterious corporation with the Hamburg postmark that got to buy up all the buildings in this part of Berlin as part of privatization and now, in turn,
is supposed to be selling them off to new owners, who tend to
remain fairly anonymous in most cases, or just absent, letting the
Hamburg corporation go on managing the buildings (I have never
found out who actually "owns" the Krügers' building, have always
paid them my rent in cash, as requested). The Krügers, of course,
would have been "unofficial co-workers" (the secret police's euphemism for informer), but I imagine them as having been rather
official unofficial co-workers, as having used their real names as
code names. The inside of their apartment is somewhat shocking:
East Germans, no matter how privileged (like West Germans, no
matter how rich), have what could pass for bad taste somewhere
else, with the bad taste in the Krügers' apartment compounded—
or, perhaps, refined—by the passage of time; nearly everything in
the apartment dates back to 1977, when the Krügers began subletting to East German businessmen in Berlin on business (they
told me about this when I first moved in, back when they also told
me their real, other address, from which, lately, they have been
claiming to have moved). I used to think of the apartment as tran-
scendentally ugly, and now I think of it as a museum exhibit ("I
am living in a museum" has become the opening line of all my
unwritten letters): the kitchen has a mid-1970s Foron washing machine (Foron was the East German state appliance line) that looks
like an oven and needs three hours to wash a load of clothes;
spread over the concrete floors there are psychedelic-colored car-

pets (1960s color schemes reached East Germany in the 1970s and then, like the outer space and atomic motifs of the 1950s, persisted; the Krügers' now absent hand towels, which looked new enough to have been mideighties replacements, were covered with little kaleidoscopic planets) and, in the hallway, a cupboard full of old Florena products (Florena was the state toiletries line), made in Karl-Marx-Stadt, and which now, whether originally toothpaste or cold cream or something called "foot cream," are yellowy wax when, in fits of boredom, I squeeze them out of their identically faded steel blue tubes; in a cupboard above the washing machine, there are old East German herbs in disintegrating plastic envelopes, with the old East German prices printed right onto the plastic, like expiration dates. The Bavarian philologist, a friend of Irmgard's up from Munich for what he called his "end-of-the-year opera weekend," called the apartment *"schrill"* (he eventually explained that *schrill* meant "shrill" in English) when he and Irmgard came by to pick me up on the way to *Der Rosenkavalier*. (The philologist and Irmgard went to college together in Munich, where they both earned simultaneous master's degrees in philology and art history and where, now, when not playing hooky at the Bavarian State Opera—"hooky" was also his word; he had been, years before, and improbably, a high school exchange student in the Texas Panhandle and spoke his English-accented English with a periodic, heavy twang—he was writing a dissertation on Gothic verb forms; Irmgard, who recently became a bank executive instead of getting a Ph.D. in art history or classical philology, loves me cautiously but proficiently; I teach English at a state-subsidized, high-tuition foreign-language school deep in East Berlin, to East Germans, some of whom have Ph.D.s in English; each of us, as it turns out, is thirty-one, and, like so many people suddenly in their thirties these days, still adolescent-seeming, arguably a little grotesque.) "Simply *schrill*," said the philologist, as he perused the thick plastic wallpaper, then the shellacked birch trunk that had been mounted on the living room wall (its splayed branches vaguely suggest deer antlers), then, on the shelves of the bedroom's wall units, souvenirs from the Krügers' trips in the early 1970s to Varna on the Bulgarian coast, including an arm-sized pen that had "VARNA" written all over it. He also said that the Krügers' apartment was just like a West German apartment in the 1950s. (In West Germany's booming-but-cautious 1950s, legend has it, West Germans sat in their apartments, thriftily and unrepentantly, eating baked potatoes and looking at souvenirs from vacations in Austria, which was the closest thing to a foreign country that they would spend money on visiting; now West Germans take vacations to places like the Maldives, and East Germans, years into their sudden freedom but maintaining a bitterness that passes for unrepentance, are the ones who have to go to Austria, which is where the Krügers like to go; when Frau Krüger shows up in the middle of the night and I am in my room pretending to be asleep, I sometimes imagine her in a dirndl.) Later, the philologist often stuck his fingers in his ears: on the underground, on the way to the opera, predictably, when the train, pre-1989 and perfidiously orange, slowed down between stations, threatening one of its humanlike screeches; then, repeatedly, and seemingly unpredictably, during the opera itself, to show, perhaps, that (as he later complained) he didn't like the conducting and didn't like the voice of the mezzo singing Octavian and didn't like the sets used in Act II during the presentation of the silver rose; up went his arms, gnawed-on thumbnails shining, index fingernails disappearing inside his head, his elbows quivering, and grazing my chin and Irmgard's forehead. After the opera, back on the underground, he suggested that we all go to Irmgard's for the fresh blood sausage he had brought from his Upper Bavarian village, where his cousin, the butcher, had slaughtered a pig on Christmas morning. On the underground all the East Germans were staring, as they always do: they heard Irmgard's High German, subjunctive-mood inquisitiveness and noticed her pink satin shoes (Irmgard, invariably, wears elegant, often inappropriate shoes, as if she were always going to the opera and never, as she prefers, to old bomb shelters and abandoned light bulb factories and converted power plants to dance to ragamuffin music);

they heard the Bavarian philologist's Bavarianness (actually, Upper—extreme—Bavarianness), and they stared at the West Germans, with exhausted contempt, with the opposite of curiosity. And they stared at me, but differently. I—I am often told—don't look German, nor do I look American, nor Jewish. As it happens, I had a vaguely Jewish childhood in a blank Middle Western suburb and am what my father was taught in the army to call "a white Jew." I am six feet three inches tall, with light brown hair, curly, but not too curly—East Germans mistake this for something else, northern Italian perhaps: they think of me, I have been told, as an Italian student and stare, understandably, at my Italianness. I think of the way they stare on the underground as alien, as cowlike or as owllike, as dead fish–like or as stonelike; they stare and stare and only really begin to seem human—by smiling—when they notice a dog riding with them, even one of the enormous police dogs, usually German shepherds, though sometimes rottweillers, always miserably panting inside their metal-and-leather, not-entirely-contemporary-looking muzzles: the new squadrons of transit police, who are all assumed to have been guards at the wall, or worse, finger their dogs' mouths through the muzzles and make cooing noises, and the passengers stare and smile. But even their smiles are strange: Germans, it has occurred to me, don't anthropomorphize; they seem to find the inhumanity in things and identify with that. I can't recall seeing a German treating his dog as if it were a child, although I have seen Germans beating their dogs in public, which, according to the BBC World Service's European Community radio tabloid, "Europe Today," is where Germans, more than any other nationality in the European Community, beat their children; on the underground, screaming children, if their parents don't slap them to shut them up, are stared down into silence by everyone else, while barking dogs are only sometimes smiled at. The attraction to German shepherds cuts across political lines: skinheads and left-wing *Autonomen* (the ganglike "autonomous ones," who are usually thought of as Communist revolutionaries, though most of them seem to be teenage runaways, flattered by the attention) treat their German shepherds fairly similarly: tenderly, but decoratively, like lapdogs. I rarely see skinheads, except on television, although I see *Autonomen* every time I leave the house, and I see their graffiti, which, lately, have become exotic, unlikely ("LONG LIVE CHIANG CHING!" "CEAUSESCU!" "THE SHINING PATH WAY IS THE ONLY WAY TO *REVOLUTION!*"); they like to hang old East German hammer-and-sickle flags from their squatted houses and bring them to their demonstrations and "spontaneous actions." (*Autonomen* have been violently against Berlin's doomed bid to hold the Olympics, and against a rumored proposal to build a huge exhibition hall on the site of an East Berlin park so that Berlin can woo a fashion industry trade fair away from Düsseldorf; they are against West German telephone booths and West German cable television; they are against American cigarettes and French car dealerships and against new, Italian delicatessens in old, decrepit East Berlin neighborhoods; they are, arguably, xenophobically East German, unlike skinheads, who are xenophobically German.) In Alexanderplatz, they often ask strangers for money, which they claim they will use to fight fascism and which they obviously use to buy beer and vodka; East Germans walking by aren't unsympathetic and sometimes smile as they give them money (the *Autonomen* have a way of distending themselves that suggests an extreme, almost organic, alienation, something animallike); West Germans, who when they are walking through Alexanderplatz always seem to be scowling, or else tittering (the ugliness of the buildings can make them giddy), walk right by; tourists run away in terror, having confused the *Autonomen* with skinheads, who wear military fatigues with combat boots, unlike the *Autonomen*, who do sometimes shave, or partly shave, their heads but who like to wear black leather pants with their combat boots. *Autonomen* don't get nearly as much air time on television as skinheads, except from Bavarian politicians who claim not to see the difference between thousands of acts of reported neo-Nazi violence this past year and protesting *Autonomen* wrapping themselves in Palestinian scarves against tear gas and throwing rocks at specially trained West German riot police, who are rumored to be advocating showing up at *Autonomen* demonstrations in tanks. Bavarian politicians are occasional guests on nationally broadcast television talk shows, which don't come from one place in particular, are always taped regionally, and, no matter how prominent the guests, always feel amateurish, merely regional (which is actually the usual effect in Germany, where every big city seems in some way provincial when compared to any of the others); the guests and the studio audiences always have to sit cocktail lounge–style, around small tables, which come with bottles of German sparkling wine chilling in silver buckets placed in the exact same spot at every table. (Germans, in fairly innocuous places like libraries and museums, are institutionally paranoid, assume they are being patronized by thieves, force people as soon as they walk in to check their coats and backpacks and purses and, if the security guards insist, anything that might suggest a coat or backpack or a purse, like a jean jacket or a large wallet; I can't be sure about television talk show sets, but none of the women in those audiences seem to have purses with them; I imagine someone knocking over a table on camera and the silver bucket staying attached to the table.) The assortment of guests on these shows can be diabolically eclectic. This week, for instance, on a special Christmas-week broadcast of a popular talk show from Hannover, the guests were a former Fassbinder starlet whose boyfriend had just died of AIDS, a former UFA star from the 1940s who had become a television soap opera star in the '70s and '80s and who seemed to have been invited to talk about her trip to Greenland, the German Interior Minister, a soccer star, and an East German journalist talking about his secret police files. Eventually, they all had to talk to each other, which the host facilitated by asking the Interior Minister about safe sex, and the soccer star about Greenland, and the UFA star about the East German secret police's unofficial co-workers as compared to the Gestapo's network of domestic informers, about which she claimed to remember nothing. After the guests had to talk to each other, there was a politically neutral musical interlude featuring those five East German sisters who are famous for holding on to poodles the same shade of blonde as their wigs; they have been West German television stars since the 1950s, when they fled to Munich from their village near the Thuringian Forest, and, on a stage behind the guests' table, they sang "The Most Beautiful Girls in the World Come from the Thuringian Forest"; the Interior Minister, as the most important guest, sat directly facing the audience, and he had to crane his neck whenever he tried to watch the sisters' lip-synching (singing on German television is invariably dubbed); I noticed that the UFA star, while she must have thought that no one was looking, gulped down her refilled glass of sparkling wine. The tone of these shows is always the same: instructive. The talk shows are often on late at night, after the *Volksmusik* programs—which feature yodelers, lately mulatto yodelers, probably sons of American soldiers, in *Lederhosen*, being condescended to, and there as some kind of political gesture—and long after the drag queens, who in Germany get their own prime-time sitcoms. The yodelers are exaggerated, seem in drag, and the drag queens wear bifocals and lecture about safe sex and "foreigner-friendliness." Germans seem to find all this rather boring and, when it comes to German television shows, only really laugh at the political satire, at, say, a puppet of Helmut Kohl fucking a Franz Schönhuber puppet (he's the Waffen-SS veteran and subsequent Bavarian television personality who leads the crypto-fascist, or openly fascist, or Nazi, Republikaner Party that, especially in affluent villages in southern Germany, sometimes gets a fifth of the vote these days, which is about the percentage that the PDS, which is the revamped Communist Party, gets in skyscraper suburbs of East German cities, like in Marzahn, where I teach, where the unofficial unemployment rate is 50 percent); afterward, the Franz Schönhuber puppet says, laughing sinisterly, "Next time, Helmut, don't forget to wear a rubber." Germans think that that is hilarious, that, and people (Italian-looking people, for instance) hurrying, obviously trying to make a train, tripping and falling down the stairs in a train station. Irmgard doesn't think anything is funny; she, too, has to find a new apartment, which is just assumed to be impossible. (German tabloids often run articles about Berlin's housing crisis, about people like the West Berlin computer programmer who—after two years of trying to find a one-and-a-half-room, sixty-square-meter apartment for less than seven hundred Deutschmarks per month so that his girlfriend could have somewhere other than the bathroom to develop her photographs when she visited from Bremen—gave up his search on Christmas Eve and jumped out the window of his parents' apartment. The tabloids run these articles dialectically, next to articles about "asylum seekers" driving up to their free dormitory housing in new BMWs; they run articles about the firebombing of asylum seekers' dormitories next to articles about Russian *mafiosi* heading westward.) She is also subletting in East Berlin, five minutes away from where I live (we met last spring, on our mutual underground platform, after weeks of regarding each other as the only other non–East German waiting for a train on the mornings of the days I teach), and I make assumptions about the man who officially rents her apartment—an art historian, who, after accepting a five-year curatorship in Italy, has returned four and a half years early and has told Irmgard that she has to leave before April. I just assume that he had once worked for the secret police; I assume that his code name had been "Leonardo" and that the West German foundation that offered him the curatorship found out about it and asked him to leave their Tuscan villa early and have occasionally asked for most of the six-month portion of his salary back. Irmgard, who was planning on staying the full five years, and moved in with, among other things, a grandmother's Biedermeier credenza that had survived air raids in Leipzig and an evacuation to Schleswig-Holstein, is desperate; her books alone—she speaks four languages and reads seven—could fill up a small van; she has begun asking people at well-placed bank branches if they know of anything and has gone home for New Year's Eve to ask her father if he would buy an apartment for her in Berlin. Irmgard grew up in a villa outside Hamburg, and she remembers her father always coming home early from the office to drink coffee on their terrace overlooking the Elbe River. She has already had, incredibly, a Jewish, German-born boyfriend, a rather moody professional viola player, who, when Irmgard and I visited Munich together, did not seem at all jealous, and in fact seemed homosexual; when he and I were alone one afternoon, he was flirtatious and a little perverse, giggling—sardonically, I suppose—as he showed me pictures of the half of his family that had gotten out (his mother's, wealthy Jews from Marburg who fled to Costa Rica) and then of the other half, most of whom hadn't; he was standing much too close to me and at one point rested his head on my shoulder. I shouldn't, and, in fact, don't, think of myself as Irmgard's boyfriend (even though we sometimes almost fuck). I am nobody's boyfriend. I can't get it up—not with other people and not, usually, on my own. (As it happens, and jokingly, I taught the expression to my students last fall, when I still could get it up, in the advanced conversation workshop that the director of the school makes me call "Idioms and Idiosyncrasies," and which, as was intended, made some of the students laugh, but which most of them, and nearly all of the middle-aged men, just wrote down absently, as though I had been accusing them of something.) So: no real sex, not much jerking off (I don't think I would teach my students now what "jerking off" means; I would be too embarrassed or too selfish; not being able to get it up makes you timid and spiteful, "East German"); some kissing and fumbling and, since this is Germany, slapping and poking, which is how Germans express affection. A mother will, somewhat gently, slap or poke her baby and call it "a little snail"; two women in high-heeled shoes, after shopping, shake hands vigorously and then one will grab the other's shoulders and let go with a shove. There isn't much sexual tension in my classroom, and, things being what they are, my temptations are not to seduce but to deceive—with idioms. I have never succumbed, except once, when I told my students that Americans in the Middle West like to say "that's like throwing a hot potato at a man without arms" when they want to describe something especially impossible, doomed to fail, a folly, etc. None of the students ever reused it, except once, in a critique of the course written by the sixteen-year-old who was the best student in the class. "Trying to teach us idioms," he wrote, "is like throwing a hot potato at a man without hands"; "without arms," I thought about writing in the margin. I have been teaching at the school, which was my reason for coming to Berlin, almost nonstop since I got here, with only a few weeks off, like now, between terms. I teach two days a week, ten hours a day (three classes and lunch) and earn fifty dollars, in Deutschmarks, per hour, no taxes. Someone else there, a twenty-four-year-old from Pittsburgh who started the term after I did, teaches five or six days a week, ten hours a day; he told me that he hasn't earned this much money since he gutted fish with a hose in Alaska the summer before he graduated from high school: at the end of each term he goes home like a drug dealer, with thousands of Deutschmarks in cash in the linings of the loden coats he brings his mother and sister. When I am not teaching, I read books, watch television, and listen to the radio, like anyone else, and I leave town. I read books by German Jews and by other Jews, by Italian and Polish and Hungarian and Russian Jews; I read them all in English translation (I learned German in high school and college and then spent years forgetting it; here, I have re-learned it, but haltingly and vindictively, more to monitor Germans than actually to talk to them), as though they had been written by American Jews; when Irmgard notices that I am reading a book by a Jew who had written in German, she sometimes brings the original over to the apartment—for my conscience, she once explained. (Irmgard speaks to me in English, which she sometimes spikes with French expressions, and thinks of my German as convincing and incomplete, which is how I think of my feelings for her.) The books by German Jews, or by Jews writing in German, or by Jews who had once lived someplace where German was spoken and then, at some point, wrote in German (I find these distinctions telling, unlike many Germans, for whom, like for most Jews, the word "Jew" is enough), overlap, derive: Walter Benjamin on Franz Kafka; Gershom Scholem on Walter Benjamin on Kafka; Kafka on Karl Kraus; Gershom Scholem on Hannah Arendt; Hannah Arendt on Benjamin on Karl Kraus or on Benjamin on Kafka; Elias Canetti on Karl Kraus, or on Kafka, though never, to my knowledge, on Benjamin or on Scholem. Lately I have been reading Aharon Appelfeld, who was born in the Bukovina—once Austrian, and, by the time of his birth in the 1930s, still somewhat German, though technically Rumanian and, in any case, utterly polyglot, though now, after Hitler and Stalin, only Ukrainian, and the stuff of legend. He lives in Israel and writes in Hebrew, and the books of his that I have read feel, up to a critical point, beyond place, outside time; I am reading *Badenheim 1939* over and over again. It's about doomed Jews interned at an Austrian, or Austrian-sounding, spa town, about to be deported east, to their deaths; initially their internment feels vaguely willful, like a hesitation, a lingering. I imagine Appelfeld's Badenheim to be some kind of inversion of the situation you find here, now—in 1993, say—in what used to be called "Eastern Europe": Americans—Jews, often —traveling, teaching English, heading eastward, through Germany, Czechoslovakia, Poland, Russia. The American Jews meet one another, or somehow end up together, linger, complain about the food, wonder at the low prices, imagine that they can't afford to leave, but feel, really, compared to the barrage of nothingness at home, freed. Except for the violence. It's impossible to follow each and every attack on what get called "foreigners." (I, apparently, being white, and American or Italian, and not, it would seem, Jewish, don't count, although a majority of Germans in a recent poll said that Jews, even the ones born in Germany like the viola player, were necessarily foreigners, making me perhaps doubly, or even exponentially, foreign, even though my coloring on someone shorter, I have been told a couple of times, looks almost Viennese; I have joked with Irmgard that if I meet a gang of skinheads in a dark alley my plan is just to sit down.) I have noticed that television networks and editorial boards of newspapers tend to follow certain attacks and ignore others, in the way, perhaps, that financial laymen—interested in their own investments or not interested at all, unless there's some sort of crash—follow financial news. At the school, in our conversation workshops, we often talk about skinheads and neo-Nazis ("right-extremeness" is what the Germans like to call it, and which they use as an all-purpose word, good for describing everything from Yukio Mishima to Jesse Helms); that is, when we're not talking about communism and the secret police and socialism ("socialism" for East Germans can be a very specific word, used to describe the things they liked under communism, like day care centers and abortion on demand and a certain feeling of solidarity in their favorite cafés and bars). At first, I had thought that the East Germans in my classroom were talking about the secret police in a way that people on American daytime television talk about, say, having slept with their fathers, but I was wrong: East Germans talk about the secret police in a tone that has no correlative to anything in my experience, and they can seem to me as if they were pioneering a new way to use the human voice, except when they are talking about everything else, when they sound, in turn, so corrupted and deluded that I have to make an effort not to let my eyes spin back in my head. When it comes to Germans and Jews, to Germans, the German problem—what euphemism should I use?—I maintain, when I read, for instance, a certain guilelessness, an openness, an insatiability; in public, so-cially, with East or West Germans, and in the classroom, almost articulated outrage, silence. I rarely talk about myself in the class-room: I don't tell people that I am Jewish or Italian or, to some people, vaguely Viennese, or bisexual, for that matter—as I haven't told them about not being able to get it up, about being no-sexual. I tell them that I am from Milwaukee, which is true enough. When I do tell people that I am Jewish, they are each, in their own way, flabbergasted; they lose their facial expressions, look, really, as if their faces have collapsed, then they promptly, and quite alarmingly, ask me if I eat pork: to Germans, it would seem, not eating pork is something truly unbelievable but docu-mented, like cannibalism. Even Irmgard, who, I would have thought, would have known better, or more, asked, while, as it happened, we were both eating bratwurst. (I covered up my irritation by telling her that people in Milwaukee, regardless of their ethnic background or religious affiliation, often eat bratwurst, and thought that I sounded like the Voice of America, which I have never heard in Berlin, though I have heard it in Poland, and which, when not filled with factoids about America, is metric and cheerful—"It's thirty-one and sunny in Tirana!") Then they often admit that they have never met a Jew before and, almost without exception, and indifferent to any incongruity, tell me that I don't look Jewish, which always ends up sounding like a compliment, and which is actually something that my mother has told me, and which she has always meant as a compliment. (My mother thinks that she and my father look Jewish, but that her father, whom she says I look like, didn't; no one now seems to know exactly where he was born; he came to America as a child from some part of Austria-Hungary and, as an adult in Milwaukee, always claimed to be Austrian, but he was probably Galician, meaning that, now, if remembered as anything other than a Jew, he would probably be remembered as a Polish Jew, or, in Germany and present-day Austria conceivably, as an *Ostjude*, an "Eastern Jew"—Orthodox, caftan-wearing, and what Germans probably have in mind when they say I don't look Jewish; they officially know what *Ostjuden* looked like from Holocaust documentaries and from television news reports about Israel, and, occasionally, from old anti-Semitic caricatures in Wilhelminian and Weimar-era satirical magazines, though, rarely, one could argue, from Nazi propaganda: the viewing—let alone buying and selling—of Nazi propaganda is *verboten*, except for specifically approved scholarly purposes and at Berlin's flea markets, where various kinds of Nazi memorabilia are kept under counters covered with old Communist memorabilia, and policemen and people shopping for other things, when they notice someone looking at, say, an old issue of *Der Stürmer*, usually turn away too quickly to take in the illustrations.) I have found that actually talking about "it"—Jews in Germany, Jews, Germans and Jews, Germans—ends in exhaustion and embarrassment, like, it has occurred to me, trying to fuck without a hard-on. As I said before, I often leave town, but usually end up going eastward, to Posen or to Warsaw, to Prague, where I take up with those afore-mentioned Americans or with Westerners of various creeds and nationalities, though really only of two professions: foreign-language teachers, who are recently graduated college students or failures, and executives, who are often recently graduated college students and, under the circumstances, successes. The feel in these places, with these people and their hard currency and fomenting privilege, is colonial, clubby. Everyone swaps notes, jokingly en-vies: Prague and Cracow and Budapest, no matter how close they were to concentration camps or what happened there under the Communists, are considered cushy, talked about as though they were hill stations; in Berlin, of course, there is a lot of action, but Westerners in Eastern Europe, who like beer but hate traffic jams and construction sites, treat Berlin as vast and burdensome, as a Bombay or Calcutta; Moscow and St. Petersburg, depending on who's talking, can sound remote but swashbuckling, Khyber Pass–like, or as terrible as everywhere else (Bucharest, Minsk, Warsaw, Sofia, etc.), strictly hardship, Aden, Guyana. People who work in places like Minsk go on internal vacations, spend the odd weekend in places like Prague—" 'Germans' in 'Austria.' " I always return to Berlin, where, I imagine, I have seen it all, that there is no wall in my mind, that I have gone back and forth, that I have run the gamut. I sometimes construct Schnitzler-like scenarios, but with a twist. For instance:

The Prostitute and the Soldier

Antje was twenty-one years old. After her mung bean noo-dles, which she had bought along with a pack of contraband Polish Marlboros from the Vietnamese family shivering in a trailer kitchen outside the Friedrichstrasse train station, she was still hungry. Her stomach was growling. "You're breath-ing in too much air," she told herself, which she had read

as the cause of a stomach growling in a tabloid article head-
lined: WHY BERLIN'S STOMACHS GROWL. She considered getting
a Turkish kebab, knowing that the Turks would give her chili
and garlic sauces and only charge her for the garlic sauce;
they always squeezed her hand when they gave her back her
change, but they never asked her to get in their cars because
she was too expensive. They were driving to Dresden, she had
heard and repeated, then into Bohemia, paying for Czech
girls in Deutschmarks (she hadn't read the tabloid article
about that, though, with its headline: THE GASOLINE COSTS
MORE THAN THE GIRLS). She was standing on the Oranienburger
Strasse, where she often stood, between her friend Silke and
another girl whom she had never seen before, and she and
Silke occasionally walked down the street to chat with the
policemen who were guarding the restored synagogue
twenty-four hours a day: Antje and Silke knew all the policemen's names, were inclined to give them discounts.
Andrej's name hardly mattered. His officer, and his officer's
wife, and even their visiting daughter, it was said, were always drunk. His officer came into the barracks, where the
floor was made out of packed mud, and forgot names, stag-
gered out. Evenings, Andrej and his friends, Dimitri and Andrej, took guns and grenades and got a ride from their
barracks near Brandenburg to the Spandau forest near the old
border with West Berlin and waited in the darkness. Boys in
cars turned off their headlights and walked into the forest.
They spoke their half-forgotten grade school Russian, and Andrej thought that they sounded like demented children; he
knew that they were drunk, though, and he didn't hate them.
He gave them guns and grenades and asked for two thousand
marks, and then they gave him one thousand, or five hundred, or two hundred and fifty marks. Tonight they had given
him five hundred marks. Afterward, he couldn't find Dimitri
or Andrej, and he walked back to the road alone, and then
down the road until he got to the train station. On the platform, and, later, on the train, he knew that the few other
people were staring at him, at his white, round face, and
would have stared at his tunic if he hadn't changed out of it
before going into the forest. He looked out the window of

the train as he rode through Berlin, and he thought that the empty silent stations looked like something out of a dream. He got off at Hackescher Markt and walked to the Oranien-burger Strasse, feeling ridiculous, thinking he should be in a car. He surprised Antje. "One hundred," he said in the German he had taught himself for the purpose. Antje heard his Russian voice and looked at his small, filthy face. He'll stink, she thought and said "Seven hundred and fifty" in her grade school Russian. "Two hundred," said Andrej, to which Antje answered in German, "Go piss on yourself"; speaking the Russian had reminded her of school, which she had hated. She walked away, over to Silke, disgusted and bored.

Like that. Of course in Berlin, these days, the prostitution on the Oranienburger Strasse cheers everybody up. Apparently there used to be prostitutes there in the 1920s, which Germans call "the Golden Twenties," but apparently there used to be prostitutes everywhere in Berlin in the 1920s, when people were fainting from hunger in the streets. Journalists from all over the world are lining up to write about the prostitutes and the restored synagogue and the construction sites and the squatted-house-turned-performance-space, and about the new, high-ceilinged cafés, which, with their bits of tile and stucco from before the war, are sometimes said to be "Jewish." For my taste, it's all too much, doubly surreal—Brueghel figures drinking beer in a De Chirico city-scape, Piranesi figures trapped in an Escher drawing; only parodying. As for the synagogue: its blue Byzantine dome looks like a gold-trimmed robin's egg or a mausoleum or, because of the rather blasé brand of police protection, a jewelry store; not exactly a target in the conventional wwhich in Germany would mean the political) sense, past that point. Once I went to a rooftop party in East Berlin given by some landscape architecture students from West Berlin who were celebrating their move east; the synagogue was the accidental backdrop for the party, at which, because the party was on a roof, and with a fair degree of seriousness, kinds of fondue were served. The landscape architecture students, who, with a couple of exceptions, were my age and older (students in Germany often stay on at universities until their middle thirties and, by the time they graduate, have crow's-feet and still innocent expressions), admired the synagogue's beauty while frying bits of meat. Landscape architects have political credentials in Germany, where people are obsessed with population density figures when they're not being obsessed with low birthrate figures, but I had to disagree with them about the synagogue, which, I said, was too ghostly to be beautiful, exactly, and which they went on to talk about with a kind of natural awe, as if Berlin were a species that could regenerate its synagogues. If the subject had come up, though, we probably could have agreed on the prostitutes, who, having arrived in significant numbers on the Oranienburger Strasse not too long after the wall fell, have certainly animated the life of the city—the prostitutes, and the hatred between East and West Germans, which, in a few quick years, has become so blunt and resourceful as to suggest something Balkan-like, eternal, and is expressed everywhere, in every setting, except on television sports programs. In Germany the sportscasters all seem to be middle-aged Bavarian women with saint's names (Magdalena, Theresa, Mathilde); when talking about German athletes of any kind and, on occasion, about foreign athletes with German-sounding last names, they can become effervescently partisan: "Heartful greetings, dear viewers. Our wonderful German air pistol team captain will soon be here to tell us about our team's super third place finish. As you must have heard by now, the South Koreans and the Chinese unfortunately have come in first and second, but I know that next time our dear Germans will be victorious." Once I turned on a sports program and learned that Germany and Israel were playing each other that day in wheelchair basketball. When the sportscaster mentioned the game, which wasn't being televised, she tried not to let her face collapse, and failed (she briefly looked inhuman, but also like something that is supposed to look human, like one of those carved apples that dries up into something resembling a person's head), although it might have been the wheelchairs, and not the Jews, that had unnerved her: Germans suffer from, as one admonishing tabloid editorial put it, "handicapped-fellow-citizen-hatefulness." Last summer, a group of people from Hamburg, including many older couples and a young woman without arms, went to Turkey on a package tour; upon returning to Hamburg, one of the older couples sued the tour operator for the price of their vacation because the sight of the young woman—in the hotel lobby, turning pages of old German magazines with her feet; in the breakfast room, eating her rolls and German sausage and drinking her German coffee with her feet— had been, they argued, objectively nauseating, and they won. After that, for a time, handicapped people, usually without arms, began appearing on talk shows, shaking hands and feet with *Bundesländerministerpräsidenten*, German rap stars, and each other. Their inclusion on the panels was meant to be civically instructive: "Frau Hannelore T. from Donaueschingen is just like any other German citizen, except for the fact that she has no arms and only one leg. God's greetings, Frau T." (People from southern Germany actually say "God's greetings" when they mean "hello," and real people on German talk shows, like criminals in German tabloids, are rarely identified by their full last names.) I don't think it did much good. A few days ago at a train station in Schleswig-Holstein, not too far from the Danish border, two men, twenty and twenty-one (and described by someone from the Bavarian Justice Ministry on a talk show the next night as thirteen and fourteen) threw a legless woman and her wheelchair down a flight of stairs. Witnesses claim to have heard the two men screaming "They forgot to gas you at Auschwitz, you hacked-up cow!"; other witnesses claim to have seen the two men push the woman down the stairs and then run away. (The numerous witnesses seemed to fall into two groups: the ones who had heard everything but had seen nothing, and the ones who had seen everything but had heard nothing; or, perhaps, only into one group, who had done nothing.) Later that night, when the men returned to the station to hang out, they were promptly arrested for attempted assault. The tabloids, possibly because of Christmas, preferred to turn their readers' attention else-where. CHRISTMAS RAGE, ran a headline today. JEALOUS POLES IN BRESLAU SET FIRE TO GYPSIES' FUR COATS. The tabloids always call these onetime German cities by their previous, now suspect, German names—which, theoretically, is what a skinhead would always do and what an *Autonome* would never do, and which I, unless I remember to do otherwise, sometimes do. I have a lot of time this week to read newspapers. No school, of course. And Irmgard is gone. I took her to the airport to say good-bye (I had planned, beforehand, to say good-bye sternly but sentimentally, East and West German–like, north and south German–like, adult-like), and she told me that the Bavarian philologist had told her that he thought I was passionless. ("Passionless?" I said to myself, as though the word hadn't come from the philologist, and then from Irmgard, as though it were a word I had already used to de-scribe myself. "That sounds like a euphemism for not being able to get it up, which is already a euphemism." Then I thought about the fact that the German word for impotence, *Impotenz*, sounds an awful lot like "impotence," or else like something nonsensical, like "in poor tense." Then I thought about the Krügers using their real names as code names, about people deceiving each other with the truth.) "Oh," I asked eventually. "Did he have his fingers in his ears again?" He wanted to know, she said, what I was doing here. He didn't ask me himself. If he did though, or if anyone were to ask (Irmgard, in relaying the question, was asking me something else, on the order of "Do you love me?" which I am sure—or fairly sure—is more important to her than fucking; the fact that we don't exactly fuck, that we just fumble around, or do nothing and go right to sleep as if I had no cock at all, doesn't bother her, as, apparently, it didn't bother Marlene Dietrich), I would have to answer: lingering, and waiting for next year's eviction, which, for the time being at least, I imagine to be something gentle and in-evitable, like a graduation.

[2]

On the radio, lately, everyone complains that the weather, which in Berlin has more to do with color than temperature, is mild and obliterating. Winter—only irreversibly begun, now, a third of the way through January—has like last winter turned everything the color of cement. The daytime sky, which hangs flat in Berlin, starting just above the buildings, is a shelf of gray cloud; the buildings—the prewar ones with their missing façades, and the postwar, poured concrete ones—are naked, colorless, behind the dead-looking trees; there are winter smog alerts because so many people in East Berlin (nearly everyone else around here, for instance, where I live) still need to heat their apartments with soft East German coal, about which, on a radio call-in show, I recently heard a new kind of East German chauvinism: "It stinks," boasted the caller, "but at least it's *our* stink." There is no snow, no sharp cold; sometimes during the day it's fifty, fifty-five degrees, as though it were a cold summer day. I remember the arrival of summer last year: the dead trees suddenly grew big pawlike leaves that shone in the white northern sunlight, and the grayness slipped behind a cool, too deep green. I once told a man who was living in Berlin but was in fact from Hamburg, where it rains all summer, that high summer in Berlin somehow reminded me of California, and he said, all smiles, "Thank you!" The extremeness of the winter—the dead-looking trees, the sour coal smell—makes me think of its opposite, of summer evenings that smell forestlike, permanently fresh, which, in turn, reminds me of Elias Canetti, who spent a good portion of the century thinking about his book on crowds, in which, at one point, he catalogues national crowd symbols. The crowd symbol for Germans: the forest and (formerly) the army; to Canetti, bark looks like a uniform; a boy running away from home and into a forest presages his joining the army; an army, in its way, is a marching forest. Last summer I sometimes brought *Crowds and Power* to the Tiergarten, but I didn't get very far until months later; the thought of Canetti writing for decades and the scent of the linden trees, which have waxy flowers that bloom for weeks and already smell processed, like soap, made me drowsy, or impatient. Canetti's crowd symbol for Jews is the exodus from Egypt—a crowd moving through a desert. Possible corollary: sometimes, to get back into or out of East or West Berlin, I like to walk across the Potsdamer Platz, which, having been bombed, walled, and unwalled, is empty, has no real season; like certain people, it persists, can seem unchangeable, as if it were defying the weather; though actually it has changed, gone, recently, from being vaguely tundralike to absolutely empty, stripped down, ready for construction like a patient shaved before an operation (in Berlin I anthropomorphize buildings, places, bits of city; façadeless houses look like burn victims, an unearthed pair of streetcar tracks near the Leipziger Strasse looks like a rash); the emptiness, when I am finally inside it, makes the Potsdamer Platz look deceivingly small, not at all vast, only a brief walk that in the middle gets longer and longer; I drag myself across. And I think, dragging (well nigh schlepping—if I am permitted a Bellowism): a Jew marching through a German desert. Before I came to Germany and read books by European Jews, I sometimes lived in New York and Chicago and read books by American Jews. Of course, even now, I don't always read books by Jews, by the Elias Canettis and the Saul Bellows; for instance, I have read that book about Marlene Dietrich by her daughter, Maria Riva. At first I read it badly, too quickly. "I remember a limbo line," I read, in the part where a teenaged Maria Riva runs away to San Francisco and becomes a dresser for a drag queen, after having spent her childhood dressing her mother. "How did I get there and why?" Of course it was "limbo *time*," which sounds like a literal translation from the German. The new term has started, and I have only been asked to teach three classes, which means I have an extra day and five hundred fewer dollars per week. More time and much less money, a recipe for musing, cross-referencing. I am not entirely unsympathetic but found the book patently loony, and I did wonder what Walter Benjamin might have made of Maria Riva (he liked to collect books by the mentally ill), and then I wondered what Canetti might have made of it, or what he might have made of what Freud might have made of it. Canetti's book about crowds ends with a long discussion of the memoirs of Daniel Paul Schreber, the paranoiac about whom Freud had famously—and, in Canetti's view, badly—written: Freud thought that Schreber, who thought that he was the only man left in the world and was gradually turning into a woman, was a repressed homosexual, which was causing his paranoia; Canetti thought of Schreber as a crowd of one. Canetti, like Benjamin, doesn't go in much for psychoanalysis; Freud is one of Canetti's negative role models, with Nietzsche, I suppose, being the other. Between the wars, during Canetti's intellectual coming-of-age, Freud and Nietzsche were read and talked about everywhere; Canetti, perilously, scrupulously, managed to avoid them. Perhaps I could describe them as his Scylla and Charybdis, as Herr and Frau Krüger have become mine. They show up now at all hours, often separately, with what look like, although they don't let me see them, interior decorator swatches. I get ready to leave whenever I hear the door click open—I always have a few minutes while they change into their bedroom slippers—and pretend, suddenly in the hallway, to be on my way out. I imagine that they will ask me to leave even sooner than the end of February, and I haven't found a new apartment. Irmgard thinks that they are remodeling and planning to rent out the apartment to a company, or to some new tenant who is paying them to redecorate; she thinks that we should take pictures while we still have the chance. The art historian's apartment is large and barren—a bed, a desk, tables, naked walls—except for his fifteen hundred books (according to Irmgard, who has brought something like a thousand herself): old East German books and, indictingly, books almost certainly banned in East Germany, like old German editions and relatively old annotated West German editions of Ernst Jünger and Gottfried Benn, Milan Kundera in French, Jean Genet in Dutch. Irmgard, having forgotten remarks I had made about Hanukkah, gave me a book about East German industrial design as a Christmas present, then she confused my remarks about Christmas: I had told her that it was customary in Milwaukee for Jews to eat in Chinese restaurants on Christmas Eve; she remembered this as Jews observing Rosh Hashanah on New Year's Eve in Chinese restaurants. When we are drinking, though, she does occasionally remember to say *"L'chaim!"* instead of *"Prost!"* I have, like Irmgard, come to prefer north German, bitter-tasting beer, and, like Irmgard, have come to think of German sparkling wine, the dreaded *Sekt*, which many Germans always drink, as insipid. Hans-Joachim—a childhood friend of Irmgard's living in Berlin and also, often, my friend—dismisses *Sekt* as "petit bourgeois" (he used to live in Paris), which, in its German equivalents— *"kleinbürgerlich"* and *"spiessig"*—Germans use to mean everything that they openly hate about themselves—the narrow-mindedness, the provincialism, the lack of spontaneity, the bad taste, which are the same things, phrased differently (loyalty, diligence, efficiency, lack of pretense), that they begrudgingly, and then emphatically, admire about themselves, that they always seem to be celebrating. At exactly midnight on New Year's Eve—in Berlin, at least—Germans carrying bottles of *Sekt* come outside in their bathrobes and bedroom slippers and let off firecrackers, or they get dressed and celebrate in groups—at the Brandenburg Gate, for instance—that turn riotlike. Some people drink too much and other people drink too little, except in Germany, where people either drink way too much, or, like Irmgard, just, with peculiar accuracy, enough. And they all smoke. Once they find out that I am American they are filled with questions about Americans (questions about being Jewish don't get much further than the question about keeping ko-

sher, which is more like an accusation), the answers to which will
not revise their ideas, which all have to do with puritanism and
violence; Americans, to a German, are a crowd of nonsmokers with
guns. Germans prefer to think of themselves as primitive and sophisticated, sitting under a tree in summer, naked and smoking a
cigarette. At beaches or in parks last summer, I kept on my swimming trunks or underwear until the end of August, when I was
used to having them occasionally off; I sometimes smoke if everyone else does, and never smoke if nobody else does. On New
Year's Eve, trying to ignore the firecrackers in the courtyards of
Herr Krüger's apartment house (who could call it mine anymore?),
I was quite sober, reading Aleksander Wat's autobiography and
considering a trip to Lemberg—Lemberg in German, once the capital of the Austrian province of Galicia and later the Polish city of
Lwów, where Wat was imprisoned after the Soviets marched into
eastern Poland after the Wehrmacht invaded western Poland
(Wat's autobiography, which is called *My Century*, is more or less
an oral prison memoir, has digressions about bedbugs), and which
he remembers as the most "exotic" of Polish cities (and where I
sometimes accuse my grandfather of coming from, or just passing
through), and which, like Czernowitz, the capital of the Bukovina,
had been something like a third Jewish and quite polyglot and is
now, also, only Ukrainian (Lvov, or sometimes Lwiw, in Ukrainian
rendered into Latin type); expelled Poles from Lwów ended up in
Breslau, now Wrocław, which had been virtually all German until
just after the war, when the Germans who hadn't already fled were
expelled. Some Poles, I have noticed, still lust after their old borders,
their old provincial cities, and this, like similar lusts in Germany, is
considered, by those who feel differently, suspect, eventually dangerous, insane. Not many younger Germans seem to recognize the
word "Lemberg" and even tabloids will use Lvov, which I have
seen described as the "Palermo" of the Russian mafia. I prefer Lemberg, which sounds more Yiddish, than Lwów or Lvov or Lwiw,
which sound Polish or Ukrainian, anti-Semitic. On New Year's Eve,
however, a trip to Lemberg when I should be finding an apartment

began to seem imprudent (when it wasn't sounding mythical; or else too specific, only having to do with me and my assumptions about my grandfather—specifically mythical), a variation on running away. Then I thought about watching a soft-porn movie called *Drei Niederlausitzer auf Dirndljagd*, which means "Three Men from Lower Lusatia"—Lusatia is in East Germany, except for the part that is in Poland—"on a Dirndl Hunt." It was a post-1989 jingoistic soft-porn movie, and a variation on the pre-1989 jingoistic soft-porn movies, which always show men drinking beer and then going up into mountains and trying to fuck women in dirndls. Once, late on a Saturday night, at a time when it would otherwise have been showing a couple of soft-core porn movies, a German network showed both parts of Leni Riefenstahl's *Olympia*, to titillate, presumably, as well as to rouse support for Berlin's Olympic bid (though, of course, on a different network at the same time, it would have been shown to rouse protest against the Olympic bid —to appall). Soft-core pornography is very popular, and even a bit wholesome, in Germany; there are soft-porn talk shows (topless women and men in their underwear talking, at some point, about politics, or showing their porn home movies, which are often too shadowy, somber) and soft-porn game shows (completely naked contestants winning and getting a free trip to Tenerife, or losing and getting a free trip to a German spa, which, because it is in Germany, would already be covered by their health insurance). A few days into the new year, Herr Krüger came to the apartment while I was at the grocery store and took out the television set; I ran into him on the stairs. The TV (the very old but perfectly serviceable West German black-and-white television that he must have bought at one of the old hard-currency Intershops, but which, because it's black-and-white, is considered highly undesirable in Germany—both in West Germany, where it reminds people of the 1950s, and in East Germany, where it reminds people of the year before the wall fell) was resting in his arms, like a horn of plenty. He said it broke while he was trying to dust in my room; when I got back to the apartment, the place where the television set had stood was outlined in dust. Since then I have been listening to the radio instead, which I had already often done, but only regularly in the middle of the night when I couldn't sleep, and then only really to the BBC World Service. The BBC World Service repeats variations of its programs *ad infinitum*, like a geometric series, compounded by the fact, which has especially occurred to me in the middle of the night, that too many of the shows have four-syllable titles. "It Made Our World," which was actually a sequel to "They Made Our World" ("they" being Alexander Fleming, Adam Smith, James Watt; the BBC, as though it were a century ago, is arrogantly, or unconsciously, or, when it comes to cricket scores, playfully, too British); "Poems by Post," "Jazz Now and Then," "Jazz for the Asking" (OK, five), "Classics with Kay," "Folk in Britain," "Brain of Britain" (the network game show), "Focus on Faith," "What Jews Believe." In the daytime, when I avoid the BBC (in addition to kinds of shows, they repeat the same shows three or four times a day, and I postpone listening until the middle of the night, when there's nothing else on) and listen to the Berlin stations, which, in the mornings, have West Berlin disc jockeys trying to chat with East Berlin callers. "Our next caller is Torsten from Marzahn." (Marzahn is Berlin's—in fact, East Germany's—most notorious skyscraper suburb; people moved out to the skyscraper suburbs, which are sometimes called "satellite cities," in the 1980s so they could have central heating and toilets in their apartments; my school is in the heart of Marzahn, near the Avenue of the Cosmonauts, on Helene-Weigel-Platz; West Germans think of it as a slum, and East Germans who live there, like my students, think of it as unattractive and cosy—a little *spiessig*, a few of them actually admitted to me—which is how lots of non-Germans think of Germany; I think of Marzahn as the land of the dead.) "What are you doing, Torsten?" "Nothing." "Are you late for work?" "No." "What do you do, jobwise?" "I'm unemployed." "Shit! When are those politicians going to do something? Uh, Torsten? Are you still there?" "Yes." And in the afternoons I listen to what get called "culture programs," which are erudite and

nearly always have something to do with Jews—musicologists talking about klezmer music, rabbis talking in accented English, which
is then overdubbed into German, about Arnold Schoenberg. On
the rock stations, in the afternoons, the DJs play the German rock
songs all the way through and interrupt the English and American
songs to broadcast the national *Autobahn* report. When I leave the
apartment now I tend to notice the radio stations that are getting
played, in taxis, for instance, or in peoples' apartments (East Germans who heat their apartments with coal overheat them and often open their windows, letting out, in addition to the sounds of
their radios and TVs, the smell of cabbage cooking in pork fat,
which, at around dinnertime, seems to be everywhere, floating just
beyond the coal fumes), and everyone else seems to be listening
to the American and English military stations, which are—were—
meant to serve the local garrisons that are now busy disappearing.
They play Top 40 music from the 1960s, '70s, and '80s, when their
disappearance seemed unthinkable, and they also have talk shows,
of a sort. The American station runs awkwardly acted demobiliza-
tion skits, like the one about the American soldier, going home
with the German shepherd he has bought in Germany, who strikes
up a conversation with another American soldier, who just happens to bring up the topic of customs forms. The British station,
which seems to be coming from specific towns, and sometimes
from specific buildings, in the former British Zone of Occupation
(the American station seems to be coming from America, or, when
they are doing their skits, from an army base that might be anywhere in Germany), gets soldiers and secretaries and soldiers'
wives to call in and joke with the DJs or play little game shows, with the
winner getting a free one-way ticket on a ferry back to England.
Actually, I think that each place with a British garrison—like Cy-
prus, Hong Kong, the Falklands, Croatia, and Bosnia—has its own
programs, but I have heard British soldiers calling into Berlin from
Bosnia, with cellular telephones, joking with the DJs, making re-
quests, talking about sunning themselves. "Sun?" says the DJ. "I
can think of a certain lady at Osnabrück HQ who would go for a

tour of duty down the Balkans. Hm, hm." On New Year's Eve, the BBC World Service wished the world a Happy New Year hourly, by time zone. I fell asleep after midnight in the Azores, during the beginning of *Drei Niederlausitzer auf Dirndljagd*. No phone calls. The Krügers have not only disconnected the telephone—which strongly resembled telephones I had seen in old UFA movies from the 1930s and '40s, which get shown on German television in the morning, when no one watches television, or very late at night, after the pornography (except on the local Bavarian station, where UFA movies are shown on Sunday evenings, like "The Wonderful World of Disney" when I was growing up)—but taken it out of the apartment. Irmgard showed up on New Year's Day, a few days early, with the news that her father thinks Berlin is a bad investment, and we took a bath together. I jerked off after she left the next morning. Irmgard has a beautiful face, beautiful breasts, but strangely huge, almost horrible, hands, fingers that don't taper, boxlike cuticles. I suppose her face is Viennese—long and white, unhappy—which betrays the fact that her father was born in Brno (Brünn, before the war, when a third of the town was German, which visitors, sometimes even Germans who were born there, cannot imagine), the son of a Sudeten German factory manager and a Czech piano teacher, who, Irmgard told me, disappeared back to her parents' apartment in Prague when the Germans marched in, and whom her father, who was eight, never saw again. I can't imagine Irmgard's father, motherless in Brünn, listening to German victories on the radio. Or: I imagine him years after his expulsion, in Hamburg, on his way to work, in his car, listening to the radio. Irmgard wears her silver-black hair down around her shoulders. She smells like expensive perfume and, vaguely, like chocolate, for which, like Gershom Scholem, she has fierce cravings. After she told me about her father, I decided to do some research on Sudeten Germans and had to go to the Free University Institute for Political and Demographic Research, in Dahlem, which is all the way on the other side of Berlin, to find a book in English. One part of the institute is a student dormitory and anarchic: almost labyrinthine, with concrete hallways that are still covered with the anti-Semitic kind of anti-American graffiti popular, I have heard, during the Gulf War (Star of David equals dollar sign; an Uncle Sam, with *peyes*, holding on to a gun), and that lead nowhere. The other part is the library, which is actually atypical for German libraries, even more extreme, with a camera filming people reading and someone spot-checking peoples' pockets as they leave for, it would seem, stolen, crumpled pages. The barred windows of the library have a view across the street of the American Army's officers' club, which, now, on the brink of closing, will apparently let in just about anybody. The day I walked by, their marquee was advertising that night's TWO-FOR-ONE LOBSTER BUFFET and that weekend's MEXICAN FIESTA. If I had wanted a lobster or to see the inside of the officers' club, I would have had to wait all afternoon; the book was short and direct, and didn't take me very long to read. In the foreword, the author played with an adage: "It was often said in the 1940s that Germans made good Nazis and bad anti-Semites, and that Austrians made bad Nazis but good anti-Semites; the Sudeten Germans, in their way both German and Austrian, made the best of both."

The Russian and the American

Lt. Colonel Franklin Howard's earliest memories: toasted cheese sandwiches; white girls in sweaters, white boys in Jeeps driving up in the afternoon; dogs barking at a pile of burning railroad ties. His mother, because she had light skin, got to work as a cashier at the girls' college down the road, and, until Franklin was ten, she brought him along on Saturday afternoons; he would sit next to her on a stool, reading. His journey from Virginia—from what he would later call a shack, where he had lived until he was eight and which had no electricity, no running water, and, for a time, no windowpanes—to West Point, and later to West Berlin, did not seem as monumental to him as the fifteen-minute drive, that first day a few years ago, over the Glienicke Bridge, where spies had been swapped, and into Potsdam, to the corner of Gutenbergstrasse and Jägerstrasse, where old stone houses still damaged from the war were roofless, had trees growing out of their windows. Franklin had written a thesis on the Potsdam Conference, and he sometimes drove to the Cecilienhof Palace to look at the conference table, though this reminded him of West Point, where he had been miserable. Or he went to an edge of the park in Sans Souci, which he had read about in a gay guide, and waited for men to give him blow jobs, which reminded him of nothing, which washed his mind clean. It was a warm day for January, and he had parked his car. He was walking down Jägerstrasse, thinking how much everything had changed since he had last been there in August—one of the roofless houses had been torn down and replaced with a new house, already covered with graffiti; had the street, he tried to remember, already been repaved? He was wearing blue jeans and a ski jacket, and knew the people walking by were staring at him, as they always did; this often reminded him of an old doll he had once found in the woods on his way to school; its marble eyes moved, could seem to follow him. Andrej (the Andrej who couldn't agree on a price with Antje; the Andrej from Novosibirsk), in full uniform, was eating an ice-cream cone, which Dimitri and Andrej, also in full uniform, were finding very funny; their hats, which still had red stars on them, were enormous, and their heads bobbed under the weight, like the doll with the spring in its neck that Andrej had bought to bring back to his sister in Novosibirsk. They walked past Franklin, and Andrej, who had probably seen black men a few times at Alexanderplatz—Angolans, or Cubans, selling cigarettes—but had never seen them in Potsdam, or (I assume) in Novosibirsk, turned his head to stare at Franklin, who saw the high cheekbones, the slanted eyes and pale face. Franklin thought: the white man in him is covering up the Asian man. (Franklin thought that the white man and the straight man in him were covering him up, suffocating him.) He remembered Andrej's face, later, in Sans Souci, standing above a kneeling streetcar conductor—his hands on the conductor's tunic, his cock in his mouth—and lost his erection.

Irmgard's father is an alcoholic and a millionaire; her childhood, in between trips to expensive hotels, was terrible. The fact that her father would come home early to drink his coffee on the terrace, Irmgard recently admitted, felt like a punishment. She seems to be trying too hard at her job, too hard to find an apartment. The other day I touched her twitching eyelid with my finger, and she said, in German, "Too much coffee." The art historian's apartment is a little closer to Alexanderplatz than the Krügers' apartment, which lies on the Berlin Mitte side of the border between Berlin Mitte and Prenzlauer Berg. East German friends of mine, Kurt and Sabine, live three streets away from me and technically in Prenzlauer Berg, although they can talk as if I lived in a completely different part of town. Kurt and Sabine—like most of the people I have met in Prenzlauer Berg who all are, actually or vaguely, artists—live in a micro-universe, or perhaps, a village, with art galleries and grocery stores and studios and friends' apartments a few blocks, or, at most, an U-Bahn stop away. Kurt is a fairly famous sculptor, which in the old East Germany was like being a CEO, and Sabine, who sometimes drew Mickey Mouses on T-shirts before the wall came down, which might have been considered subversive, is his girlfriend, though now she spends her time taking care of her two children from two men other than Kurt, both painters, and both of whom live, with their new girlfriends and new children, around the corner, in the same apartment house; Kurt and Sabine claim they seldom see the two men and their new families, except at art openings, when they avoid each other. Kurt actually grew up in a village north of Berlin and got into art school because of his father, who was a carpenter and Communist Party member; Sabine's parents were physicists, and necessarily party members, in Berlin. I sometimes assume that either Sabine or Kurt, or both of them, had been working for the secret police in Prenzlauer Berg before the wall came down, when, apparently, half the people in any given crowd, at the parties and art openings and poetry readings, in the lines at the grocery stores, in the handful of favored cafés and bars, had been informers, and the other half had been informed upon, often by their closest friends, and sometimes by their families; this, of course, makes everyone there now seem either detestable or pitiable—at least to outsiders like me. (To insiders, I think, the situation is more simple and more complicated; obvious and unfathomable.) Two falls ago, when I first got here and became fast friends with Kurt and then Sabine (and then Sabine, but not really Kurt, and now, more Sabine but also Kurt), when lots of people were reading and talking about their secret police files and learning who had informed on whom, the painters and sculptors and poets and actors who had been informed on weren't talking to the informers, who began to go to bars and openings and grocery stores in parts of West Berlin, though now they have begun to reappear, sometimes shamefaced, sometimes not, usually better dressed. Kurt and Sabine claim they never want to see their files and find out who informed on them, and they don't seem to have felt the need to disappear. I have talked to them each, separately, a few times, about the secret police, and they both got emotional before getting philosophical; when they got emotional, their dialects became thicker, and when they got philosophical, they spoke in a literary-sounding German grander in its way than Irmgard's; I ended up not understanding enough, nodding. I went over to see them today to find out if they knew of any apartments, and they were laying down carpeting. Kurt's father was there without his new prosthesis (he lost a leg on the Russian front), on the floor, telling Kurt where to pound the nails in. Like many people, he refuses to give up, or even tone down, his communism, and he was wearing a hammer-and-sickle pin on the strap of his overalls; his real leg was sticking out, and his upper body, in spite of his age, still seemed muscular; he looked like one of those parodies of socialist realism that you sometimes see these days—a worker-athlete going over a hurdle just underneath the floor. Kurt told me that his father's old prosthesis had been the wrong size, which nobody realized until after the wall came down and his father went, begrudgingly, to a specialist in West Berlin; the years of walking that way had twisted his spine, and he was, especially when he wore his new prosthesis, in horrible pain. I had heard about Kurt's father but had never seen him, and, looking at him this afternoon, I tried not to think of his predicament as symbolic, which I had thought before; I tried to think of Kurt's father's face as registering the pain, as unrecognizable to people who knew him. "People in pain," said Kurt, when I asked him about it later as his father napped, and whom I think of as wise when I am not thinking of him as an informer (I imagine that one precludes the other), "live in a different country." Kurt is an alcoholic, and the biggest change in his life since the wall came down, he has confessed more than once, has to do with alcohol, with the fact that he now drinks French and Italian wines instead of Bulgarian wine. He is seldom nostalgic, as such—not for the old privileges of the state sculptors' union, not for his old bars, which have closed down or have changed beyond recognition. He is gentle, well-read, and exhausted, and on the occasions when he tries to stop drinking, violent (the one time I saw him sober, he knocked over his glass of tomato juice and then threw the glass across the room); he seldom leaves his apartment, which is enormous enough to include a large studio, and thinks, sometimes, of Sabine's children as his own. Sabine, who is thirty-two (five years younger than Kurt, who has a baby face but looks fifty), is more cynical and more lively, reads a little less, and talks sometimes about leaving one or both of her children and going to South America. In her apartment, or near her apartment, she is utterly confident, matriarchal; once, when we went to see a movie in West Berlin, which she had suggested, thinking it was being shown in East Berlin, she became a mouse, disappearing inside her coat. She goes to West Berlin, which still unnerves her, a few times a year to buy panty hose. She and Kurt think of me as a Jewish-American-bisexual giant, as alien (but neutral, not West German), and their tone of voice, which is amused with their friends, is, with me, to whom they feel they have to explain things over and over, a little strained; considering I live three streets away, and think of myself as seeing them often, I seldom see them at all. They knew of countless apartments—of apartments in Prenzlauer Berg, without toilets but with telephones, with coal stoves, with no stove, without windows. They could afford to install central heating in their apartment because Kurt sold a sculpture to a Swiss collector and because they don't seem to spend money on anything else, still eating canned food and wearing tattered oil-black and oxidized-blood red clothes, as if the wall were still up. Their taste in clothes, which, among their friends, is fairly standard, strikes certain people from the West— including me, at first, always, and still, sometimes—as austere, elegant, and strikes people like my students in Marzahn, who wear new, Western department store, brightly colored outfits, as old-fashioned, or as what poor people would wear. The young West Germans who have moved to Prenzlauer Berg either dress like *Autonomen*, who have squatted many of the more derelict houses there, or like people who could be friends with Kurt and Sabine; this complicates telling the West Germans apart, even though most of the *Autonomen* are in fact West German, which is not exactly acknowledged, or at least not held against them by East Germans and not held in their favor by West Germans. I have noticed, actually, that East and West Germans, unlike Jews and homosexuals, cannot always identify each other, but, like gentiles and heterosexuals with regard to Jews and homosexuals, always think they can, with their assumptions seeming narrow-minded, vicious. Bisexuals don't recognize each other as such—they recognize people as heterosexual or homosexual—but assume each other's existence, like East and West Germans before the wall came down; Americans in Eastern Europe are obvious, or less obvious, somewhat disguised, like me, but once recognized, obviously disguised, in drag; tall people strongly dislike being around people who are too tall (there are many West Germans who are too tall, and strangely, almost no East Germans) and are drawn unconsciously to people who are slightly shorter. East Berliners like to tell one another apart. People in Marzahn, for instance, who were either born in Prenzlauer Berg or who moved to Berlin from East German towns and villages, like to recognize people from Prenzlauer Berg, which they think of as a slum; West Germans who don't know Berlin think of Prenzlauer Berg as chic, as the place in East Berlin where they would probably live. I think of Prenzlauer Berg as a place filled with pensioners, or people who look like pensioners, too stubborn or too poor to have moved out to Marzahn and Hellersdorf (the other, and newer, satellite city, farther out and by pre-1989 East German standards, swankier), carrying home cauliflower in nylon-netted shopping bags; I walk past the century-old tenement houses that look five hundred years old, that seem, on smoggy winter nights, to be something beautiful, austere, but walking past in the daytime I think that the black stains on the houses are from air raids and not just from coal smoke, that the pits in the stone are from coal smoke as well as from bullet holes, that the scale of the buildings is oppressive, that the whole borough, much of which had been built to house factory workers, and where three times as many people had been living before the war, looks like an evacuated slum, like the old forgotten people who are living in it; I think of people having waited fourteen years for a telephone, or having informed on someone, perhaps in their own apartment, to get a telephone, and now waiting four or five years for the city to finish putting in the new cables (it has been much easier for people in Marzahn and Hellersdorf to get telephones, though, I suppose, nearly impossible for them to sublet their apartments to people from the West for three or four times the official rent), and, in the meantime, waiting outside graffiti-covered, pink-and-gray, otherwise stablelike, newly installed West German telephone booths, like cattle. (Yet now I, too, have to wait, unless Irmgard is home, and I can use her phone; I stand in line, staring at the hair on a head in front of me.) And I think of Prenzlauer Berg as being across the street, somehow not where I live, somewhere else. Prenzlauer Berg is supposed to be the place in Berlin where Americans like Burt Kaminsky live. He tried to turn an old back house tenement apartment that was missing a wall into an art gallery; he put up a barbed-wire fence where the wall should have been, and people came until the weather turned cold, then the woman who had owned the building before the war kicked Burt out of the apartment, where he had also been living, using a battery for his electric blanket and coffeemaker. Now, when I see him on the street, or in a bar, he asks me for money, usually for exactly ten marks. His stories about his father and himself (his father has Alzheimer's disease, and Burt, after spending most of his father's savings on cocaine, hired a hustler he met on Eighth Avenue to take care of his father during the day while he was in Brooklyn at art school; the hustler beat up Burt and then Burt's father and stole Burt's car; Burt, after leaving his father at a veterans' hospital, took the last of the savings and came to Berlin to open up the art gallery) make me forget about Nazis and Communists, for a while. Burt is evil and yet somehow, while he's talking, blameless, unlike Germans, who are probably more like conduits for evil but who seem especially evil (or at least culpable) while they're talking. (Many of the things that I think about Germans could have been anticipated, decided on before I came here, are clichés, but clichés that, when enacted daily, seem extraordinary, death-defying—a trapeze act; or else, perhaps, life-removing.) Burt and I both lived in the East Village in the 1980s, never really knew each other, recognized each other here in Berlin on the subway. (I met Sabine and Kurt at the gallery, just after I got here, and, eventually, Hans-Joachim and Irmgard, then others.) As a child, and later, in college, I had an inner life as well as what I think of as an outer life (a function, a context); in high school, when I was miserable, and after college (but before Berlin), when I worked at a series of relatively similar, and similar-sounding, entry-level, though really dead-end, jobs, and was also miserable, I had an inner life but not much of an outer life. Here in Berlin I am distracted by the context, have too much of an outer life, not much of an inner life by comparison; when I go to other places in Europe (am away from here; away from away from home), I have no inner life whatsoever, except last fall, when I went to Paris and had a disastrous visit with a woman I slept with several times in college. (I consider college to have been the happiest time of my life, often for formal reasons: my college town, Madison, was a big city on a smaller scale, utopian; Prenzlauer Berg, with its bullet holes and old secret police informers and *Autonomen*, is a marred utopia, but the scale and pace of life reminded me for a while of Madison, though now it reminds me of Marzahn, which is, of course, a dystopia; I think of my life in Berlin as neither happy nor unhappy, but rather outside my life, with trips away from Berlin more—exponentially—outside.) Annette, the woman I had slept with fourteen years ago, and I had kept up our friendship, usually by telephone, and she wasn't the only one. I can still feel close to other women I slept with a few times twelve or fifteen years ago, though I seldom feel close to the men I have slept with often, or a few times, or once, and who seem to have disappeared as though the earth had opened up and swallowed them. (This is, of course, typical, and once admitted, a consolation—because it's true—in an imperfect world; a truth that men can feel close to instead of having to feel close to each other.) Annette now lives in New England, where she is a women's studies professor and, rather recently, a successful feminist romance novelist (she writes the books during her vacations and, she claims in interviews, during committee meetings); she was in Paris for the first time, on sabbatical, though she had been to other European cities on book tours; I had already visited Paris once, the summer after I graduated from college, on the verge—I now like to think—of disappearing for years. Just before I left America and especially just after I arrived in Berlin, I had often called Annette, which could cost two or three hundred dollars a call and may be why the Krügers took out the telephone what I now realize to have been exactly two billing periods before what will be my eviction date. Annette is, increasingly, a solipsist, but a generous one; she assumes that everyone else has had the same life and has the same feelings about it as she has had, that having been a graduate student in women's studies and now going on book tours to Italy and believing that romantic love is a kind of salvation (she reads *Madame Bovary* in the way Emma Bovary would read a romance novel) are fairly widespread conditions, like being tall. On the telephone over the past few years (we hadn't seen each other in three years and hadn't really spent more than an afternoon together in five years) she could be forthcoming as well as anecdotal, not only, though probably mostly, interested in herself; in person, in a sublet apartment on the Quai d'Orsay, overlooking the Esplanade des Invalides and the Pont Alexandre III, none of which existed for her, she repeated her stories for the tenth, or twentieth, time, the way people repeat things to themselves, and which, uninterrupted by telephone etiquette, suddenly sounded all the same, meant to be self-deprecating but were in fact self-aggrandizing, humiliations that turned triumphant—encounters with the new women's studies department chairperson, or with her English or Italian literary agent, or with her tax attorney, always retold with puns and twisted clichés that sound almost funny on the telephone, or if you think them to yourself, but which in person are disjunctive, not at all funny, little black holes. (Her romance novels aren't especially funny, are turgid and upbeat, controversial.) Or she would just go into monologues, remembering to warn herself about being audited, about the toxicity of Parisian car fumes, about gaining weight (she would cut up a single éclair into little pieces and amortize it throughout an afternoon), about the weather (she was afraid that it might rain when she went out, and she would have to redo her makeup), about going out alone at night, which, she said, the women of Paris—as though they were the women of Riyadh—just didn't do; she talked about the subtexts of Hollywood movies, and, self-deprecatingly, about her book reviews, then self-aggrandizingly about her books, about how none of the critics got the *Meet Me in St. Louis* references in her last novel; she spoke intimately about the movie stars who wanted to buy the film rights to her books, or the ones who were just fans. One evening I said I was going out to buy a German newspaper and ended up staying away all night; I went home with an unemployed Alsatian copywriter (he and I did, in fact, speak in German) whom I had met at a discotheque on the Champs-Elysées at six o'clock in the morning, though we were too drunk to fuck—actually, I probably wouldn't have wanted to fuck, although I still could fuck back then—and showed up at her apartment the next afternoon, hung over and with a dozen pieces of pastry; she cut up an éclair as I wolfed down most of the others, sweating. I told her about going home with the copywriter, and she told me that she had thought about calling the police, then she asked me if I was "in love" (she's in love with a fifty-year-old, never-married family court judge in Boston, who visits her every other weekend), then she told me, for probably the hundredth time, about the married Spanish professor she had had an affair with in graduate school; she thought of graduate school as claustrophobic—"girdle-wit school"—and remembers the affair itself, which went on for years, as degrading and exotic, like something out of a Jean Rhys novel. She told me that my going home with an Alsatian copywriter was something out of a Jean Rhys novel—which she had also said a few months before about my teaching English in Berlin—then told me I should probably go to graduate school. During our visit, I felt imperiled, as though she wanted my soul, but scaled down, diminished, as some lesser version of her own; I thought of those Austrian and Prussian provincial cities rebuilt to look like Vienna and Berlin; I thought of being buried alive. Then, after I went to stay in a hotel and didn't call her, I began to hate her (years before, of course, I had been a little in love with her) and tried to pretend that I had never known her; then I thought that I was hating her irrationally, like a relative. When I got back to Berlin and finally did call her, we spoke as though we hadn't just seen each other; she described the apartment she had been staying in as though I had never seen it, and I avoided the subject of Paris altogether, as though meeting her there would be a bad idea, because, perhaps, we would want to do different things—hating the idea of meeting her as opposed to hating her, I thought. My memories of Paris, now, have to do with food, with eating an ice-cream cone in the Luxembourg Gardens a week after graduating from college, and, nearly a decade later, eating alone in restaurants, and going on a perverse sightseeing trip to the "Pétainiste" grocery store in Neuilly that Hans-Joachim had told me about, which specializes in German food, looks like a German grocery store, and attracts a clientele presumably not unsympathetic to Jean-Marie Le Pen, and where, in any case, the young housewives looked like Jean-Marie Le Pen's daughters, who look rather German and sometimes make appearances as "celebrities," along with disenfranchised Bohemian aristocrats and Leni Riefenstahl, in the pages of German *Illustrierte* magazines. Aleksander Wat talked about the "Chineseness" of the Parisians, by which he meant the constancy of their habits, the way they eat their meals and build a mandarin political class—a stability that makes Paris, compared to the rest of Europe, seem unchanging, outside time, a little provincial. Though actually Paris had changed in the years since my other visit; the Champs-Elysées was all boarded up and looked, when I left that discotheque at eight in the morning, like East Berlin, like the Karl-Marx-Allee. Berlin itself, of course, is still very provincial, even by German standards, but unique, which has to do with its constant instability, which distracts people, when they think about it, from the fact that they can't buy anything, that people wear old or ugly clothes, that all the movies are dubbed, that the national newspapers are published elsewhere, that the restaurants are terrible. German food often reminds me of my childhood, of Milwaukee, which used to be stable to the point of being inanimate, is still authentically—to some people, even exotically—provincial, and, because of its consistent Germanness, unique. The entire time I was growing up the city had the same mayor, whose last name was Maier, and the fanciest restaurants were downtown and served German food, though now Milwaukee, which has had the fastest growing violent crime rate in America and is famous for a serial killer, has a deserted downtown, and it's hard to imagine restaurants of any kind because no one leaves their houses at night. I remember as a child going to a German restaurant downtown on Thanksgiving—when lots of the other people there, like my parents, were Jews who didn't feel like staying home—and eating potato dumplings and liver dumplings and

sipping my father's Oktoberfest beer and listening to a string quartet play Strauss waltzes. Thomas Mann's son, Klaus, visited Milwaukee in the 1930s and wrote in his autobiography that
Milwaukee was more German than Germany. Klaus Mann's mother's father was Jewish, which makes Klaus Mann, according to Jewish law, non-Jewish, and, according to the Nuremberg laws,
half-Jewish, and half-Jewish according to the parlance some people
use when they talk about these things, especially Germans, who,
if they are talking about some dead person also famous for being
German, will say "half-Jewish" and sound somber and self-recrim-
inating, even pious, or merely German, by which I mean, in this
case, precise to the point of being wrong. I heard a radio program
about Klaus Mann, who is in vogue in Germany these days, in
which he was described as being half-Jewish, though the program
had everything to do with his being homosexual, nothing to do
with his being Jewish. Canetti, in his notebooks, forty or fifty years
after the fact, recalls a meeting in prewar Vienna with Klaus Mann,
who spoke so rapidly and unoriginally about American literature
that Canetti couldn't remember anything he said. The recollection
is a kind of warning, like much of Canetti's writing, which conjures up vanished places not out of longing, never sentimentally,
but to warn you that they once existed. Maria Riva, who also writes
about vanished places (prewar Europe, prewar Hollywood), is sentimental about time spent away from her mother, longs for her
mother's absence (yet perversely seems to have remembered everything her mother ever said); her book—which celebrates the survival of her inner life as it chronicles the decline of her mother's
body, and which ends, almost logically, with her mother's
funeral—gloats, which is a warning of a different sort, a vanity.
The past, in Canetti, is even a greater burden than the present,
while the past, in Riva, is what no longer burdens her—this makes
them each, in their way, very German. Marlene Dietrich apparently had a fondness for German food, which in Riva's book is
meant to be sinister, but which has been written about as proof of
her Germanness—as a vindication—in some of the recent news-

paper profiles of Dietrich, who, because of what happened in Baden-Württemberg a few weeks ago, has often been in the news. A movie theater owner in Stuttgart decided to begin the new year by changing the name of his theater from the Thalia to the Marlene Dietrich. On the Sunday of the first weekend in January, after the last showing of *How to Marry a Millionaire* (he had opened with *The Blue Angel* and then went right into a Marilyn Monroe retrospective), masked "right-extremist-youth-bands," after spraying *"Jud Sau,"* which means "Jew sow," on the sidewalk in front of the theater, attacked the theater owner, who was in the box office counting his weekend gross. They punched him in the face a few times, took his money, and threw a single Molotov cocktail at the stage, which the theater owner, in spite of a broken jaw, put out with a fire extinguisher before the fire department could get there. Then the controversy began, which I had to follow by newspaper. There were many Germans (35 percent, in the poll I read about) who thought that renaming the theater had been a provocation, and slightly fewer (28 percent) who said they think of Marlene Dietrich as a traitor. Then, on a television talk show that I didn't see, an actor from a soap opera said that he didn't think Marlene Dietrich was a traitor, that she was a great star, the only real star that Germany has ever produced. Now he has started getting hate mail; one letter was from the *Bürgermeister* of a village near Stuttgart who said that neither he nor anyone else in the village was going to watch the soap opera again. I was talking about some of this with Kurt and Sabine, who didn't seem very interested. Kurt said that he hadn't known that Marlene Dietrich was Jewish; Sabine told me that Marlene Dietrich had been bisexual, which she said only to me, as though it were a compliment. Kurt's father, who must have been born around 1920, said he remembered in the 1930s when Marlene Dietrich had been the girlfriend of John D. Rockefeller (who, I think, would have been in his nineties in the 1930s), which was the sort of thing that German *Illustrierte* magazines wrote about under the Nazis. Later I remembered that many Germans think of Rockefeller as a Jewish name. The last time

I tried sleeping with a man (it was early last fall, and I felt nothing, pretended to be drunk), he and I talked beforehand about my being Jewish; later, when we were in bed after not really having sex and talking about not being able to remember each other's last names, he asked me if I was related to the Rockefellers, who, he said, were the only American Jews he knew of. He was from Swabia, near Stuttgart (though you can't make a connection between what he said and what happened there without seeming, and even feeling, a little crazy), and, when I first saw him at one of Hans-Joachim's parties, but not at all, weeks later, when I saw him in a bar, he looked rather Jewish, reminding me of a particular counselor at the Jewish summer camp I worked at in New Hampshire. I took a job there as a counselor when I was a teenager in order to get away from the world of my suburban high school, which, as it happens, wasn't at all Jewish, and where I had no friends, but also no enemies, where I eventually just didn't exist. My mother, like her father had been, is ambivalent about being Jewish and has sometimes claimed to be Unitarian, which she associates with the department-store-owning Gimbel family, who apparently converted; my father, whose presumably Orthodox parents died when he was a baby, and who subsequently grew up in a state orphanage and then with Yiddish-speaking Orthodox foster mothers, is not ambivalent, exactly, about being Jewish, but has probably come to associate it, like my mother, with being poor; these ideas (to be discussed this week on the radio, it would seem, on a show called "Gustav Mahler and Jewish Self-Hate") now seem quaint, more German than Germany (where the thousands of new Jews from the old Soviet Union may be poor but know very little about being Jewish, and have to learn the rules of Judaism at the same time as they are learning the German language, from Germans), or just remote, as far away from the present as my parents and their suburb are from Berlin Mitte. I don't know if I'll be in town for that radio program, though; I think I'll go to Poland for a few days and come back the day before I have to teach. Poland is baroque, intricate. Last time I was there, in Posen, I went to an outdoor market and saw a man who seemed to have been to a close-out sale at an elastic factory—he was selling brassieres, small trampolines, and trusses all made out of the same patterned elastic; at least I think they were trusses: as someone (though no one in my family; no one I have ever met) might say, "I don't know from trusses." He was standing next to an old woman who was sitting behind a pile of dried peas, and she was next to a man selling French structuralist philososphy in Polish translation; it was September and people were carrying around large sunflowers and picking out and eating the seeds, then spitting out the husks onto the street. Poland, which of course used to be the land of the dead, is lively but skewed—land of the liars and the lied-to. The food at the dairy bars reminds me of the food in the East Village, which reminded me of food I ate as a child with my father, when he and I would visit the neighborhood he grew up in and eat at a delicatessen that burnt down after Martin Luther King was shot. I think that Germany is the land of the dead—all of it, a kind of Marzahn. And not only do I think that Jews shouldn't live in Germany, I don't think Germans should either; I think, as some mixture of a zionist and a humanist, that everybody should leave, start over. Yet here I am, planning a departure and a return. I consider the fact that I feel the way I do and am here earning all this money (though of course much less than I had been) as monstrously hypocritical—eating the hand that feeds me. In Kurt's apartment, I thought about leaving Berlin for good, then I thought about asking the school for a ten-mark-per-hour raise. I remembered my summer camp, where there were Jews from all over the country; southern Jews, many of whom were related to one another, told us that, in the South, gentiles use the expression "to Jew down," which means to bargain (I never learned such expressions, grew up without anti-Semitism, except the Jewish kind; my mother used to call what remains of my father's family— cousins he never knew very well—"kikes"). I wondered, as a point of regional grammar, if one could "Jew someone 'up.' " This struck me as ugly, and I thought: You are almost about ready to leave here, though without thinking it seriously, without wondering where I would go, where I would end up.

[3]

At the party at Hans-Joachim's, the subject, really, was the new Europe. At one point, all of the male guests at the party had two first names (except for Mike, although I think he might spell it "Maik," who is an unemployed puppeteer from East Berlin)—Jan-Friedrich, Sven-Wilhelm, Hans-Dieter, Hans-Joachim—which, like old Germanic names (two of the women there were named Hydrun and Isolde, another man was named Wulf), were popular in West Germany in the early and middle 1960s, just after the wall went up. I think Hans-Joachim has had some kind of sex with most of the men, who were coming and going, often trying to ignore each other in intervals, bringing food or flowers, like characters, I thought, in a Feydeau farce as directed by Rainer Werner Fassbinder. I have never tried having sex with Hans-Joachim because I haven't had the courage. Hans-Joachim is HIV-positive, which is off-putting, although probably less so in Germany, where AIDS has been highly politicized and where politics has to do with a fierce like-mindedness, a slight deviation from which might land you someplace else entirely; either you would have safe sex with Hans-Joachim, regardless, or you wouldn't know him; knowing him and not having sex with him because he is HIV-positive would be like firebombing his house because he is HIV-positive. I worry, increasingly, about making the right impression politically, am becoming, in this sense, at least, more German, and might consider very safe sex with Hans-Joachim, though after taking into account my present state I assume that he wouldn't have the patience. Hans-Joachim, who has just earned master's degrees in art history and architecture and city planning in five instead of the usual seven or nine or ten years, and who also has no wall in his mind, rides back and forth between East and West Berlin with condoms and AZT in the glove compartment of his Peugeot, going on dates and to "safe-sex parties." He says he doesn't go to the safe-sex parties for sex, though, because so many of the men there are having unsafe sex; he goes to watch. At his last safe-sex party in East Berlin, he met a shepherd from the East German part of the Harz Mountains, living in Prenzlauer Berg, and, needless to say, unemployed, whom he had invited to his party but who never showed up; I was curious and waited all night for the shepherd. Just about everyone there—again, except for Mike and myself—was a West German who had moved to Berlin after the wall came down, and who seemed, that night, to have just returned from some other country in the European Community. Hans-Dieter was back from Holland, where, he said, there were new garbage cans equipped with microchips that made it easier for the state to fine people who weren't properly sorting their garbage. Hans-Dieter is quite serious about ecology but, when I asked him, said he would never join the Green Party, or any other party, which is typical for younger Germans, who seem to have politicized everything in their lives except their politics. Johann, another childhood friend of Irmgard's and Hans-Joachim's, was back from London, where, he said, the newest kind of gay bars also had straight people in them, which everyone else at the party at the time agreed was a good idea though unlikely to catch on in Berlin, where gay people, like other people, are triply, even quadruply, segregated (by East and West, of course, then by borough, by demographic group, by specific inclination, like the bar off the Karl-Marx-Allee meant to attract the working-class leathermen of Friedrichshain). I talked about something I had heard on the BBC World Service about news broadcasts in Finland being read in Latin. Mike, who obviously felt uncomfortable, was prattling. Eventually he repeated a story told to him by a friend who designs costumes at the opera house in Schwerin, which is supposed to be the most beautiful

opera house in East Germany, about a Bulgarian tenor whom some
skinheads had mistaken for a Turk; the skinheads knew that he
was an opera singer and, when they attacked him in the parking
lot of the opera house, cut his tongue before setting fire to his car.
People at the party shook their heads, then someone else, who had
just been in Italy, told everyone about the male prostitutes in
Rome, who are apparently all Albanians now, and "*homophobisch*,"
robbing their customers at knifepoint without even having sex
with them first. Isolde, who works for the Treuhandanstalt, which
is the scandal-ridden government agency that is supposed to be
privatizing East German industry and is housed in the old Luftwaffe building near the Potsdamer Platz, was just back from a
meeting of the European Parliament in Strasbourg, which she pronounced "Stras*bourg*," in French, sounding ridiculous, rather than
in German ("Strassburg"), as most Germans do, which would have
sounded too—perhaps ridiculously—German; she said that the
music in the discotheques in Strasbourg was more humane than
the "techno" music that gets played in Berlin. (Irmgard won't go
to the bunkers and factories when they play techno music—which
sounds to me as if someone had left a microphone on the end of
a moving piston—because it gives her migraine headaches; she
hadn't come to Hans-Joachim's party because she had a migraine
and was staying home at the art historian's apartment with some
aspirin that Johann had brought back from England, which had
codeine in it and which, according to Isolde, who was admonishing, is banned in Germany.) Someone else had been to Antwerp,
where, I said, the Flemish right-extremist party had gotten a higher
percentage of the vote than any other right-extremist party in any
other major European city. Wulf said that the town hall of his
parents' village—which is near the Black Forest, Hans-Joachim
later said when I asked, chastising me for not picking that up
from his accent—had been turned into a processing center for refugees from Bosnia, and, in recent local elections, a third of the
village had voted for Republikaner candidates. Then Jan-Friedrich
said to me, switching to heavily accented English as though he

didn't want to be misunderstood, that what was happening in Antwerp was because of the Jews; he said that there were lots of Jews in Antwerp; you know, he said, who wear dresses and sell diamonds. Caftans, I said, which Hans-Joachim—who is teaching himself Czech, which will be his sixth language, I believe, not counting Latin and Greek—translated into German as *Kaftan.* Jan-Friedrich said that he had learned about what the Germans had done to the Jews in school, of course, but, after reading what a rabbi in Israel had said about homosexuality and AIDS, he decided that what the Jews were doing to the homosexuals was just as bad as what the Germans had done to the Jews. I said, in German, that that was completely idiotic. Wolfgang, someone from Hans-Joachim's HIV-positive sports group, who had spent the fall in the hospital with pneumonia and who still looked—well—as if he had been in a concentration camp (Germans, I have noticed, avoid this analogy, while Americans use it all the time; I try to remember to avoid it), said that lots of people, not just Jews, were prejudiced against homosexuals. I said that I was Jewish, and Jan-Friedrich said that he hadn't known, looked embarrassed, apologized, said that he had known that I wasn't German, and was probably either English or American, though at first he had thought, because of my German, possibly Dutch, but not that I was Jewish, that I didn't look Jewish; he smiled. I said I had to go to the bathroom; I went into the bathroom, closed the door, turned on the tap, and looked, suddenly, at the row of Hans-Joachim's prescriptions and thought of the cover of the paperback edition of *Valley of the Dolls,* which I read when I was about eleven. I associate my childhood with blockbuster novels, with sitting alone in my bedroom and reading *Exodus* and *Hawaii* and *QBVII.* (I have a sister who is thirteen years older than I am, and I grew up, I assume, as an only child.) Hans-Joachim doesn't look at all sick, has just begun to feel tired, although he has terrible skin, which has to do with his being German, to some extent: he has psoriasis, which is more common in Germany, I heard on "Europe Today," than anywhere else in the European Community. In the summertime, he is always in the sun; he now keeps a canoe on a lake in East Berlin and rides around old industrial canals where a lot of former minor party functionaries still have their dachas, in bikini underwear, with a speaker-equipped Sony Walkman, listening to jazz and burning the lesions off his skin. I went with him once last summer and remember the beefy-faced, almost Russian-looking, old party members sitting on old East German lawn furniture and staring at the West Germans in their new motorboats, and at us, as we listened over and over again to Dinah Washington singing "Mad About the Boy," and Chet Baker playing "Daydream" and "Ev'ry Time We Say Goodbye"; there was a little canal-side café, with its own dock, where Hans-Joachim ordered a "Queen Louisa" ice-cream sundae while the radio played a Muzak version of the theme from *Gone With the Wind*. I remember not really being able to keep up with Hans-Joachim, who, like many German men, is quite muscular, looks like an athlete, instead of a bookish architect who speaks with a lisp. I am not at all muscular, have, at times, tended toward lankiness, except in Germany, where I drink beer and eat sausage and have gotten fat, become fleshy around the hips, grown small breasts; I am tall and broad-shouldered, which goes against a funny lilt—a fagginess, really—in my voice that I sometimes blame on having spent too much time with the southern and eastern Jews at that Jewish summer camp; I don't sound at all like my parents or my sister, who have midwestern twangs, with, in the case of my father, and even sometimes in the case of my mother, Yiddish intonations, and I can lead people to assume that I am from New York, or somewhere that they can't identify, and probably homosexual. My childhood didn't really end until I was in high school, when I joined the ski club to avoid being a total outcast; in college, people I knew played Frisbee, which seemed to be a part of a whole, connected to reading books and taking drugs and living in apartments; in New York, and then in other places, I used to walk the length of the city, preferably alone and sometimes in the middle of the night, afraid. Here in Berlin, which is still relatively empty and, considering the kinds of cities I used to live in, not at all dangerous, I walk often, though increasingly less often. Hans-Joachim has been hired by the city to help standardize the memorial plaques on houses in East and West Berlin, which, by my standards, is a highly political job having to do with deciding which socialist heroes get remembered and which get forgotten, although Hans-Joachim claims to be apolitical, even when it comes to AIDS, and something of an aesthete, intent on keeping plaques made out of stone and getting rid of ones made out of concrete. He hasn't started the job yet and has even more time on his hands than I do and, to pass the time, has sometimes given me tours of Berlin, explaining the architecture and, incidentally, pointing out the places where men have anonymous sex with each other; or probably the other way around. Hans-Joachim has eroticized the city in the way that I, arguably, have de-eroticized it: I walk through Berlin as though it were a necropolis, abandoned, overrun by something else; when I am walking, I rarely notice people, or at least, don't notice them as sexual objects; I notice their faces, which I think of as medieval, or as peasantlike, or as animals' faces, and I hear the sounds of their shoes on the cobblestone pavement as timeless, reminding me of a noise a pair of shoes might have made on that same cobblestone pavement x or y number of years ago, or I hear their walking as heavy, ungainly, as making noises that hooves might make. When I first arrived in Germany I was sexually attracted to Germans for two reasons: an extraordinarily profound expression on certain Germans' faces and something mysterious about most Germans between the ages of twenty and forty, about their manner, which I came to think of as androgynous (Germans under twenty and over forty, except for the ones with profound expressions, can look rather blank, neuter.) I now recognize this expression as something else, as yet another kind of blankness, an attempt, really, to look inconspicuous, as if their thoughts were no different from everyone else's, as a kind of a failed, even ignoble, ordinariness that reminds me of those people in Dante not even interesting enough to get into Hell, the masses who "lived without praise or blame," a description, by the way, which I can imagine going over as a compliment in Germany, as a description of humility. (I read Dante—or, in Dante—after college, autodidactically and idiosyncratically, as though it were a travelogue; in spite of my attempts to remain insatiable, I am really something of an autodidact, which is an inversion of bookishness; autodidacts, who often read the same books, or types of books, over and over again, make a fetish out of wisdom, fancy themselves one or two books away, or already past, knowing everything; bookish people make a fetish out of books, can never read enough, never want to get to the end, avoid wisdom to lust after more knowledge; Germans, famous for their philistinism and pedantry, "don't know" from wisdom; I am trying to teach myself to be more bookish.) The androgyny of Germans—a toughness, even in the most otherwise feminine women, and something soft, not yet finished, in the men—is only mysterious to me now in the sense that I wonder if Germans see themselves that way. I have noticed that Germans claim to be attracted to people who don't look at all German or to people who look extremely German. I am sexually attracted to people who remind me of people I have slept with in the past, although I am rarely still attracted to the people I actually did sleep with, who now seem—having been refracted through other people—too familiar, and make me long for someone else, something new. Germans, lately, often disgust me, although I am sometimes attracted to Germans who remind me of Germans whom I was attracted to when I first got here, who, in turn, didn't remind me in any way of anybody I slept with before, or I am attracted to Germans who do look like someone I slept with before, and, in that case, probably don't look very German and almost certainly look vaguely Jewish. I am especially attracted to men's hands and women's backs. I am probably more attracted to women after I have slept with a man and more likely to sleep with a man just after I have slept with a woman, a cycle that necessarily repeats itself, but then sex, like learning, has a lot to do with repetition, even impotence, which, from a certain distance, is a repeating abstinence, a kind of celibacy, empty, like the moment before a revelation. Now, of course, that I am not really having sex, not fucking, I could think about sex—especially about fucking, about the act itself—all the time and have, especially in the last couple of days, although before, when I had sex as much as anybody, I thought of fucking as just one more thing to do, and to be avoided entirely, even with a condom, with men. So: I want to be with a woman when I am with a man and with a man when I am with a woman, and I want to fuck when I can't and don't care when I can. This amounts to an eroticized *Wanderlust*, a yearning to be intimately elsewhere, and more like absence than detachment. My mother—who picked up Yiddish from her mother, who was a Russian Jew and not ambivalent about being Jewish—uses Yiddish words, though less often than my father, and she used to tell me when I was a little boy and couldn't sit still that I "had *'spilches,'* " which is like having ants in your pants, being impatient, and is perhaps a Yiddish equivalent of *Wanderlust*. In Polish, *spilches* means "needles," which I learned on a train in Poland, where people are too friendly, when a woman asked me what I was doing in Poland; I explained that I was working in Berlin but wanted to get away, that I had *spilches*, which also, eventually, let her know that I was Jewish, a fact that I sometimes flaunt and at other times recognize as a disguise. Instead of going to Poland this week, I went to Hans-Joachim's party, looking for some sort of sex, perhaps, and for a new apartment. (When I am not thinking about leaving Germany, I think about moving to West Berlin, which, compared to East Berlin, can seem more German, or less Russian.) I never got around to asking if anybody knew of an apartment because so many other people there asked first. Jan-Friedrich, who claims not to sleep with men, came to the party, he actually said, because he is looking for a new room in an apartment—a situation that Germans pedantically call a *Wohngemeinschaft*, or "living-together-society"—and he thought that homosexuals would know about empty rooms in other homosexuals' apartments; he said that he wouldn't mind living with homosexuals as long as they were *ordentlich*, which

Germans use to mean "orderly," or "sane," or "essentially like me"; Gypsies, who are despised, are usually accused of being *unordentlich* even before they are accused of being criminals. Hydrun came, she said, because she knew that I would be there and hoped that I would know of empty, telephone-equipped apartments in Prenzlauer Berg that Americans on their way back to America were leaving behind. The point of the party (parties always have official purposes in Germany, where people are expected to throw their own birthday parties) was to celebrate Hans-Joachim's remodeling of his apartment, where he has only been living for a few months, and where, perhaps, he can only stay until the end of the summer. The apartment, which is in Wilmersdorf, which people associate with old Wehrmacht widows and turn-of-the-century lavishness, is huge—105 square meters, according to Hans-Joachim (Germans always know the exact sizes of their apartments but, seldom, their neighbors). He had put in new tile and new appliances and stripped off most of the old wallpaper and paint in the living room, which takes up about half of the apartment and has what must be a twenty-five-foot ceiling, leaving the stone wall looking naked, almost destroyed, which is something of a fashion in Berlin; I thought that Hans-Joachim's now grayish brown walls looked unusually ravaged, like a centrally heated street in Prenzlauer Berg. I was very serious or not at all serious about finding some kind of sex at the party, as I am very serious and not serious enough about leaving Germany. Germans, incidentally, are considered terrible lovers. I heard a joke on "Europe Today" about the European Community: instead of blending the best of Europe, which would have been English diplomacy, French food, German efficiency, and Italian sex, the European Community blends the worst—French diplomacy, English food, Italian efficiency, and German sex. Germans in bed, and predictably, are violent, or awkward to the point of seeming violent, except for Irmgard, who is tender or neurasthenic; I, apparently, am absent. When I met Irmgard and we were fucking almost every day, she told me that, even while we were in the middle of fucking and looking into each other's eyes, I seemed to be *"anderswo"* (she talks about sex in German), which means "elsewhere." Later I came across "elsewhere" in Gershom Scholem's *On Jews and Judaism in Crisis*, in which he suggests that "being elsewhere" and, simultaneously, a "desperate wish to be at home" describe the pathology of the Jews' relationship to Germany. I felt that he was also describing me, and my predicament, which has often been a desire to be at home somewhere else, but then away from there too—in exile from a place I haven't yet visited. I only really have to stay here until March, when the term ends, though of course I could just quit and leave before that. I don't feel as if I am going anywhere. The smallest journeys, even going to Potsdam on the S-Bahn, can overwhelm me with feeling (usually regret and relief), but now I feel nothing, fill up my head with constant, dispassionate, almost clinical thoughts about fucking, with a kind of stick-figure pornography. Actually "nothing," as such, according to theosophic Kabbalah, can be a form of fullness, of "pure absolute being." I read in Scholem's *Major Trends in Jewish Mysticism* that the Hebrew word for "nothing" has the same number of consonants as the Hebrew word for "I." These sorts of numerical coincidences can be quite meaningful in the Kabbalah, about which I arguably shouldn't even be reading, considering that I don't know a word of Hebrew. My mother, who is a Reform Jew, had one ambition for me as far as Judaism was concerned: to go to "religious school" on Sundays and be "affirmed," which would have been, had I not dropped out to take skiing lessons, an excuse to throw a party, and which Germans Jews incorporated into liberal Judaism, American Reform Judaism's direct ancestor, as a way of being more like German Protestants; my father, who grew up Orthodox and lost the argument with my mother over whether I should be Bar Mitzvahed—is it more correct to say "be a Bar Mitzvah"?—worries less and less about these things and likes to joke that he is a " 'reformed' Jew." (Strange coincidence: the surname of the most famous Reform rabbi in Milwaukee while I was growing up was Pastor.) I have relearned my German—which is very good for five minutes, then unpredictably inconsistent,

weird—from talking to Irmgard and Hans-Joachim and from reading tabloid newspapers and books by Elias Canetti that I couldn't
find in English translation: I use Irmgard's verbs and Hans-
Joachim's adjectives; the nouns are mine, Canetti's, and the *Bild
Zeitung*'s. The faces and names and buildings of Milwaukee can be
impeccably German. There is a suburb west of Milwaukee called
New Berlin which people in Milwaukee pronounce New *Ber*lin,
with the accent on the first syllable, which is how Germans pronounce Berlin when they are trying to speak English. My parents,
and now my sister, who bought a house a five-minute drive away
from them, live not too far from New Berlin in a suburb called
Brookfield, which, because of its compound-nounness, suggests
something German to me. I think my parents and sister must be
the only Jews for blocks, though all of my parents' friends are Jewish and live on the other side of town, in suburbs near the lake.
My parents only sometimes (actually, more and more) use the
word "goy," and have often used the word "gentile." My sister
married a gentile whom she went to grade school, high school,
college, and law school with, but whom she claims never to have
spoken to until their fifteenth high school reunion; now, when
she's not working, she spends a lot of time around people she went
to high school with, who must be, without exception, gentile,
though she works for what my parents would call a "Jewish" law
firm. My father often uses the word *zhlub* to describe sloppy Jewish
people, like the Jews he went to high school with who never made
it; my mother would use the word "dutchy," which must come
from "deutsch," to describe comically dressed gentiles, like some
of her neighbors, who, in spite of their wealth, remain, like so
many wealthy West Germans, decidedly something else. My father
is an accountant; my sister is an accountant as well as a lawyer;
my mother, at one time, worked as a bookkeeper; when I dropped
my Introduction to Accounting course during my second semester
at college, my parents suggested that I see a psychiatrist; when I
am suddenly around Americans in especially foreign places, like
Warsaw, and get excited, my voice changes, can revert to a mid-

western twang. I sometimes think about going back and living in Milwaukee, but think this feverishly, like Leon Samitzky, the character in *Badenheim 1939* who was born in Poland but left fifty years before and talks, strangely and exuberantly, about going back. Actually, I think of living in Milwaukee as a personalized torment. Would I want to return, I wonder, just so I could leave it? (Yes, I'll think, so I can go again from there, someplace else; to leave it.) At Hans-Joachim's party, I thought about changing something other than my location, like, for instance, my taste in music. I have been listening to the same music for years, a mixture of the music my sister listened to when she was in high school (my sister is sentimental about everything except her old records), and the music that was popular when I was in college; wherever I go, I always seem to have cassettes of the Beatles' White Album; Elvis Costello, Joni Mitchell, the Roches; Crosby, Stills, Nash and Young, and Neil Young; Rickie Lee Jones, and others. I like greatest hits albums and live albums and new compilations, which, in addition to being more portable, can be, because of the order of the songs, familiar but surprising, a new version of the past. I don't enjoy this music as much as I have—like in the few years after college when I would be sitting around wherever and listening to it and suddenly I was back in Madison—and sometimes, in fact, can't stand it, though I often use the songs as teaching aids in the classroom, making enlarged photocopies of the lyrics off the cassette liner notes and playing the tapes on the school's new, unbelievably expensive, West German stereo system. "History repeats the old conceits, the glib replies, the same defeats," which is from Elvis Costello's "Beyond Belief," and, one would think, a sentiment most Germans could understand, but the words themselves, or Elvis Costello's particular English accent, or something, makes "Beyond Belief," like many of the other songs I have played, fairly inscrutable to East Germans, even to the ones with Ph.D.s in English and comical English accents picked up from the BBC World Service's English teaching programs, which many of them seem to listen to and which are scrupulously snobby about American English vs. English

English. Everyone likes the Beatles, though. Well, not everyone; only very few, actually. Germans, especially East Germans, like to learn by rote, which they're used to; they like to go over exercises in their old Cambridge First Certificate Grammar Review Workbooks, the answers to which they seem to have memorized, and not learn the lyrics to "Sexy Sadie" or "Martha My Dear" or "Both Sides, Now." Students, apparently, have complained (the classes are expensive, work out to about thirty or forty marks per hour per student; one of my students—although I have never found out which one—actually asked for a refund), or, in a few cases, told the school that they liked my class because they didn't have to do any work. (When I am not playing songs, I often show videos of American movies or give impromptu lectures about American cities I have lived in.) It has occurred to me that East German students like doing their exercises in the way that I like listening to the same songs over and over again, although, in my case, less, much less now, so that I use my cassette player, which I bought just after I got here and can't disappear one day with the Krügers, desperately, numbingly, as though it were a prayer wheel, or as though someone else were making me listen to these songs—which usually have something to do with being young, with that kind of real feeling, and which remind me of the fact that I am feeling nothing—as some kind of punishment.

The Black Man and the White Man

Olaf remembered nothing about his childhood, or, rather, about his real childhood. He remembered waking up in the orphanage in the middle of the night and having to go to the bathroom, which smelled like the vinegar they used to clean the toilets, which is what his entire army barracks, years later, would also smell like. He had never met his real mother, who, he was told, beat him up so badly that he had to be taken away from her and put in the orphanage, where he remembered orderlies hitting him over the head with broom handles for no reason whatsoever. He had begun to hear stories about East German orphanages, about parents applying for passports to go to the West and getting their children taken away from them, or about parents going to the West the summer before the wall went up, when Olaf was born, and locking their children in their apartments before they left. "Aren't you curious?" asked Silke, the veterinarian whom Olaf worked for on Saturday afternoons, to be near the animals. (His dream: to leave Berlin; to work on a farm.) This was his second, other job; his first, real job was in a new West German–owned dry cleaners near the Lichtenberg train station; after a week of smelling dry cleaning fluid, the smell of animal fur was, for Olaf, like the smell of fresh bread. (For a year just after getting out of the army, he had worked happily in a bakery.) And he could talk to Silke, who thought he should have requested to see his secret police file when he had had the chance, and possibly sue the government for what might have happened to him. He had grown up believing that the state had saved him from his mother; now he lived as though Silke, on Saturdays, were saving him from the dry cleaners, from white shiny boredom. He often told Silke about having sex with men, what they smelled like, and tasted like; he told her about the black man in the toilet on the Strasse der Pariser Commune; "I had never had one before," he said. "He was American and spoke better German than I can. And he had such big lips! And hairy arms, just like an ape. 'You're just like an ape,' I said. And he got mad. So I still haven't had one."

I force myself to go to the opera, where either I drink too much beer while waiting for the opera to start and spend the opera wanting to go to the bathroom, or I spend the opera imagining some other staging entirely; at Christmas, when I saw *Der Rosenkavalier* with Irmgard and her friend from Munich, I thought about a *Der Rosenkavalier* set in Vienna during the late 1930s, with Baron Ochs as a Jew who, during his humiliation in the third act, is forced to scrub a paved section of the stage; I imagined a Marschallin coming on at the end to say her *"ja, ja"* on the arm of a Wehrmacht officer.

Going to the opera, which I only did a couple of times in America (I remember going to see an opera in Los Angeles—where, for a while, I worked on the staff of a game show for whom I sent consolation prizes to contestants who had lost—in shorts, and some man who had that awful southern California Okie accent said to me, "Gee, what do you wear when it gets hot?"), reminds me of Professor Whitlaw, who is the most proximate cause of my being in Berlin. I was living in Chicago, working as a paralegal in a sort of dummy corporation set up to distribute the damages won in a class action suit (actually I had just quit that job by telephone and was lying on the floor on my futon, thinking of Chicago as a cemetery, of its buildings as gravestones, thinking of myself on the floor as underneath the corpses), when I decided to drive up to Madison and sit in the student union; that afternoon I drove up with the car windows rolled down, and then sat in the student union and played the same songs on the jukebox that I would have played if I had been in my apartment in Chicago, the songs I had played on the jukebox ten or twelve years before, though now it was a CD jukebox, the songs I had tried to find on the car radio during the drive up. Then Professor Whitlaw walked by and recognized me. He had been my intellectual history professor, and, at the time, I had thought, before I graduated and forgot about him, my hero. Professor Whitlaw was a Kantian and a frustrated political philosopher who taught two courses each semester: in the fall he taught "Ancient [political] Thought" and "Medieval [political] Thought," and in the spring he taught "Modern [political] Thought" and "Contemporary [political] Thought"; he acted as though the history of Western philosophy was the history of Western political philosophy and the history of Western political philosophy was more or less an anticipation of, or followup to, Immanuel Kant; he concluded each semester's classes with the same prepared address, which he titled "Why I Think Kant Is Right and Other Philosophers You Have Read This Semester Are Less Right." In my senior year, after having taken all four of Professor Whitlaw's classes in reverse chronological order—for which

I rewrote the same paper about Friedrich Nietzsche, called, that first, and each subsequent, semester, "The Politics of Aesthetics," and for which, each time, I received the same B+ with a similar comment (example: "This a well-written, sympathetic view of F. Nietzsche. Thank you. F. Whitlaw.")—he would take me out to lunch to Chinese restaurants off campus, where he would talk about places he had visited and operas he had seen in Europe twenty-five years before as a graduate student, and about his teenage daughter, who apparently sat at home all day, reading novels and refusing to eat; Professor Whitlaw weighed hundreds of pounds and only read political philosophy, and his dream, I think, was to teach political philosophy in the political science department, with the occasional cross-referenced course in the philosophy department, and not intellectual history in the history department, which cross-referenced courses from other departments but rarely from its own. Many of the courses I took in college were cross-referenced, or somehow overlapped; in my senior year, I took a graduate seminar on the history of film of the 1930s for which I could have received credit in the history, economics, or communications departments, and which wasn't all that different, really, from a course I had taken the year before in the history department on American cultural history from 1914 to 1945, except that we spent more time in the graduate seminar on *Snow White and the Seven Dwarfs*. (In college, I learned confusions of varying refinement; in life, I have learned that failure is a particular road outward.) That day, after Professor Whitlaw had sat down and I went through the litany of my various entry-level jobs, which I talked about as though they had all been the same job, a cross-reference between youth and oblivion, he suddenly got excited and told me about a former graduate student of his from Germany who was now a politician in Berlin; he had written Professor Whitlaw asking for names of recent graduates who might want to move to Berlin and teach English; it was like a deus ex machina, like, I have come to learn, the ending of a baroque opera (or, if my present story were an opera, what happened before the curtain went up). Two weeks later, Professor Whitlaw was in a car accident—a rear-end collision, killed instantly; nearly three weeks later, I received a letter from him that he must have sent the day, or the day before, he died, with the names and addresses of places he had visited thirty-five years before and had mentioned to me in passing nearly a decade before (I had stopped eating lunch with him a few months before graduation, actually standing him up for the last lunch, hadn't told him about going to Europe the first time): a Parisian hotel, which I tried calling from Annette's sublet apartment after she told me to leave; a Bavarian confectionery to which I tried taking Irmgard when we were together in Munich; names of political philosophers in this or that European capital; though, strangely, not the name of his ex-student, which he had promised to send me when I had an address in Berlin. The official letter a month later offering me the job was from the director of the school in Marzahn, who had gotten my name from the Berlin Senate, who at some point must have gotten it from Professor Whitlaw; the ex-graduate student seems to have vanished, as have nearly all the places and people on Professor Whitlaw's list, some of which might have actually disappeared decades before: the Parisian hotel was a bank; the candy shop in Munich was a subway station; the names of political philosophers in Berlin, Frankfurt, and Vienna belonged to no one, and their addresses led nowhere. Of course, after I accepted the job and left Chicago a few months later, I, too, might seem to have disappeared. (Or: I disappeared years before, after graduating from college, and have reappeared here, in East Berlin.) For a while I tried to relearn German by memorizing parables of Franz Kakfa, which read like antitravelogues, can seem to be about the futility of travel, or, even, and almost technically, about the failure to arrive, like his parable "Das nächste Dorf," "The Next Village," in which the narrator's grandfather tells him that life may be too short to travel from one village to the next—even without (the grandfather warns) taking into account accidents. Running into Professor Whitlaw was a kind of accident, both for him and for me, and I sometimes think that he got into the car crash on the way home from mailing me that letter, then I tend to go to the opera, which I imagine to be a kind of penance, or, at least, which I don't enjoy as much as I think I should. I would never go to the opera with Hans-Joachim, who has known for years that he is HIV-positive and, without fail, shows up at places hours late, as though, it has occurred to me, this might postpone his dying; or he'll show up what he thinks of as days late and what I think of as unexpectedly, or else as ghostily, like Professor Whitlaw's letter. He thinks that, because I am an American, I find sex shocking, that I am shocked that men watch each other jerk off in the toilet across from the KaDeWe department store; what did shock me, apart from the smell (I walked in once and gagged, which I remember happening when I was a child and I asked my parents to take me into a pet shop at a shopping mall) was the juxtaposition, the simultaneity: there is the toilet and the department store and the restored pre–World War I subway station, forming a kind of triangle with, in the middle, a plaque that lists the names of the better-known concentration camps, above which there is an inscription: ORTE DES SCHRECKENS, DIE WIR NIE VERGESSEN DÜRFEN—places of terror that we will never be allowed to forget. The chosen verb—*dürfen* (to be allowed to) —interests me, as though remembering itself were the punishment. AIDS, for Hans-Joachim, is what Nazism is for West Germans, a cliché and a taboo, outside conversation; for East Germans, Nazism is just too remote, two villages away. I think of Hans-Joachim, whose sex life with men, unlike mine, predates AIDS (Hans-Joachim started having sex with men when he was a teenager in Hamburg, when, he told me, he would go to porno theaters off the Reeperbahn and give blow jobs to married men who reminded him of his father; I started having sex with men during my last year of college, with friends who reminded me of other friends), as a kind of pagan in Hell, damned, but not evil; I assume that he has safe sex with men because he once told me that he does, and because I assume that that is what I would do if I were in his place; I assume that Kurt and/or Sabine were working for the secret police because I cannot be certain that, had I been in their place, I wouldn't have done the same. Sodomy, in Dante's version of the Inferno, is considered a form of violence, much worse than never having been baptized; working for the secret police, I believe, would have been a form of treacherous fraud, the worst kind of sin, with its practitioners, like Judas, spending Eternity in the Inferno's ninth circle, close to Lucifer. As for me: I am just passing through, not unlike Dante, or, rather, like an American. I remember my American Legal Culture course, in which we learned that, in Anglo-American tort law, there is no general duty to rescue. Interesting coincidence: Dante's life overlapped with the life of Moses de Léon, the Spanish Jew who probably wrote the *Zohar*, or *Book of Splendor*, which is the most important literary work of the Kabbalah. Gershom Scholem wrote a memoir at the end of his life called *From Berlin to Jerusalem: Memories of My Youth*. The straightforwardness of the title conceals other meanings, could be described, perhaps, as Kabbalistic: the title's second half, for instance—"memories of my youth"—contradicts the first half, suggests a return to Berlin; Scholem—who was born in Berlin Mitte, as it happens, and was a remarkably early reader of Kafka, and who was also aware, decades before the Nazis came to power, that German Judaism, *"Deutschjudentum,"* was a contradiction, an impossibility, that there was no place in Germany for a Jew—wrote his memoir, as he wrote many of his books, in German, and claims never to have lost his Berlin accent, may even have spoken Hebrew with a Berlin accent; as his title suggests, Scholem made his home in Jerusalem, where the Messiah will reassemble the Jews at the end of time, but, even though he was a zionist interested in Messianism, he was not a Messianic zionist, was increasingly despondent over what Israel was becoming and died, coincidentally, in 1982, the year Israel invaded Lebanon; Scholem's Berlin: impossible to have lived in though never entirely left behind; Scholem's Jerusalem: never entirely arrived at (also, arguably, an impossibility). As for memoirs: I would not title mine of the other night *From Milwaukee to Berlin*, which sounds too general, like an airline flight, or specifically deceiving, like a lie, as though I were pretending that my family had once lived in Berlin, that I were, somehow, returning here. I think I could honestly call that memoir, considering how it ended, *From Wilmersdorf to Berlin Mitte*. All the guests had left; Hans-Joachim looked exhausted, like an old man, I thought. (When they get tired, adolescent-looking people in their thirties, like other people in their thirties, like people in their forties and beyond, look old, closer to death than not; people in their twenties, when they are tired, can still look like children; Hans-Joachim is twenty-nine and looks like a child until he gets tired, when he becomes ethereal, or skeletal.) I helped him clear the table and then stood around while he called a cab (although I probably would have stayed over if he had asked me). On the way back to East Berlin, the cabdriver, who was from West Berlin, got lost. He drove accidentally down the Rosa-Luxemburg-Strasse and then, after I pointed out the mistake, down the Hirtenstrasse, which doesn't cut through to the Alte Schönhauser Strasse, where the Krügers' apartment is. We drove past the small playground of the nursery school that had been in the newspapers a few days before; the nursery school teacher had been working for the secret police throughout the 1980s reporting on little children's parents, which the tabloids in West Berlin were gloating over and the broadsheets in East Berlin were mourning over. (It is out of my way, but I have walked down the Hirtenstrasse, by mistake, while trying to walk to Alexanderplatz, and I must have walked by that school, might even have seen that teacher holding hands with children too young to have parents denounced by her.) The cabdriver went past Rosa-Luxemburg-Strasse, back to the Karl-Liebknecht-Strasse, not realizing that, because of the construction site, he wouldn't be able to turn left at the Wilhelm-Pieck-Strasse (Berlin Mitte has been famously reluctant to rename its streets), and then, cursing East Germans, drove down the Prenzlauer Allee and made an illegal turn over some streetcar tracks so he could make a right turn onto the Wilhelm-Pieck-Strasse, and eventually, a left turn at the Alte Schönhauser

Strasse, which still has a no-left-turn sign at its corner (East Germany, comically, was famous for discouraging cars from turning left). I told him just to stop, that I would walk, but the cab fare was still nearly the Deutschmark equivalent of thirty dollars, which I think must be the most I have ever paid for a cab that wasn't going to or from an airport, though I remember once taking a cab from Washington Heights, where I had just slept with a black woman from the office I was temping at (she is the only black person I have ever had sex with), to the East Village, where I was sleeping on the floor of my old college roommate's apartment. I don't remember how much that cab ride cost, but I thought, as I walked through the first, and then through the second courtyard, which the room I sleep in overlooks, that even now, several years later, a thirty-dollar cab ride from Washington Heights might have gotten me all the way to Brooklyn. The Krügers had been in the apartment while I was gone and had replaced the carpet in the hallway with taped-down plastic, which made the bedroom—which, except for the bed, still looks like a living room—seem quite separate from the rest of the apartment and, even more than usual, like a museum exhibit: a composite room showing how certain families were living while I, somewhere else, was finishing up my childhood.

[4]

The demolition of the Berlin Wall—rather than its construction, as is generally supposed—was Kafkaesque and Orwellian: after having been torn down, the wall is still falling slowly, though its nominal disappearance gave birth to many dying—actually, stillborn —metaphors (the wall's construction was an exaggeration, a monstrosity, a technologically refined paranoia, essentially— almost merely—German, "German" being something of an unkillable metaphor, or perhaps a metaphor reborn). The "tearing down of the wall" (though most people often say "fall," as though it had happened naturally, during some kind of natural disaster) has become a metaphor for "the end of communism," which, some people now argue, had been foredestined in Hungary in 1956, years before the wall went up, and which, in predictably contemporary fashion (a substitution of image for idea, an anti-Platonism), has become in turn a metaphor for the tearing down of the Berlin Wall, for what people watched on their television screens in November of 1989. Germans use the expression *"die Wende,"* or "turning point," to describe the wall falling down, though seldom to describe the end of communism as such, more to describe themselves and their disrupted habits; Irmgard told me that her mother, for years, has politely referred to menopause as *"die Wende."* The real turning point for East Germans, they will invariably claim, came on November 4, five days before the wall fell, when a million people showed up at Alexanderplatz to demand, among other things, a more perfect—which, for some of them, might have meant a more literal—kind of socialism. West

Germans think of July 3, 1990, as the real turning point (the point of no return, in this case); on July 3, the Deutschmark became the official currency in East Germany, and East Germans got to swap their East German marks at a one-to-one, or, as the amount got larger, at a two-to-one rate, instead of at the ten-to-one rate they were worth, and everyone now agrees that this all happened much too soon, that July 3 should have come months later (last summer July 3 was remembered with disgust or embarrassment, or simply ignored, as though it had been forgotten). The most embittered East Germans talk about the real turning point as having come over a period of time, in the months after November 9, when protesting East Germans began changing their banners from "We are *the* people!" which sounded democratic, to "We are *one* people!" which sounded nationalistic. October 3 is "the Day of German Unity," the official national German holiday commemorating what a German can describe as the "unification," "reunification," or "unity" of Germany. Germans who were against unification say "unification"; like many non-Germans, they didn't approve of a powerful Germany in the center of Europe, and they don't like to concede that the previously unified Germany had been, after all, Hitler's Germany; the fact that they say "unification" reveals their political failure (a negligible amount of Germans ended up being against unification and in any case found other ways to describe it) and their love of fantasy, makes them seem internationally minded, conceals their (utter) Germanness. Now, years later, nearly everybody says "reunification" unthinkingly, or because they want to remember the other German unification under Bismarck, or, to put it politely, because the association with Hitler is not a preemptive one. Politicians and news broadcasters say "unity," which, in its literal English translation, "oneness," probably sounds the most German (the most threatening, the most awkward). When it came time to pick a Day of German Unity, November 9 was, of course, the most obvious and the least likely choice: before 1989, "November 9" was practically a euphemism for Kristallnacht, which began on the night of November 9, 1938, and is remembered, because of German indifference, as the turning point in the Nazis' persecution of the Jews, as the beginning of the Holocaust; before 1989, November 9 was a national day of shame, soberly observed on television documentaries and in newspaper editorials, and, occasionally, in the Bundestag itself; now, people write *Volksmusik* songs about November 9 with titles like "On the Ninth of November My Heart Was Full of Pride!" On November 9, 1918, Kaiser Wilhelm II abdicated, and November 9 has also been occasionally remembered as the anniversary of the death (in German, one word, *Todestag*, literally "day of death") of the Germany unified under Bismarck. (The Kabbalist—for lack of a better word— in me wonders: Is there a connection—other than the obvious, German, one—between the beginning of the Holocaust and the end of communism?) The official Day of German Unity—October 3 —seems arrived at arbitrarily, makes people a little nervous, isn't generally celebrated except on television and in newspaper editorials and at an official government-sponsored party, usually in some medium-size city that many non-Germans might never have heard of; banks and stores are closed, though, as they are on Sundays, when the whole country seems to disappear from itself, and which, in the figurative sense of the literal English translation, is a kind of *Todestag*. Most people, except politicians and newscasters, still say "East" and "West" Germany, as most people in Berlin, except the most nationalist-seeming taxi drivers, still insist on "East" and "West" Berlin, though sometimes hesitantly, the way Germans in certain circumstances speak their dialects. To distinguish between East and West Germany, the politicians and newscasters have to say *"die neuen und die alten Bundesländer,"* or "the new and old federal states," which sounds like newspeak, or, rather, like its opposite—an overly specific, too long euphemism. The German language, of course, is filled with such euphemisms: the woman who runs the school where I teach used to run foreign-language courses at one of the adult education schools (they're called *"Volkshochschulen,"* or "peoples' high schools," which sounds like a onetime Nazi, or Communist, neologism); her

Prussian-sounding title was *Fachbereichsleiterin der Fremdsprach-kurse*. When people want to mean the old East Germany and not the new one, they say the DDR, which was the German acronym for the German Democratic Republic (which wasn't democratic, and wasn't a republic, but was thought of at the time, and is still remembered, as even more German than the BRD, or Federal Republic of Germany, which is, in fact, a federal republic, though generally thought of as too Americanized to be German in the evocative sense of the word, which is really the only way Germans themselves like to use it). The old East Germany, of course, like any socialist country, was a mine of euphemisms, some of which people like to chuckle about now, like *Kartoffel Stäbchen*, which means "potato stick," and which, in its plural form, was what politicians and restaurant owners and scrupulous citizens in the DDR were supposed to call french fries, which Germans had always called, and still call, *Pommes frites*, which they pronounce in strangely perfect French or Germanize by just saying the first word, *Pommes*, as though it were a German word. (*"Pommes,"* when pronounced in German, sounds like a Yiddish word not derived from German, like *tsoriss* or *bubkes*.) While I am on the subject, and though I am sure President Kennedy was understood, *"Ich bin ein Berliner"* means "I am a jelly donut." A German jelly donut, which is filled with cherry, or apricot, or prune preserves and covered with glaze or powdered sugar, is called *ein Berliner*, except in Berlin, where it's called a *Pfannkuchen*, or pancake; *"Ich bin Berliner"* means "I am from Berlin," while *"Ich bin ein Berliner,"* told to an audience of Berliners, means, possibly, "I am a jelly donut from out of town." I like to think of the demolition of the Berlin Wall (which people can no longer bear to talk about; words like "reunification" and expressions like "the new federal states" and "the end of communism" and "after the wall" seem to have become euphemisms for hopelessness, which, in Germany, shows up in people as an exhausted brutality, as a kind of cold explosion) as "the rebuilding of an absence," which sounds like a metaphor for dying, rather than a dying metaphor. "Dying metaphor" is Orwell's phrase for words or phrases that have lost their evocative power. "Kafka-esque" and "Orwellian" are virtually textbook examples of dying metaphors (along with, though to a lesser extent, "textbook example"), but "dying metaphor" itself sounds like a phrase Walter Benjamin might have used, especially in his letters to Gershom Scholem, to describe the phenomenon of Franz Kafka. (Scholem and Benjamin were "good men of excellence or virtue," I like to assume, and therefore, perfect friends in the Aristotelian sense; I think of myself as essentially friendless, or, rather, don't think of the word "friendship" as describing my relationships with people, especially here, and would, instead, defer to something I read not too long ago, but didn't underline and can't find again, in an English-language Midrash reader, which ran: "It is of greater value to be a stranger than to be kind to strangers.") Benjamin actually wrote in one letter that Kafka's writing represents "a tradition fallen ill," which is a theme in Kafka's story "The Great Wall of China," in which the Chinese emperor and his authority are as vague as rumors. The real wall in China and the wall in Berlin, I once remember reading, had something in common: they were the two man-made structures on earth visible from outer space. The wall in the Kafka story, which was certainly inspired by the real wall in China, remained unfinished after having been completed: it was constructed in sections rather than continuously and there were said to be gaps, as though the wall were a series of walls, a labyrinth rather than a barricade. It isn't especially imaginable in the Kafka story that the Great Wall could be torn down; its demolition, like its construction, would seem beyond human endeavor, would remain necessarily incomplete. Germans, famous for accomplishing the unimaginable (both the Holocaust and the subsequent German ability to pretend that it didn't happen—to shop and to piss and to jerk off near a Holocaust memorial—are unimaginable, are metaphors for death these days, in fact, familiar enough to be dying metaphors), not only managed to build a perfect, unbreachable wall, they even managed to tear it down, as far as the rest of the world is concerned, in a matter of months; tourists walk around

in a daze and have to ask "Where was it?" "Was it there?" "No,"
they are told by Berliners who lived with the wall most of their
lives. "It was there. Or maybe over there." The wall's location,
which, after all, couldn't have changed, has become a rumor, while
the wall itself, changed to the point of disappearing, still exerts its
powers, which people acknowledge by pretending that it's still
standing even as they're driving through it. In the Kafka story, the
remoteness of the wall, which feels as vague as the authority that
commissioned it, is said to unify the Chinese; the Germans, divided as much as ever by their now absent wall, no longer have
their division in common. I, too, pretend: I walk around Berlin as
though I had a purpose for being here. January is almost over and
I only have little more than a month to find an apartment (February shouldn't even be called a "month." Who doesn't find the
first of March unsettling? Who doesn't wake up on March 1 and
feel that time has bent and who, every fourth year, doesn't greet
February 29 as an ordinary day, and then, after admitting its ex-
traordinariness, find it even more unsettling than a March 1?) and,
after this term ends in the middle of March, no job. Frau Kohlenberg, the ex–*Fachbereichsleiterin der Fremdsprachkurse*, told me that
they were cutting back on the number of courses, though this was
a lie according to Brett, the guy from Pittsburgh; the truth is that
they don't think I am a very good teacher because half of my "English for the 'Federal Certificate of Fluency' Examination" class
failed their exams (the results came back last week). After I pay the
last month of rent to the Krügers, and if I don't eat or drink or go
anywhere, I will have only 1550 Deutschmarks to find a new apartment and a new job, or to buy a ticket home; I decided to call my
parents, as though they could save me. My parents used to be
beneficent and smothering, now they are enfeebled and remote;
they think of my teaching job as a form of success, and I couldn't
tell them that I had been fired. When I called, they had just come
back from a discount drug outlet, where they had been buying
diapers for themselves (my mother has kidney disease and occasionally needs to be catheterized, and my father has had his en-

larged prostate nipped and is pretty much incontinent); "we just got back from a 'togetherness trip,' " my mother said, using the sort of expression she occasionally picks up from daytime TV, and by which she meant "buying diapers." I had a vision of them much sicker than they are, bedridden, and imagined myself back in Milwaukee, driving to the discount drug outlet to buy the diapers; to kill time, I would drive to an outlet on the other side of town, then drive along Lake Michigan and smell the breeze; I thought of the Kafka story "The Judgment," in which Georg Bendemann, the Kafka stand-in, is taking care of his presumably bedridden father, who, at the end, rises up, stands on his bed and condemns Bendemann to death by drowning, after which Bendemann goes and jumps off a bridge. My father got on the phone; "How do you feel," I said at first, then I told him that the school was having problems, that it would probably close, and he asked me if I had any money saved. ("You earned close to fifty grand last year, no taxes, that's like eighty grand here, and what have you got? You've got *bubkes*.") Eighty grand is what my sister earns. I told him I wouldn't have a job. ("So you have to teach at that school? Who says you can't teach at some other school?") His voice thundered through the old East German exchange that the post office at Alexanderplatz still uses, telling me, for the hundredth, thousandth, time—like, I thought, some senile judge— that I should have never dropped accounting, that I had nothing to fall back on, a phrase which, that day, I took literally for the first time, although my father, who only means things literally, must have always meant it that way; I saw myself leaning back against nothing, falling backward, ending up in Milwaukee in my childhood bedroom. He said other things that I don't care to remember, that I have to forget every time he tells me, mostly having to do with all the jobs I have quit, which he likes to list in chronological order, and dramatically, as though he were pandering to a jury that had already made up its mind. I remembered something that I had thought about occasionally, though not since I had come to Germany, a parable I had heard at that Jewish summer camp, about someone whom I have remembered as having been called Moishe.

Moishe the Tailor

Moishe, a tailor, had a wife and three sons. On the first Shabbat after Simchas Torah, he was feeling a little confused and decided to go for a walk. There was a birch forest down the road from his village, and, although he had not been in the forest since his youth, he walked there in the dying light of the afternoon. In the forest, he walked and walked; "I can't stop," he thought. Darkness fell, and the birch trees looked like pillars of ashes in the moonlight; Moishe continued his walk. "I've never been *this* far before," he thought, with a fear and excitement he had not known since his youth. Deep in the forest, there was a distant light; Moishe was walking toward the light, when he suddenly heard singing voices. Moishe thought that the voices were singing the most beautiful song he had ever heard; as he walked closer to the light, he began to hum the melody. The light was coming from a cossacks' campfire, around which cossacks were singing some sort of cossack folk song. One of the cossacks heard a noise in the woods and ran boldly into the darkness, where he found little Moishe humming. He dragged Moishe by his caftan back to the clearing, and, all at once, the cossacks decided to burn the Jew. They tied him to a tree, then they put straw around his pathetic, worn-out boots, then they put a log from the fire on top of the straw. Moishe was still humming; the fire had singed his beard, burnt through his boots, but his eyes were glazed with joy. One of the cossacks, possibly the leader, reminded the others of the old cossack legend that it was a sin to kill a madman. They all looked at Moishe, who was humming their song louder than before, louder than all of these cossacks together could have sung it. They poured water on the fire, untied Moishe, and left him on his back, humming, with his face turned toward the dark sky. Two days later, his sons, half-insane with worry, found him in the clearing; he was still humming. They took him home, and his wife put him into bed and fed him; "all he does is hum," she told her sister. Months went by, and Moishe wouldn't stop humming. Moishe's wife and her sister went to see the Rebbe, who decided that Moishe would have to be sent away. That afternoon the Rebbe wrote a letter, and, weeks later, a cart came to take away Moishe. Men carried Moishe's bed, with the humming Moishe still in it, out of the house and put it onto the cart. As the cart started to move, Moishe stopped humming. "Where are they taking me?" he asked his wife. (The villagers gasped, looked around for their Rebbe.) "We thought you were mad," said Moishe's wife. "All you did for months was hum." "I heard a beautiful melody," said Moishe. "And I didn't want to forget it."

I don't know where this parable comes from; I don't remember much about the girl who told it (it was late at night around a campfire; the girl was one of the head counselors and, conceivably, a rabbinical student). I sat outside the socialist post office at Alexanderplatz, having just finished talking to my parents, and remembered the parable. What could it mean? In my interpretation, I am Moishe, and my father is everyone else (Moishe's sons, his wife, the sister-in-law, the Rebbe, villagers, the men who come at the end) except the cossacks, who are German, and their melody isn't beautiful, but ugly, the ugliest melody that my Moishe has ever heard, which, as I sat there, seemed to explain my reluctance to leave Germany. In Kafka's version of psychoanalysis, as expounded in a famous letter to Max Brod, the father's Jewishness is at the root of the "father complex": the son, to outdo the father, tries to become even more assimilated (more German); Kafka's version describes the son's inevitable failure by more or less comparing the son to an insect caught on a piece of flypaper, with the flypaper representing the father's Jewishness. Elsewhere in the letter, Kafka talks about the wit of Karl Kraus (the Viennese satirist who is no longer often read but often read about; his writings, which have been replaced by memories of reading his writing, are no longer really satirical, but legendary, lush) as a kind of Yiddish-German, or *Mauscheln* (the letter is sometimes called "the *Maus-*

cheln Letter"); in the letter's English translation, Kafka's Karl Kraus sounds like my father (" 'He writes? Who about?' "), or, for that matter, like my mother's father, who died when I was sixteen, but who used to come to our house on Saturday afternoons to eat *Sulze* (which is a gelatinous sausage, eminently disgusting, especially popular in Berlin, not unheard of in Milwaukee), to smoke a cigar, and to scream about cars ("What Pontiac?" he'd say to my father, who likes Pontiacs. "You need a GM car like a hole in the head!"). In the camp counselor's original parable, Moishe might have been called something else. My name is not Simon Lurie. I was given my middle name, Henry, after my grandfather's sister, Henrietta, who died when my mother was a child, although my mother once told me that she had planned to name me after my grandfather's younger brother, Samuel, who died in Austria-Hungary of diphtheria at the age of five, and whom my grandfather kept a picture of next to his bed, but her brother beat her to it and named my cousin, who is a year older, Sophie, which she hates, insisting that people call her Amy, which is her middle name; none of us grandchildren were given "Jewish" names; my father, perhaps because of the orphanage, doesn't have a middle name and doesn't know his Jewish name; thanks to his real parents, is named Israel, which is, of course, very Jewish-sounding; he doesn't mind being called Izzy, which is fairly Jewish-sounding. He claims not to remember the orphanage but vividly remembers the Jewish foster homes, which, now, when I think back on his stories, sound like a combination of Charles Dickens's novels and Molly Goldberg's radio show, which I learned about in one of my history classes after having heard about it from my parents (my mother didn't like it; my father did). My father doesn't seem to know anything about his parents except that they came from Latvia and were named Luriansky when they first got to Milwaukee and then, just before he was born, changed their name to Levine, which got changed to La Vine at the orphanage. Simon, which is a possible permutation of Samuel, is the name of the best known of Jesus' apostles (Simon Peter), and of the least known (Simon the

Zealot); Lurie, like Luriansky, like Levine, suggests a connection to the Levite tribe, and, in a slightly different form, was the name of the great Kabbalist Isaac Luria ("La Vine," of course, sounds French, or vaguely black, or like the name of a drag queen, ridiculous, except when preceded by my father's name, when it sounds comically, and, because of the long *i*, vaguely elegantly, or emphatically, even ridiculously, Jewish). A *Mauschel* was a Jewish peddler—is derived from Moishe, or Moses—and *Mauscheln* was his language; in my version of the parable, Moishe was named after Moses, the law-giver, and after nobody in particular—after the giver of the law and after a taker, even a squanderer, of the law; after a first and a last. Kafka, according to Walter Benjamin, didn't actually write parables ("that is their misery and their beauty, that they had to become *more* than parables"); Isaac Bashevis Singer wrote parablelike fantasies that can read as parables without morals. Lesson in futility: trying to talk about Franz Kafka with a Czech person; lesson in the fantastical: listening to a Polish person talk about Isaac Bashevis Singer (eventually the other party and I just have to pretend that we are talking about the same writer). In Prague, Kafka is in vogue, appears on T-shirts, is a sort of Mickey Mouse for the Disneyland that Prague has become; in Warsaw, Isaac Bashevis Singer is in every bookshop window, conceivably surrounded on both sides by anti-Semitic graffiti, usually Jewish stars on the end of a gallows. Czech people can read Kafka and forget that he was a Jew, let alone a German-speaking Jew, and apparently find him very funny, the way Kafka's German-speaking Jewish friends did when he read them his stories out loud; Polish people seem to read Singer, whose world they view as impossibly remote, the way Germans read Grimm's fairy tales. In visits to Prague and to Warsaw, I always end up at the new vegetarian restaurants—for the food, I tell myself, as though I weren't going there to get away from the Czechs and the Poles (and the French and the Italian and the German businesspeople, and the Australian and the German tourists), and to find Americans. At the vegetarian restaurant in Prague, which is near the Church of St. Ludmila, and which with the discotheque and the performance space and the CD shop forms a kind of Complex Americana, I always order the veggie melt and can relax, because the music (Elvis Costello, Rickie Lee Jones, R.E.M.) is playing loudly enough for me to ignore the American college students, who are in Prague teaching English and going to poetry readings and auditioning for English-language productions of *Grease* and going to the "networking workshops" run by one of Prague's English-language newspapers. (But, I have to confess to myself, as I eat the veggie melt and wish that I had ordered the vegetarian pizza, haven't I come here to do just the opposite? To talk with these people?) In Warsaw, the vegetarian restaurant is in the New Town, near the Church of the Visitation of the Blessed Virgin Mary; unlike the vegetarian restaurant in Prague, the vegetarian restaurant in Warsaw doesn't specialize in vegetarian versions of student union food made with local ingredients (i.e., red cabbage), but in vegetarian versions of Polish food—cutlets made with lentils, tofu shaped like a duck breast and then roasted and covered with plum sauce—though the American Peace Corps workers and English teachers, sitting on the patio and talking about their graduate school applications, are usually eating salads. Warsaw's New Town had been built about a century after its Old Town, which was built in the thirteenth and fourteenth centuries, though both were simply razed to the ground by the Nazis; now the New Town and the Old Town are the same age, rebuilt after the war and praised for their resemblance to the real ones (what I like to imagine happening at the vegetarian restaurant in Warsaw: an American tourist claiming that his roasted tofu tastes even more like roast duck than the roast duck that he had eaten at his hotel), with the resemblance augmented, according to one guidebook, by accruement of pollution on the buildings' façades, which the guidebook referred to as "patina." Across the river from the Old Town, there is a district of Warsaw called Praga, or Prague, where, I assume, Canaletto worked on his paintings of Warsaw's Old Town, which were used, like his paintings of Dresden's Old Town were used in Dresden, after the war in its

reconstruction; the Prague district of Warsaw used to be quite Jewish, like the rest of Warsaw, and was where the Poles sat watching
the Germans level the Warsaw Ghetto after its uprising, and where
the Red Army sat watching the Germans level the rest of Warsaw
after *its* uprising. Many of the buildings in the Prague district—
where, until the end of communism, there was an infamously
rough black market and where guidebooks still warn visitors not
to go, as though the wall were still standing—never had to be
entirely rebuilt but seem to have been bombed and neglected to
the point of no longer looking like buildings; they look like mountains, with doorways looking like caves, not unlike the New Town
of Dresden, some of which made it through the firestorm, and
which looks incalculably older than Dresden's Old Town, which
the city is still busy rebuilding. Prague (the Czech city), which was
not at all destroyed, and Warsaw, which was mostly entirely destroyed, feel like inversions of each other (Prague, the Czech city,
and Prague, the district in Warsaw, which, compared to the other
Prague, was pretty much destroyed, seem to have nothing in common except their name, and, perhaps, vague connotations of intactness), except when you're wandering around Prague looking
for evidence of Franz Kafka, where, in spite of the fact that most
of the places where he lived and worked are still standing, something having to do with him seems to be entirely missing, destroyed (the Jewishness, the Germanness; all gone, except in
versions presented for, or brought in by, tourists), not that I would
want to find it; if I read Kafka before I go to sleep or to get back
to sleep after I have woken up in the middle of the night, I don't
feel well the next day, have what I will remember to have been
nightmares. Prague and Dresden (which was partially entirely destroyed, though, really, considering what survived, essentially destroyed) are also inversions of each other (Berlin, which was also
essentially entirely destroyed but was entirely differently rebuilt, is
an inversion of itself; hermaphroditic), though Dresden and Warsaw, like East and West Germans "after the wall" (or rather, "after
'after the wall' "), are just too different to have even their oppo-

sition in common. Professor Whitlaw told me that he wanted to visit Dresden and Prague, although I don't recall his ever mentioning Warsaw; he often talked about wanting to visit Kaliningrad (once Königsberg, the city where the Prussian kings were crowned and where Kant spent most of his life, a capital of high—not in the linguistic sense—Germanness, and, after having been completely destroyed, was rebuilt and repopulated with a fairly exact version of Soviet society; compared to all these other cities—Dresden, Lemberg, Breslau, Warsaw, etc.—even more absent from itself, more negated) and place a wreath on the postwar grave of Immanuel Kant; I remember his telling me that Intourist had once told him that visas to Kaliningrad, which was a gigantic military installation and "closed" to foreigners, were only granted to previous visitors: "One never goes to Kaliningrad a first time," he enjoyed saying. I read in a newspaper article that the people who actually live in Kaliningrad want to change the name to something else (Kalinin was a Stalinist stooge), back to Königsberg, or else Kantgrad, though I imagine the place as being essentially unnameable, with any name being a legalism, a technicality, a substitution for a name; I imagine the place—about which I have seen serious, mournful television documentaries and sentimental television documentaries meant to pander to old, exiled East Prussians; and about which I have seen four-color picture spreads in newspaper travel supplements, in which remnants of redbrick buildings seem to be growing out of the ground, like vines—as unimaginable, as unnameable as the God of the Jews. According to one travel article, all of Kaliningrad looks like the part of the center of Dresden that was not rebuilt to resemble its prewar self —unrebuilt, and the ugliest place I have ever seen, unseeable. I have stopped in Dresden a few times on my way to or from Prague, though I never made it to any of the "alternative" bars on the other side of the Elbe, in the New Town, one of which was something of a gay bar before skinheads blew it up this week. It has been a bad week for me, for gays in Dresden, and for Catholics in West Berlin: a priest at a Catholic church in Charlottenburg was exposed in last Sunday's newspaper as a secret police informer; the twist in the story—apparently many priests and pastors in East Germany, and in places like West Berlin and Bonn, had worked for the East German secret police in numbers not much smaller than artists, athletes, and politicians—was that the priest, who is my father's age, had also worked for the secret police under the Nazis. Or perhaps it wasn't such a bad week—at least for me. After Frau Kohlenberg told me on Friday that I wouldn't be teaching next term, I felt briefly relieved, almost ecstatic; I waited for the S-Bahn and looked back over Helene-Weigel-Platz, which looked like a gray hole in the air, and thought that I would only have to go back there six more times, then I wondered what I would do for money, where I would sleep (Irmgard is moving out of the art historian's next week, and going to Hans-Joachim's apartment, to sleep in the huge, stripped-down living room until she finds a new apartment). "I have to think clearly," I told myself on the train, and decided to visit the houseful of Americans I know in Prenzlauer Berg: I met them all at once last winter, at the last party Burt Kaminsky gave before he was evicted, and either I follow them around or avoid them. (In Warsaw and Prague, where the Americans are innumerable, or at least more conspicuous, I am ambivalently—inevitably but hesitantly—American; in Berlin, where Americans are less conspicuous, or just less enthusiastic, older, I am anti-American or American.) I consider them to be like me (indolent, bad with money, promiscuous, which I would be if I could, messy) but more so, worse in every respect, which makes them disgusting or comforting, too American, or just American enough. The atmosphere in their apartments (they have taken over a whole back house of apartments in the most decrepit part of Prenzlauer Berg, on a street that doesn't seem to have ever been rebuilt after the war; all of the street's buildings still have their prewar advertisements—for cobbler shops and bakeries and fruit-and-vegetable stands, for a mustard factory, for a photographer's studio—which were painted right onto the stone and are slowly peeling off; I think of the old advertisements as "city skin") can remind me of Madison, or make me feel as sternly impatient as someone's father; sometimes I want to tell them to clean up their apartments, to get a job, to grow up. They are all, actually, older than I am, and make "sculpture" or plan improvisational performance pieces, or practice stand-up comedy, and they only have money after a "performance," when they invite their friends to pay ten marks to watch them, or when one of them is working as a bartender somewhere in West Berlin; they live on rice and beans, which they sometimes have to buy with empty beer bottles, and shoplift their cigarettes; occasionally, after they have invested in some drugs, they have lots of money, and throw parties, or buy new televisions. They have been drifting this way for years, first in West Berlin, then, astonishingly soon after the wall came down, in East Berlin, where they have preserved their West Berlin habits far better than real West Berliners (a real West Berliner: a West German who came to West Berlin in the '70s or '80s to drift, to do nothing, and who now finds that the West Germany he was trying to get away from has followed him). Kerwin, at thirty-nine, is the paterfamilias and the stand-up comic; he imagines himself to be a post-1989, black, middle-class Lenny Bruce, though his performances in real life are more intense, more convincing. He has at various times, though, not, I believe, simultaneously, been a graduate student in set design, a male prostitute, a female impersonator (he passes around pictures of himself dressed as Diana Ross or as "Miss Shirley Bassey of Cardiff, Wales"), a cocaine addict, a drug dealer, an office manager and father of two, a de facto housewife in Hamburg, a teacher of army brats in West Berlin, and now, in East Berlin, he has formed a nonprofit organization for the promotion of American stand-up comedy and is waiting for "contributions" from wealthy West Berliners, or for money from the multicultural fund of the Berlin Senate, so that he can pay his back rent and get a couple of fillings replaced. He likes to kiss people on the lips, especially, I have noticed, when he has a cold; I don't like to kiss anybody, really, and am a little paranoid about getting colds (I always wash my hands after riding on the U-Bahn, as I had washed my hands after riding on the subway in New York and on the El in Chicago—thoroughly, and now, here, I suppose, also sentimentally); "I have a cold," I said, when I went there after school and he leaned over for a kiss. "Do you think I care?" he said, and then tried to stick his tongue in my mouth when he kissed me. "Oh, admit it. You half-straight boys just love us black folks." He stuck his hand under my sweater and grabbed a handful of flesh. "Simon says, 'Eat candy bars.' " He had answered the door at Karen's apartment. (Karen is from Long Island and Jewish and makes Jewish plastic surgeon jokes in her performance pieces—"I used to be Jewish until I had my breast reduction surgery; now I'm half-Jewish"—and has a pierced nose, is cantankerously thirty-five, generous.) Kerwin and Al, Karen's boyfriend (the sculptor, though they all help him with his sculptures), were watching "The Oprah Winfrey Show" on a satellite channel. Kerwin, who talks to tele-visions, said at a woman in the studio audience who was asking a question, "Girlfriend! Don't you know where to buy yo' glasses." (Kerwin grew up in a white suburb of Seattle, has to affect his black acccent.) Al, who was drinking a beer, laughed, then Karen, who was cooking vegetarian chili, walked into the living room with her glasses upside down. The apartment usually smells like garbage (Karen and Al found their mattress on the street; in a dumpster, they found dozens of pairs of old ladies' shoes that Karen likes to stumble around in, and basketfuls of old East German books that Al eventually wants to use in his sculptures) but now also smelled of hashish and cigarettes and black beans and East German coal, and only vaguely of garbage. Al, I assume, is also thirty-five; I don't think we have ever had a conversation alone, and he is usually silent—stoned, actually—around other people; Karen talks about her performance pieces, or, if Al's not around, about other men she has crushes on, like the two West German students living across the courtyard; Kerwin claims to be celibate, by which he seems to mean only sleeping with other Americans in the house (Karen, a few times; not Al; Toby and Henry, who, according to Kerwin, are also "half-straight white boys"; not Tabitha); every few months he goes to a gay bathhouse in West Berlin; once, when I saw him the day after, he said, "I fucked my brains out last night. What did you do?" Kerwin, when it comes to Germans wwhom he calls "Germs," except for his "ex-husband" in Hamburg, whom he calls "Lutzi"), can speak in what I think of as scatalogical homilies. "They just want our Jew-black-Puerto-Rican asses" is what he has to say about neo-Nazi violence. Germans on the U-Bahn look the way they do because "they all have their heads up each other's asses." Germans and Turks have a lot in common because German and Turkish middle-aged women are all "big-assed mammas." When I told Karen and Kerwin about losing my job (they already knew about the Krügers' kicking me out), Kerwin said, "Oh poor baby! And I know you were saving up for rabbinical school," then they both said that I could move in with either of them and stay as long as I wanted, rolled me a joint "for the road," offered me a beer; Kerwin came up behind me and rubbed my neck and shoulders. Once there was a party at Kerwin's apartment where half of the people in the room seemed to be Americans in their thirties dressed, pretty much, as East Germans (except for Luis, a friend of Kerwin's, who really is a drag queen, at Dollywood, one of the tourist-trap drag shows in West Berlin; Luis does Helmut Berger in *The Damned* doing Marlene Dietrich in *The Blue Angel*, which was Kerwin's idea—he calls it "deconstructionist"—although I imagine that the West German tourists just think he's doing Marlene Dietrich, which I said to Kerwin, who said, "Deconstructionist! That's what I mean!"), or Russians whom Toby had met, who made lots of money selling Soviet memorabilia at the Brandenburg Gate and, that day, had bought themselves Ralph Lauren clothes at the KaDeWe and were dressed, I thought, as certain American college students had dressed in the early 1980s, except that their clothes were too pressed. I still wear old Ralph Lauren button-down shirts and polo shirts, which I have been buying, or, actually, which my parents or sister have bought for me, since high school, and, that night, considered my own Ralph Lauren shirt and blue jeans as a kind of drag, felt dressed as myself ten years younger, or dressed as a nouveau riche Russian, or conceivably, as myself fifteen, or fifty, years older (I looked at the Russians in their brand-new, familiar clothes, and I thought: I have been wearing these clothes all my life. These are the clothes I am going to die in); and not, properly speaking, in drag at all—dressed, merely, as myself.

The Employer and the Employee

Susi just loved the Kurfürstendamm. She loved getting up early on Saturday mornings, when a man from West Berlin came to manage the dry cleaning store and take the week's gross back with him to the West, and she rode the S-Bahn all the way from Hellersdorf to Bahnhof Zoo; she loved to watch the city change—like a caterpillar into a butterfly—from the concrete blocks of Hellersdorf and Marzahn to the bright crowds of the Ku'damm. (Susi hated Hellersdorf, but she liked her apartment; she loved cleaning her apartment on Friday night, and then waking up on Saturday and drinking her coffee in her clean kitchen.) She always bought something on the Ku'damm, sometimes only one thing—a hair ribbon, a bracelet from someone on the street—and then wore it to work on Monday to see if Olaf would notice. She often tried to make jokes with Olaf about Silke, the veterinarian whom Olaf worked for on Saturday (though, starting in April, he would also have to work at the dry cleaners on Saturday; Susi kept reminding herself to tell him), or about his dark blond hair, which she called "dirty." "Your hair is so dirty," she would say first thing Monday morning. "It just stinks!" (Actually Olaf took two showers a day, smelled like soap.) "Filthy dirty," Susi would say, sticking her nose in Olaf's hair, breathing deeply. And Susi liked to cook from recipes she would cut out of West German women's magazines. On the U-Bahn, on her way to work, she liked to daydream about having Olaf over for dinner on a Saturday night; she would make salade niçoise with ingredients she had bought that morning near the Ku'damm at the KaDeWe (and saved up all week to buy). He would arrive at exactly eight o'clock. (Olaf always got to work at exactly nine-thirty, as though he were standing outside the door until he had to go in.) Susi would play classical music on her new cable radio system; they would joke about work. Everything would be wonderful, until Olaf finished his salad: then he would pick up the bowl, hold it to his lips, and drink the dregs of the salad dressing. (Susi's father and brother always drank their salad dressing.) Susi would never be able to think of Olaf the same way again; the evening would end before ten o'clock, in strange silence. At the door, Olaf would shake her hand, and show up at work ten minutes late on Monday (Susi was always early; she was, after all, supposed to be the manager). Sometimes, when Susi was alone, like last Saturday night, when she made herself salade niçoise with ingredients she had bought at the new discount supermarket in Marzahn, she, too, would drink her salad dressing, but only because no one else was there, and because it reminded her of her father, who died when she was fifteen.

Like everyone else in this town, it seems, I sometimes get my head shaved; well, not entirely shaved—I ask for the two-millimeter attachment to be put on the clippers first. I go to Kreuzberg, to a place called Kaiserschnitt (which literally means "Caeser's cut," though would be translated as "cesarean section"; Germans think that getting your hair cut at a place called Kaiserschnitt is hilarious), where they specialize in short haircuts, which is how people all over Europe are wearing their hair. In London, at one of those mixed gay bars, there is a skinhead night, and you can only get in if your head looks shaved ("Oh I'm sure *you* could get in," Wulf said to me at Hans-Joachim's housewarming party); they even keep clippers at the door. Real skinheads and *Autonomen* also shave their heads, though the skinheads never have sideburns, and the *Autonomen* sometimes leave a ponytail, which they dye a bright shade of whatever (usually blue or red). Once after getting my hair cut at Kaiserschnitt (which, that particular day, I had found especially enjoyable: I was late for my appointment and had to run there and was sweating, and the tall woman with the bleached crew cut—instead of the menacing, bald, businesslike owner, who doesn't even seem to have any stubble—shaved my head; she touched my sweating

head with gentle firmness, without any hesitation; I made a connection between the way Germans take off their clothes and shake
hands and bump into each other, and, for a moment, I liked being
in Germany, liked Germans' almost prosaic brand of physicality,
liked having that woman shave my head, in spite of the connotations, found it erotic, though to a real German, there is nothing
less erotic than a mere nude body, nothing more erotic than a
disguised one, the more in drag the better), I took a cab back to
Prenzlauer Berg, and the taxi driver told me to be careful because
late at night an *Autonome* might confuse me with a skinhead and
beat me up; "I have sideburns," I said, touching a shadow of side-
burn on my face. "And besides. I'm an American." The words
"skinhead" and *"Autonome"* function in peoples' subconscious as
euphemisms for "Nazi" and "Communist," as though 1992 could
really have been 1929; in conversation, the words "skinhead" and
"Autonome" suggest juvenile delinquency, *West Side Story* rather
than *Cabaret*. Germans love *Cabaret*: it makes them feel important,
glamorous; they talk about *Cabaret* the way people from Milwaukee talk about the Milwaukee Brewers, or, perhaps, about the Milwaukee Braves. Kerwin is somebody's idea of Sally Bowles, though
not a German's idea (Germans are buoyantly racist; they still refer
to a certain kind of cream-filled chocolate-covered cookie as a "nig-
ger kiss" and love to watch minstrel shows on television). And not
my idea: a few months ago I saw *Cabaret* on television dubbed into
German, and thought that, considering what is going on in Germany, there was something disgusting about *Cabaret* (I thought of
a scale version of a concentration camp made, perhaps, out of
sugar cubes; a period version of contemporary events), deciding
that a German might watch *Cabaret* and think that 1992 could
never have been like 1929 and feel off the hook, entertained.
Karen, who dropped out of film school before coming to Berlin,
did an autobiographical performance piece called "I Am a Video
Camera." Actually all of her performance pieces are autobiographical, and they are all done in English (none of these people, who
have been here for years, speaks German), not understood by the

Germans who show up and already memorized by the Americans, who are Karen's friends and have watched her rehearse for weeks, and, in any case, have already heard her stories (for purposes of narrative closure, I have thought of Karen as a failed, Jewish version of Annette, with the failure making all the difference). The other day at her apartment, we all tried to think of a title for Kerwin's new piece (he is planning on branching out from stand-up comedy into performance art), and I thought of that moment in Canetti's autobiography when he finally meets Karl Kraus in Berlin (Kraus, in Vienna, had been Canetti's hero, and would remain— even after Kraus supported the Catholic fascist Dollfuss and then, as if consequently, died—an obsession, a vanishing standard) around a table at which people are trying to come up with a title for the as yet untitled *Threepenny Opera*. (Of all the accounts of Weimar Berlin that I have read—or could even imagine—I like Canetti's the best; he makes Berlin, which he visited in 1928 and describes in a chapter called "The Throng of Names," sound like a place pulling itself apart, as though it had put itself into a centrifuge, as though a centrifuge were a ride at an amusement park; "reality," Canetti writes of Berlin, mournfully, characteristically, with detached horror, "was not at its center." Now that Germany is no longer divided, no longer has a missing center, the legacy of Nazi Germany—the fact of it, its lingering reality—is somehow at the center of everything: as negative example, as dreaded inevitability, as the wall at the end of every road, as what people spend a lot of time avoiding, as the force pushing people apart.) I suggested "Egyptologists Should," which was the last thing I heard on the BBC World Service before the electricity in the Krügers' apartment went dead (the will not of the Krügers, but of the city, which, that day, after a mistake the previous month, when the electricity had also gone dead, was relaying television cables on the Alte Schönhauser Strasse): Kerwin, in his piece, was doing a bit about the BBC World Service, which he calls "the World Service," which I like to kid him about. (After a year and a half of living in Los Angeles, I still can't bring myself to say "L.A.," have only just begun to say "KaDeWe" instead of "Kaufhaus des Westens," which is a little like saying "the United States of America" instead of "America"; I tend to think "secret police" instead of "Stasi.") He decided on "Black Faggot," which he said was "political." In spite of his efforts to the contrary, there is something about Kerwin that suggests white middle-class propriety (he can remind me of my sister's husband, who tries to ingratiate with sarcasm, who just wants to please), a stubborn normality. My political coming-of-age had to do with the United States' invasion of Grenada, which, that night in Madison all those years ago, seemed cataclysmic, and then promptly seemed forgotten. I went to Washington to a protest march with a previous year's roommate and two friends of his from his chemistry class; the two friends, one of whom had a car, had never been out of Wisconsin, and they took pictures of everything they considered noteworthy, including the gas stations we stopped at; in Washington, the night of the day of the protest, I was more disappointed by the lack of national news coverage than they were. My sexual coming-of-age—the loss of my virginity—took place at the Jewish summer camp and was forgettable and prophetic: I lost my hard-on not too long after getting inside the girl. She was a "camper" and not a virgin. The campers at the camp were freshmen and sophomores in high school and the counselors were juniors and seniors; sex between campers and counselors was forbidden and expected. Later, in college, I had sex with a virgin, which I remember as brutal and exciting; I remember the girl—her name was Helen Levy—gritting her teeth, and afterward, when she noticed a little bit of blood on her bedspread, she jumped up and ran into the bathroom to soak the bedspread in the tub. Later I was living with a social worker in New York who didn't mind having sex during her period. She had gone on a vacation to Mexico with some people from her office, and came back at three in the morning a day early. I sometimes sleep in those Ralph Lauren shirts, and had one on (a blue long-sleeved oxford) when she surprised me. She started to menstruate while we were fucking: I was on my back, and afterward there seemed to be blood everywhere—on the sheets, on my shirt, soaked into my pubic hair, dripping a little down my leg when I finally stood up. I still have that shirt, although the blood gets fainter with each washing, and it is actually beginning to fray from being washed in the Foron washing machine, which has a tub that looks like a cheese grater and a half-hour spin cycle. The camp's atmosphere was occasionally theatrically Jewish. Three days a summer, a woman called Mrs. Shumacher, who was from the Flatbush section of Brooklyn and a central casting version of a Jew, took over the entire camp to reenact scenes from Jewish history: in June, she staged an Ellis Island Day; in July, an Israel Day; and in August, to coincide with the anniversary of the destruction of the Second Temple, a Holocaust Day. The campers would be cast as immigrants, Israeli soldiers, concentration camp inmates, and partisans; the counselors, unless they were taking their days off, as most of them tried to do, had to be guards and doctors, ineffectual diplomats, philanthropists, terrorists (I was a counselor at the camp for two summers, missed both Ellis Island Days and both Israel Days, and was cast as a concentration camp guard for both Holocaust Days, didn't lose my virginity until a week after the second year's Holocaust Day, the night before everybody went home). The "programs," as they were called, always ended with the campers and counselors and camp directors and the resident rabbis assembled in the dining hall for Mrs. Shumacher's lectures on Jewish history, which, on both Holocaust Days, ended disquietingly, with new rumors of even worse crimes. If I were seventeen again, at the camp this past summer, about to go to college and relive the best part of my life, it is probable that Mrs. Shumacher, or whoever had taken her place, would stage a Berlin Day, and I would be cast, regardless of my hair length, as one of the skinheads, who would probably be thought of as adults rather than teenagers. I always had to play a concentration camp guard because that first summer, at sixteen, I was already taller than all of the other counselors, certainly taller than the rabbis and the camp directors (though not as tall as most of the kitchen staff, who all came from the same housing project in the Bronx and spent their afternoons playing basketball on a makeshift court outside the kitchen), was highly prized by Mrs. Shumacher: a convincing adult. On that first Holocaust Day, I rose to the occasion, tried to remember my potential namesake, my great-uncle Samuel: I imagined him surviving his diphtheria but not coming to Milwaukee, staying in Europe, there in 194-whatever; the next year, when I wasn't thinking about the girl I ended up fucking, I was giggling like a five-year-old.

[5]

The apartment was on the twenty-first floor and had a picture
window, which, because of its relative largeness, and because of
the apartment's extreme smallness, was like a fourth wall, a vortex:
I could see out in every direction (though, perhaps, only really in
one, essentially eastward), felt a part of the expanse (though was
virtually trapped; the apartment's single room—there was a closet
for a bathroom, a corner for a kitchen—was a little taller than I
am, as wide as my outstretched arms, empty, though roomy
enough for a small bed and an ordinary chair, or too small to look
empty; I was thinking of Leonardo da Vinci and of a prison cell
until Kahula pulled up the blinds and the view came in to get me).
"Great view, man," said Kahula. "Move in any time you want,
man." I wasn't really listening to Kahula; I was looking at Berlin,
which, with its strict prewar building codes, has houses of varying
styles and in varying states of decrepitude but usually only of one
height, and which, that day beneath me, looked like a crowd of
people bent at the waist. I identified ignoble landmarks: the
Franco-Prussian War victory column, the Daimler-Benz tower and
its enormous revolving star, the East Berlin television tower; the
delicate steeples of all the bombed, rebuilt churches looked like
progeny of the television tower (or like spikes on so many Prussian
helmets, or like reeds in a wilderness); the famously bombed-out,
unrebuilt church, the Gedächtniskirche, looked like an ordinary
church with part of its steeple stenciled out; the synagogue, too
new and disturbing to be a landmark, looked smaller and less hallucinatory, unplugged; the cranes that are rebuilding East Berlin

and building up West Berlin, and that usually look merely birdlike, or just threatening (most people think of the cranes as destructive, as building up the city until there is no place left for them), looked like bent church steeples hovering over all the prostrate, faceless houses; a blackening midafternoon light, heading westward, pausing, it seemed, at Berlin's eastern border, as though a city could have a frontier, made the meager skyline—the landmarks; scattered clusters of office buildings; low-cost cinderblock housing, in the east (though I couldn't see as far as Marzahn), and in the west (buildings like the one Kahula's apartment was in)—seem already lit up for the evening, or darkened somehow, like shadows of heavenly objects; I could just make out the empty space where the wall had once stood—arguably Berlin's only noble landmark—on what must have been the border between Wedding and Prenzlauer Berg: it was a simple stretch of darkness, a shadow of nothing. Kahula's apartment was in the north of Berlin, more importantly, in Reinickendorf (I used to divide Berlin up into its boroughs selfconsciously, sarcastically; now I do it without trying, without even noticing, veining it, like Berliners, who naturally divide the city into east and west and then into its boroughs, with inner frontiers), where I had never been and which I had thought of as Berlin's largest and most anonymous borough, though near the other, western border of Wedding, the borough once famous for its Communists ("Red Wedding"), and now famous for its Republikaner voters ("Brown Wedding"), and where I imagined taking Annette —she had always been promising to visit me before we saw each other in Paris—because there is a bus there called Wedding *Crematorium*. Buses and trains in Berlin are named for their final destinations and consequently have names like "Spandau" and "Wannsee," highly suggestive names to some people—suggesting war criminals and their crimes—and, initially, to me; the longer I stay, though, the less suggestive they become, or the more they suggest something else: "Wedding *Crematorium*," I imagined telling Annette, "is where people get divorced," though of course it's where people get cremated. While not listening to Kahula, I considered Wedding, famous for the extreme tastes of its electorate and for its burnt corpses, for that kind of initialness and that kind of finality. Burnt corpses can't vote, though they can, I considered, with a particular magazine article in mind, sell short, at least in East Germany, *in den neuen Bundesländern*. I was thinking of wronged Jews resurfacing, claiming their once aryanized, then nationalized, properties, then selling the right to litigate those claims to West German real estate companies who try to evict the East Germans living there while negotiating expensive out-of-court settlements with the Treuhandanstalt, conceivably in the recesses of the Luftwaffe building (the real estate companies usually only make their profits later, in tax credits that come from eventually tearing down the buildings and starting again—scorched-earth finance, it is occasionally called); or more precisely, I was thinking of the people pretending to be wronged Jews, of those would-be Jewish would-be litigants who not only got their Jewish names from tombstones, but—"stupidly," as the investigative reporter who wrote the article put it—from death camp archives, preferring names of families that seemed to have been entirely eradicated, incinerated. In Berlin, to do the initial research, and then the filing of the various court papers, the parties involved would have to go to Berlin Mitte, to the Rotes Rathaus, or "the red town hall," where the redness has always referred to the color of the late-nineteenth-century bricks—fashioned into a distinctive neo-Renaissance campanile that I could also make out from the picture window—and not as a comment, ironic or otherwise, on the Nazis and Communists in Berlin's and East Berlin's subsequent municipal governments ("burnt-sienna Rathaus," I imagined Annette saying, after following my train of thought, amusing herself, horrifying me, reminding me that, after all, expansion ends in contraction—that we are two different people, one unknowable to the other; that a view begins somewhere specific and ends nowhere in particular). "Great," I said. "Thanks a lot." "Forget it, man," said Kahula, and gave me a set of keys. "Just don't forget to send me the post, man." Kahula is from South Africa, though he has spent years elsewhere;

I found out about him and his apartment through Svetlana and Peter, the couple who own a comically exclusive video rental store in Charlottenburg, where I have rented videos to show my students. Svetlana and Peter are disastrously cosmopolitan: Svetlana's father is Slovak, and her mother is Russian, though, because her father was a diplomat (installed after 1968), she grew up in Western Europe, Africa, and Asia, and speaks English with a French accent (she learned English in Morocco), German with a Danish accent, other languages with accents that I don't recognize, and apparently a superannuated form of literary Russian pretty much confined to Khrushchev-era intellectuals like her mother; she claims not to speak Slovak, which she says isn't a language at all, or she claims to speak it with a Russian accent; she says she prefers not to speak Czech, because she speaks it with a Russian accent, which, she says, is in bad taste; Peter's grandfather on his mother's side was a famous and, in retrospect, famously Jewish art dealer who left Germany for Paris in the 1920s, went to Brazil by way of Portugal months before the Germans invaded France, briefly came back to Germany after the war, went to Denmark, married Peter's mother, a Danish countess, divorced her after Peter was born, and went to Switzerland, where he married and divorced four more times; when she was seventeen and visiting her father in Switzerland, Peter's mother married a Swiss German whose father, Peter told me, was famous for making a fortune in the Second World War investing in grain futures for the Wehrmacht; Peter's mother, after Peter was born, left her husband and moved to Cologne, where Peter grew up, though they spent their summers in Denmark; Peter speaks every language with a German accent, except German, which he speaks with a vaguely Danish accent; Peter met Svetlana in Copenhagen in the mid-1970s, when her father was at the Czechoslovak embassy; they speak to each other in English, with occasional Danish endearments, though they both claim to think of Danish as the ugliest language they know. Peter calls himself Marcus, or, if he has to, Marcus-Frühlmeier (Marcus was his famous grandfather's last name; Frühlmeier was his infamous grandfather's last name); Svetlana calls herself Frühlmeier. Peter's conceit: that he is a Jew; Svetlana's conceit: that she is not a Slovak. In practice they both have imprecise—international, I suppose—tastes which can seem inextricable from their fierce, exotic (or perhaps just arbitrary) prejudices: Peter hates certain kinds of Danes, all Germans, non-German-speaking Swiss, Alsatians, and Americans, while Svetlana hates Slovaks, Czechs who don't live in Prague, Poles, Germans, Hungarians (especially ethnic Hungarians in Slovakia), and, it can seem, on occasion, Jews; Peter seems to think of me as typically Jewish and atypically American and has occasionally demanded that I come to work at his video store, because, he says, "we need another Jew," while Svetlana has never publicly referred to my being Jewish and claims always to forget that I am American; in any case, they prefer to talk about themselves, often at the same time; they have been in many countries and speak several languages but end up seeming diminished by where they haven't been, mockable in languages or dialects they don't understand (Yiddish; American slang from recent Hollywood movies, which they never see and won't buy to rent out); they look ageless, though are really about forty; they are both bone-thin chain-smokers who always seem to be eating; their qualities seem more contradictory than cosmopolitan, confusing, in states of cancellation—disastrous: they seem utterly unknowable, to themselves and to everyone else, and I have thought of them as person-sized black holes. After I looked at the apartment and was riding down in the elevator with Kahula, it occurred to me that he had no conceits, then, on the U-Bahn back into town, I thought that his conceit was that no one was staring at him. (My conceit: that I am leaving Germany. Another conceit: that I am staying. And another: that I wasn't staring at Kahula.) Kahula has cornrows; he is a jazz musician who sometimes plays in Berlin, though he met Peter and Svetlana at an art opening. Peter gets invited everywhere, especially, he claims, now that he calls himself Marcus, and afterward accuses people he has met of anti-Semitism; Svetlana often sleeps all day, staggering into the store at four or five in the

afternoon; I imagine her sleeping even later, going to an art opening with pillow creases on her face. (Sometimes on the days I
wouldn't teach, I would sleep until two in the afternoon, return a
video to Peter and Svetlana, meet Hans-Joachim for coffee, then
Irmgard for dinner, see Kurt in a bar, and end up back in the Krügers' living room, feeling that I had been everywhere, that I had
run a gamut, moved my hands up and down the city's body, then
I would fall asleep and dream, as I have nearly every night since I
have been here, that I am back in school, usually in high school,
though sometimes in grade school, and about to take a test that I
haven't studied for; similarly, the view from that picture window,
so vague and intricate, sometime later reminded me of my parents'
house, which also has a picture window, which looks out onto
neighbors' houses' picture windows, which all look flat and blank,
like trompe l'oeil depictions of the void.) Svetlana, also, often
leaves town, as I used to do (Peter doesn't; if he hasn't been invited
somewhere, he sits in his store after closing, smoking hash-laced
cigarettes and eating liverwurst with a spoon), though seldom ends
up going where she will have claimed to have been going; she says
she is going to Amsterdam, waving her train ticket in the air, but
then will have gone to Istanbul; she buys a plane ticket to Greece
and on her way to the airport changes her mind and takes the
night train to Copenhagen, returns from a long planned trip to
Copenhagen with the tan she picked up in Morocco. I met Svetlana and Peter last spring when I was trying to find undubbed
videos to show my students. (After having dubbed all their movies,
Germans rent dubbed videos, can seem surprised that undubbed
videos exist; they re-record popular songs into German, with the
singers trying to make their voices sound like the real singers; on
the radio, I have heard a German Barbra Streisand singing "Leute"
and a German Louis Armstrong singing songs from *Das Dschun-
gelbuch*. Another conceit: that this surprises me, that it continues
to appall; the new view from the apartment, for instance, even
before it reminded me of Brookfield, was already familiar, consum-
mating.) Yesterday, while looking around Prenzlauer Berg for

boxes to move with, I ran into Burt Kaminsky (he asked me if he could borrow my scarf; it is the end of February, quite cold; the air is saturated with coal smoke, and the city has issued an especially severe smog alert, though the day I visited the apartment was before the cold had set in, and the sky, though still solid gray, was not much lower than it usually is; now, in the nightly fog, the bent-at-the-waist houses disappear above street level, might be as tall as skyscrapers), and I realized that Svetlana and Peter are probably the only people I know here whom I hadn't met through Burt. (I gave Burt my scarf, and then regretted it, forgot that I had no money and no job, but remembered that Kahula had said that I could pay my rent a few weeks after moving in, remembered Milwaukee and Madison, where the cold is much worse, and felt a little invincible, and studentlike, as if I were expecting my parents to buy me another scarf, as if I were going home next weekend to get my teeth cleaned.) On the subway, Kahula and I didn't talk about Svetlana, with whom Kahula may or may not be having an affair; we talked about cities where we had both been, like Paris and Vienna and Prague and Frankfurt, then, finally, about where we were from, about Brookfield and Soweto, at which point the conversation petered out, contracted. If I absolutely had to live in Germany, I told Kahula, I would live in Hamburg, where I said my girlfriend was from. The mother of Kahula's child is from East Berlin, though she lives in West Berlin; the woman whom Kahula had previously married in order to get a West German passport is from Hamburg but now lives in East Berlin, near where I have been living; he was planning on moving in with her because the immigration authorities, he said, were "beating me down." He had just come back from Moscow, where he had played in jazz clubs, and which he described as "a real big place, man." I said that certain cities suggest other places, like Los Angeles, where I said I used to live. Los Angeles makes you want to go to Mexico, feels like the beginning of Mexico. And Berlin? Berlin makes you want to go to Russia, feels like some stopping-off point on the way to Russia. Kahula shook his head. I was trying to get off the subject of cities and on to places: I hate the way people talk about cities—the way I talked about cities with Kahula and the way he talked about cities with me; Peter and Svetlana talk about cities incessantly; or rather use them, often in combinations, like adjectives, or perhaps like letters of an alphabet; I especially hate the way Germans talk about German cities, as places unto themselves, universes (people in Berlin sometimes talk that way about individual boroughs and about the people who live in them; they talk about *Marzahner* and *Charlottenburger* and *Kreuzberger* as though another borough were another planet, apocryphal, exotic; I think of talking that way as the other side of a final frontier, as what I'll sound like after I have disappeared, though when I went over to get some boxes from Kurt and Sabine, who of course not only distinguish between boroughs but between parts of boroughs, moving to Rei-nickendorf felt like a real departure—a defection—and saying good-bye felt final, like a farewell). It has occurred to me lately that I have been in too many cities and in too few places (I never made it to Mexico, which, when I was living in Los Angeles, probably never really meant more than "Tijuana," and I have never made it to Russia, which I think of as never having been to Moscow or to St. Petersburg, or perhaps just to St. Petersburg, which East Germans, almost without exception, still call "Leningrad," and which West Germans gleefully call "St. Petersburg" and which one American businessman in his middle to late twenties whom I met at the train station in Warsaw called "St. Pete"; Svetlana says "Peters-burg," talks about "the soul of Petersburg"; Peter, derisively, says "Leningrad," or on occasion "Yeltsingrad"), too concerned with specific, rather than general, destinations. And I am haunted by the phrase "ideal city," which I saw on a poster in Charlottenburg in the window of a bookstore near the video store. The poster was a composite of cityscapes painted by Piero della Francesca, per-fectly harmonious city squares, without any people; it has since occurred to me that perhaps I have been searching for a more gen-eralized, "ideal," city, which I then anthropomorphized, under-stood to mean a search for an ideal friend. (My idea of the ideal

friend: someone who doesn't irritate, who has been everywhere
but no longer needs to talk about it; someone who doesn't con-
found; who has been emptied of cities; whose emptiness can
soothe.) I considered buying the poster and putting it on the wall
of the apartment in Reinickendorf—on the wall opposite the window, as a mirror of Berlin's mess—but decided I should wait; after
all, maybe I wouldn't take the apartment; maybe I would leave;
then I thought about putting up one of Ludwig Meidner's apocalyptic landscapes. (Ludwig Meidner was a German Jew who lived
in Berlin though he was born in Upper Silesia and attended school
there in Katowice—which is to say, practically Auschwitz—toward
the end of the last century, when Upper Silesia was still German,
not to mention Prussian; he painted his apocalyptic landscapes—
views of cities enduring what look like simultaneous earthquakes
and air raids, and what now look like atomic blasts, with stick
figures fleeing in all directions—in 1912 and 1913, and his major
collector these days is a Jew from Milwaukee who used to own the
Milwaukee Bucks basketball team and whose daughter, I believe,
knew my sister, and who, from a distance, is admired by my parents for the obvious reason: his money. I admire Ludwig Meidner
because he was prophetic, which, in the long run, isn't always a
durable quality, can in retrospect become a kind of obviousness.)
Ludwig Meidner's landscapes, I thought, would be a less distorting
mirror of Berlin's mess (and of mine)—or distorting in some other
direction. In Vienna, while writing his novel, *Auto-da-Fé*, which
ends with a bibliophile oor, if the word exists, bibliomane) setting
fire to his tens of thousands of books and not at all incidentally to
himself, Elias Canetti often looked again and again at—was, in
some sense, in the writing of his novel, accompanied by—reproductions of Matthias Grünewald's famously gruesome *Isenheim Altarpiece*; the reproductions, he recalls in his autobiography,
horrified visitors, but he seems to suggest that he didn't notice
them while writing the book, rather before and especially after, as
if, for a time, they were expressing themselves through him. Walter
Benjamin had a print of the *Isenheim Altarpiece* on the wall of his

study in Berlin; he claimed to be overwhelmed by its "quality of expressionlessness." (West Berlin, without its disfiguring wall, is like other destroyed, rebuilt West German cities—expressionless, faceless; East Berlin looks daily more and more like West Berlin; Meidner's figures have contorted bodies instead of facial expressions; "the ideal city" has no people; Kahula's apartment has a bathroom and a telephone but no mirror, just the picture window, which conceivably reflects—turns into a sort of vast mirror—at night; the single room's walls are blank, brief, as if there were only a ceiling and a floor, as if the window were a mere line, a crack.) Gershom Scholem mentions Walter Benjamin's opinions of the *Isenheim Altarpiece* in his book called *Walter Benjamin: The Story of a Friendship*, a title that, obviously, refers to their friendship (and to their subsequent distances and silences—to their estrangement) and, eventually somewhat obviously, to Benjamin's inner contradictions, which Scholem at one point discreetly refers to as "the polarization in Benjamin's view of language," as if Benjamin's intellect itself were a consuming friendship, a rivalry, between two poles—between metaphysics and materialism (Jewishness and Marxism; Scholem and Brecht), between Kafka and Brecht, between Proust and Kafka, between Paris and Berlin; between history-as-contemplated and history-as-endured. Scholem first saw Benjamin in the late autumn of 1913, in Berlin, when he was sixteen and Benjamin was twenty-one, at a somewhat polarized discussion at the Café Tiergarten between members of Scholem's zionist youth organization and Jewish members of the German Youth Movement, of which Benjamin was a prominent member and for whom he served that day as spokesman. Scholem remembers Benjamin as speaking extemporaneously but in a "style ready for print" (new, but simultaneously finished; polarized, yet also whole; Athena-like). I think of two people as ultimately unknowable to each other, and think of cities as clusters of unknowability; I think of love as an open border (or as an opened-up border; an intimacy marked with the memory of something else) and of hatred as irrespective of borders. I think that the first-time meeting of people who will come to love each other is like a first visit to a city you will eventually live in (or stay in too long)—a surveyance; loving is a form of staying, of reluctantly leaving, of being surrounded by what you have found. Elias Canetti's parents—two Ladino-speaking Sephardic Jews from Bulgaria—fell in love in Vienna, and German became their private language, their language of love (and the language in which Canetti would write his books; the language in which he would write in 1944: "The language of my intellect will remain German, because I am a Jew"). Svetlana and Peter met at an embassy party but fell in love in Tivoli on a summer night, speaking to each other, they have told me more than once, in German, English, and French; they now use Danish endearments but reminisce, argue, and talk to their customers, whom they call clients, or friends (they imagine they run some sort of salon out of their video store), in English, which is the language or the other language that most of their films are in— the old Hollywood films, of course, and the French and Italian and Russian, and even the German, films, which have been imported from Britain or Scandinavia or Holland or Hong Kong and all have English subtitles. Kurt and Sabine wooed each other in East Berlin in 1987 or '88, to the sound of Nina Simone singing "My Baby Just Cares for Me" on a West Berlin radio station; they are both monolingual. Burt Kaminsky and the hustler used money as their language, and Burt seems more upset when he talks about the hustler stealing his car than when he talks about the hustler beating up his father. (When money becomes a language, stealing is a curse, a euphemism for hating; after fighting with my parents about something else—although what else could we have fought about? "You can go wherever you want," one of them would tell me. "But not with my car." "You can do whatever you want, but not with my money"—I would steal from my mother's purse, from my father's wallet; my parents use money as a language but only really to talk about money: they will describe a family's house or car or country club membership with an exact figure, which is a way of describing how much money the father earns, which is a way of describing how much money the family has, which, if it's enough, could then be used to buy whatever any of the family members wants, which would cost so many other exact figures; like novelists writing novels about writing novels.) Irmgard and I first noticed each other on an underground platform, among Germans, silently waiting for a train; we often don't say much to each other, ignoring unasked questions. I first met Annette in a student dormitory cafeteria, where she was making jokes about the toast at breakfast ("Break first," she said to me, after I put a whole piece in my mouth); she feels loved when someone laughs at one of her jokes and feels she is loving whenever she laughs back; with us now, and for some time, for years, the laughter has been uncomfortable, like a forced cough, like a debt repaid too late. I first saw Berlin on a fall day, during a heat wave, what Germans call *"Altweibersommer"* (old women's summer, in a reference to menopausal hot flashes, as though a year were a woman, and which Germans who know its derivation find very funny; Annette, when I told her, was horrified). In Berlin, negation is a language: the city is a boomtown and a ghost town; once Prussian and Jewish, and now neither, though still talked about as both; Communist and capitalist, or Fascist and Communist oor Fascist and Communist, Republikaner and PDS-isch); westerly winds smell of the sea and easterly winds smell of the steppes, of endlessness, but sharply, of salt, of mud; the city always looks gray, is in shades of gray, like a gray-on-gray kaleidoscope; it was away from all the places I had ever been, though now it reminds me of those places, as though a finishing line could collapse into a starting point; or in the way a place becomes a city, and a city a room, and a room a bed, and a bed the moments between sleeping and waking (though not necessarily between night and day), a wakeful darkness. Lately I make jokes in the Berlin dialect, just by speaking the Berlin dialect: *"Yanz yut, wahr,"* I said to Irmgard about the food the other day, when she paid for lunch because I have almost no money left, meaning *"Ganz gut, nicht wahr?"* (Rather good, isn't it?), though of course she had heard me say this before and came up with a kind of exhaled smile, a grunt. Canetti's parents, as he would have it, betrayed each other linguistically: his father betrayed his mother by making the family move to England, where she didn't speak the language; and more subtly, and possibly fatally (it could be argued that Canetti's father died upon learning the details), his mother betrayed his father by taking an extended vacation at an Austrian spa town, where she talked in German about literature with the spa doctor, who then suggested that she run away with him. (A Jew writing in German is, in its way, a kind of betrayal. My reading books by German Jews in English is a way of being truer to myself than to everyone else—a more immediate truth, a way of not disappearing.) Irmgard no longer has contact with her philologist. (She has expurgated him, I joked with an imaginary Annette.) She says that he has been a student too long, that they have nothing in common anymore. I have a forged international student ID card claiming that I am twenty-five years old and a graduate student in history at the University of Wisconsin: I can get into museums and concerts for half price; I could fly half price and then stay in student hostels, but actually I prefer trains and cheap regular hotels (or preferred; I haven't left Berlin, haven't even gone to Potsdam, in months; I used to leave town about once a week, though Irmgard thinks that I used to leave town about once a month; the Krügers, I recently overheard, think I sleep twenty hours a day). When I was traveling and often meeting variations of myself, there was an order to my noticing how much new people and I had in common, a grammar of conspicuousness: I would first notice whether people were American, then whether they were Jewish, then where they were from in America (or, if they weren't American, where I could assume they were from), then whether they were English (or French or German teachers) or something else (executives, tourists, members of a film crew), then the ways they were, or were not, sexually compromised; or else in that order, but exactly reversed. I never wondered if someone had a fraudulent international student ID card (in my case doubly fraudulent), except once, when I met a man whose

biography so overlapped with mine that the actual differences between us were unbearable—deranging—as soon as they became
apparent. He was exactly thirty, from a suburb of Chicago called
Northbrook, without a midwestern accent, Jewish, teaching English in Leipzig, and read books about homosexuals in the way that
I read books about Jews, and he had a fake international student
ID card but, after I asked, said a little boastfully (bitchily) that it
hadn't occurred to him to lie about his age; I thought that he
looked very Jewish, especially after he said that he had never really
thought about being Jewish and what was he supposed to do anyway, hate all Germans just because of what happened what he
called sixty or seventy years ago? We were in Prague, in the vegetarian restaurant, at opposite tables, talking across the aisle about
what we seemed to have in common: about the division of post-
reunification Germany (he argued the East German point of view,
as a result, it seemed, of several positive experiences with East
German gay men and one negative experience with a West
German bisexual high school teacher; I tried to argue the East and
then West German points of view on one hand, and a German-
hater's point of view on the other, citing as evidence the Krügers
and a woman who works in the bakery around the corner from
their apartment—who, in counterpoint to the Krügers, had been
ruthless before becoming too friendly); about cities we both had
lived in (he said there was more to do in Chicago than in New
York, by which he seemed to mean that he preferred the bars on
Halstead Street to the bars in Chelsea; I said Chicago was more
racist, that there was nothing to do except eat out in restaurants
or go to new suburban-looking movie theater complexes on the
edges of housing projects); about the food (which I found ironic,
considering the fact that we were in Prague, and which he found
delicious, considering the fact that we were in Prague; we had even
both ordered the same kind of veggie melt). He was much shorter
than I am, with glasses, and had gone to the University of Michigan, which is usually considered a similar, and then much better,
school than the University of Wisconsin; at first, especially before

we had actually spoken, he had been flirtatious, even a little las-
civious; after we had been disagreeing for half an hour, I went to
the bathroom, and he was standing at the cash register when I got
back, waiting to say good-bye. "Good luck at that bar," I said. (He
had come to Prague, it seemed, to go to a certain gay bar that he
had found in a German-language Central European gay guide,
which he at one point had asked me to translate because he was
still learning German.) "Good luck at the cemeteries," he said. (I,
rather pedantically, dispassionately, explained the difference between the two Jewish cemeteries in Prague after he told me about
visiting the old Jewish cemetery, which, even after I explained the
difference, he could only be bothered to call "the Jewish Cemetery," and trying to find but not finding Franz Kafka's grave, which
is in the new Jewish cemetery; after speaking dispassionately, I felt
a rumbling: when he turned his back and started walking out, I
felt like running after him, knocking him down.) He didn't say so,
but I assumed that he would eventually go to graduate school in
gay studies. I haven't thought about graduate school; I have been
too busy watching the particulars of my life here disappearing:
Brett has taken over the last few weeks of my classes; the Krügers'
apartment is so torn up that I haven't been able to use the kitchen,
and there are often workmen in the bathroom; I almost never
see Irmgard now that she is at Hans-Joachim's; I seem to spend a
lot of time at the Laundromat (the Krügers' washing machine is
disconnected and surrounded by a hacked-up floor, as though
someone had been excavating it), where I read other people's
newspapers and magazines. Most of the people at the Laundromat
are students or alcoholics. Germans, as a matter of course, have
their own washing machines though rarely their own dryers,
which are considered to be a waste of energy (they have washing
machines in the way that Americans with washing machines have
dryers); at the Laundromat, I read in a West German tabloid that,
in a recent national poll, cleanliness and thriftiness were named
as the two most typical German virtues, and Bismarck was named
as the greatest German, then I read in a West German broadsheet

that the same poll had been conducted in 1932 and the pollsters
had gotten the same answers, then I read in a new East German
broadsheet that the same poll had been conducted in 1938 and
the pollsters had gotten similar answers, with, by then, Adolf Hitler
overtaking Bismarck as the greatest German. The last time I went
to the Laundromat I saw a group of East German college students
who seemed like American high school students; they walked in,
took off their coats and sweaters, then took off their pants, tennis
shoes, and socks and put them in washing machines, put on their
sweaters and coats, and sat in the car in their underwear, with their
bare feet hanging out the open car windows; later they seemed like
East German college students, or just like East Germans, or Germans, moving in synch, as a pack, taking out their clothes and
putting them in the dryers in uniform, elegant, animallike ges-
tures. On the underground, I once saw a group of East German
college students start talking to a group of West German college
students, and then they extended their conversation—about how
all politicians are "shits"—to other people on the train; they extended the conversation around me: it was early last summer and
I was prematurely wearing my madras-plaid Bermuda shorts,
which in Europe are to being American what having a lisp in America is to being homosexual (Germans, Hans-Joachim notwithstand-
ing, don't seem to have lisps, or have lisps that turn out to be
subdialects; Hans-Joachim's lisp seems to go away when he is
making fun of other Germans' dialects), hyper-American; I don't
think I could fit into those shorts now—as the particulars of my
life disappear, I am getting larger, spending my last bits of money
on cake and cookies and sausages and beer, as though I were eating
my money, or growing to fill in the empty space; I had to spend
fifty marks on new, 38-inch-waist blue jeans at the used-clothing
store on the Potsdamer Strasse. In a *Trendmagazin*—which is an
upmarket version, that reads like a satirical version, of an
Illustrierte—there was a fashion spread about neo-Nazis, including
skinheads, biker Nazis, youngish Republikaner voters, and certain
kinds of students, like the members of a conservative, ecologically

minded student organization in Bavaria, and latter-day *Burschen-schafter* with old-fashioned dueling scars: what clothes they wore, what books they read, what music they listened to, what kind of people they hated. The *Burschenschafter* liked wearing Ralph Lauren clothes and listening to Richard Strauss; they hated "left-wing intellectuals and 'cosmopolitans,' " which the magazine decided to put in double quotes, as though they wanted their readers to know that they knew that the *Burschenschafter* meant "Jews." Kahula's apartment building was originally a student dormitory, and is now an undesirable student dormitory being gradually converted into a high-rise slum for people who have actually been granted, or about to be granted, legal residence in Germany, and for guest workers, or for their children, most of whom were born in Germany—in other words, for dark-skinned people who can't find anywhere else to live. (Apparently the building has become a little infamous; Hans-Joachim knew exactly where it was and said that it belonged in one of those towns outside Paris, where people from Mali live in one building and people from Niger live in the next one, and so on.) That day with Kahula, I noticed the *Studenten* rather than the *Asylbewerber* and *Gastarbeiter*. Noticing, it has occurred to me, is a form of accompanying (when you first arrive in a city, are at the train station, the crowds seem to be dispersing, heading everywhere else, into the city; you want to follow all of them, be everywhere at once, but stand perfectly still, are only everywhere as long as you are standing still), in the way that up is a form of down: an origin. Now, when I am waiting for the S-Bahn, and trains on their way to other cities pass by on the inner tracks, I read the placards, with the trains' destinations listed in blurring black letters that look like dashes, like marks on a drum score, and I feel as if I am on the trains, watching myself depart. I sometimes look in the windows of those trains, can usually only make out the businessmen reading their newspapers, or the many very serious, adult-looking students, which is what the *Burschenschafter* in the *Trendmagazin* looked like. In Los Angeles, on the stalled freeways, I would look into the cars next to mine, and once I saw

someone I knew from college in the next car (someone whom I
didn't like very much, hadn't spoken to in years, never really knew
in the first place, whose name I had to find out from Annette that
night on the telephone), though usually I saw carloads magically
overflowing with Mexicans, ten or fifteen heads in a compact car;
one of my most vivid memories of New York is of a summer night
in an un-air-conditioned apartment in Fort Greene in Brooklyn,
with all the windows open; I was trying to watch a civil rights
documentary on public television while all the black people in the
neighborhood were out on the street, smoking dope and listening
to rap music, screaming. Professor Whitlaw read while he drove,
and wrote, I remember him telling me, while he walked (I would
read newspapers when I rode on trains to other cities, until I got
nauseated, then I drank beer and fell asleep; I haven't driven a car
since I got here, can't really remember what I do while driving,
listen to the radio, I suppose, turning the dial until I find a very
familiar song; when I watch television, I am often absolutely still,
as if the picture were moving for me.) I think he used to bump
into things—told me that he did, or perhaps I actually saw him
do it once. Germans, admiringly, would call him *weltfremd*, or
"world-strange," which is a kind of naïveté reserved for describing
people who would seem to have better things to do than think
about reality as such, and perhaps the only example in which the
word *fremd* (which means "strange," "alien," "peculiar," and
"weird" all at once; immanently strange) is used approvingly.
(German, of course, is filled with small words that mean too much
and that are combined into eventually enormous words that don't
mean anything; verbs congregate at the ends of sentences after
clauses that, until then, have somehow been describing nothing;
meaning and action aren't distributed, coagulate—or are periodic,
set in relief, like braille). *Fremdgehen*, "to go 'strange,' " means "to
be unfaithful," sexually speaking; I have thought about being unfaithful to Irmgard, about having been impotent with other people, about whether I could use the word "*fremdgehen*" to describe
that (Germans, as it happens, are quite forceful when it comes to

other people making mistakes, as they are about giving directions—they cut you off in midsentence, grab you by the arm; finish your thought as well as correct you, follow you down streets; scream out their kindness). Except for our lunch the day after I looked at Kahula's apartment, I haven't seen her at all this week. She seems to be disappearing, is seldom at the bank; she often stays at Hans-Joachim's, calling in sick and reading his old college textbooks, which, of course, aren't all that different from her old college textbooks, which she has put in storage outside East Berlin in a converted Soviet barracks that the property developer now calls a "storage park"; the day Irmgard and I had lunch, Hans-Joachim, as it happened, was also pretending; he has decided to quit his job and become, legally speaking, bedridden; I went to his apartment to pick up Irmgard, and, in preparation for an impending visit from the appropriate city agency, he had rented a wheelchair and a hospital bed, had drunk too much the night before, had bought a plastic portable toilet; he was in the hospital bed when I arrived, looking blurred, I considered, still like himself, but at some future date; later I thought of a photograph that my parents had taken at my sister's college graduation of me dressed up in her cap and gown; "bedridden" in German, I learned, is *"bettlägerig,"* which, Hans-Joachim explained, comes from *"Bett"* and *"Lager"*—a bed-sized concentration camp, I said, which I thought of as unfunny and inappropriate, and which, with its inner rhyme—"Bett KZ"; the *z* getting pronounced "zed" like in French and in English English—made Irmgard and Hans-Joachim laugh. Irmgard and I first went to the Gemäldegalerie in Dahlem and then had our lunch at the student cafeteria nearby, where I used my student ID to get her a fifty-pfennig discount on my sauerbraten and whole wheat spätzle. During lunch Irmgard recounted for me how unhappy her student days in Munich had been. I told her about the last time I had visited the museum, when one of the older museum guards (who in Germany are always pensioners, which used to mean old Wehrmacht soldiers, and now also means onetime members of the Hitler Youth: old German men in modified uniforms, yelling sotto voce when someone gets too close to anything, herding people out at exactly fifteen minutes before closing; famously merciless) followed me around, trying to show me where the Caravaggios were, telling me, after learning that I was American, about his internment in a POW camp in Georgia during the war; he liked Georgia, he assured me, grabbing my elbow in front of one of Caravaggio's leering boys, leering back confidently, as though in synch with someone; he often goes back to Georgia, he said, on vacations. Tastes, of course, can be a kind of prison: Irmgard, who, having spent years of her life—not to mention the previous few weeks with Hans-Joachim's art books—thinking about the history of European painting, ran through the museum like a trapped animal, only pausing to catch her breath. I wasn't looking at the paintings either; I was thinking about myself in the apartment in Reinickendorf, with the blinds drawn, at night, listening, say, to Neil Young singing for the ten thousandth time "You can't be twenty, on Sugar Mountain." Germans, these days, of course, are inclined to like literature that negates them, though "like" is perhaps too weak a word, or the wrong one; "abide by" might be better. Kafka, Benjamin, Canetti, Paul Celan; when it comes to literature in German at this end of the twentieth century, Germans are a little like the mouse in Kafka's story "A Little Fable," (" '*Ach,*' said the mouse. 'The world is getting smaller every day. At first, it was so big, that I was afraid, I ran and ran and was happy finally to see that there were walls in the distance to the left and to the right of me, but these walls are rushing toward each other so quickly that I am already in the final room, and there, in the corner, stands the trap, into which I must run.' 'All you have to do is change directions,' said the cat, and ate him up."), with the cat being books by Jews who have written in German. I think of literature—especially literature by Jews writing in German—as a precipice that can be climbed upon and jumped off of, like a diving board; I worry that I am underneath the diving board, already in the water, jumping up and down, but in water, actually floating, somehow mocking. (One of my earlier memories: jumping off a diving board backward, afraid of hitting my chin on the edge; or perhaps—even arguably: watching someone else jump off a diving board and wondering whether—even, perhaps, when—he was going to hit his chin on the edge.) Paul Celan, it could be argued, betrays the German language just by writing in it; he cuts it up into little pieces then puts it back together, hacks it up, which is what seems to have happened to the bodies he writes about; in Celan, body parts become, or rather stand in for, whole people, are a sort of reduced essence; he constructs verbs out of expressions of time (in Celan, it is possible in a single word "to get Januaried," "to be Novembered"); when he uses conventional verbs, he likes to use the subjunctive form, which in German is made by adding an umlaut wwhich turns vowels into diphthongs, complicates them) and an ending onto the past tense, and which, in Celan's version of the German language and sometimes in the German language everyone else uses, could be described as what it very much sounds like—a derangement of the past. ("Betray" is of course the wrong word, perhaps I should have said "made his own," or perhaps "ingested.") Celan, of course, is from Czernowitz, the capital of the Bukovina; he was born in 1920 (his father died of typhus in an internment camp and his mother was killed with a shot in the neck), which is the year my father was born; after surviving the war, he moved to Paris. Everywhere else in Europe suggests Paris, and Paris suggests everywhere else, is everybody's destination, an ascent; this was especially true of provincial Jews in Central Europe (when there still was a Central Europe and there were still Jews there), of Kafka, who never went but who could write in his diaries about a touring car driving through a medieval square in Prague and letting off a smell of gasoline that registered as a "breath of Paris" as it blew across his face; of Bruno Schulz, who, after years of planning, finally went in the summer of 1938 (during what he called in his letters "the dead season"), and for whom a visit to Paris was a little like what an engagement to Felice Bauer was to Kafka—nullifying; Schulz didn't like leaving the goriness of provincial life in his native Drogobych (the Polish, then Austrian, then Polish, now Ukrainian, town; or Galicia, which can also have an older connotation, literally means "of the Gauls"), even when remaining there became a form of suicide; he was shot down in the streets of Drogobych in 1942 by the SS, and many of his letters' recipients were murdered in the camps; Germans, recently, have discovered Schulz, who wrote in Polish but could also write in German, and they do things like stage puppet versions of his novels and novel fragments. (Schulz wrote an introduction to the Polish translation of *The Trial* which was eventually published as an afterword, and in which he sounds like Benjamin writing about Kafka, or, for that matter, like Milena Jesenska—Kafka's Czech translator and correspondent, who wasn't Jewish, but who died in a concentration camp, like Kafka's sisters —in an obituary she wrote about Kafka, but not at all like Annette, who, years ago, after having read "The Metamorphosis," announced "it's all about money," unlike Schulz and Benjamin and Jesenska, who might each argue that it wasn't all about anything, that it was, to use Schulz's phrase, "hermetically sealed on all sides," whole and unfathomable, but possibly like my parents, who of course haven't read Kafka, but who think that everything, in any case, is always about money.) Drogobych—like Paris—is spelled just about the same in other European languages (or actually differently but always seems to be spelled the same), doesn't need to be translated, or is untranslatable; Czernowitz's variations—in Rumanian, Cernăuți; in Ukrainian (in Latin type), Chernovtsy—can sound completely different, like entirely different cities; Lemberg, Lwów, Lvov, and Lwiw sound subtly and, eventually, pedantically different, inflected; Kaliningrad sounds accidentally similar to Königsberg, or intentionally similar to Kalinin, which is a region and its eponymous city deep in Russia also named after Kalinin, confusing; Milwaukee, like Chicago, sounds like one of those Indian names that Germans find exotic; Brookfield, when it is not sounding like a translation from the German, sounds American—archetypally suburban, lush, unhappy, a puritan baroque; or merely like other suburbs, not Jewish, or ironically

Jewish; Brookfield has no nickname that I know of, although Milwaukee's suburbs near Lake Michigan do: Fox Point is called "Lox Point" and Whitefish Bay is called "Whitefolks Bay"; I, too, have no nickname that I know of. Because of Celan, and more, I think, than all of those other cities, Czernowitz is a code word for a vanished kind of Germanness (Kaliningrad is a code word for a vanished Germany). The Germans have adopted Celan, who I don't think actually lived in Germany, who only seemed to go there to pick up literary prizes (he died in Paris in 1970 by throwing himself in the Seine), though reading him, especially his later poems, produces a sort of aphasia in Germans (and in me, usually from going back and forth too often in my bilingual edition), some of whom regard him as almost maliciously inscrutable: "Celan is read but not loved," is what Hans-Dieter (actually he prefers "Dieter"), Hans-Joachim's friend, who is studying philosophy, had to say about Celan, and also that he practiced a "negative metaphysics," which is practically the same thing as calling him a metaphysician ("No one conjures our dust," Celan can write, with dreaded assurance, or with a sort of mystical dread, in a poem called "Psalm"), which is like saying he is too sentimental to take seriously. I said that if German civilization were a sentence, Paul Celan would be the punctuation mark, or the white space next to the punctuation mark (not adding that if German civilization were a German sentence I was only interested in the end of it: in the verbs, as it were; in the part that destroys—though some people choose to misread that destruction as a contradicting of what came before, as an argument rather than a slaughter; in the gory parts), to which Hans-Dieter said, "Now *you* are sounding like a metaphysician." Metaphysics, he said with extreme pride, doesn't exist in Germany, deferring to Martin Heidegger by way of Kant's *Critique of Pure Reason*. I agreed, confusing, in my mind, metaphysics with human decency and assuming that he had confused, in his mind, metaphysics with Jewishness, with my assumption proving rather prophetic when he later accused me of being *"moralistisch,"* which I had once heard used on a radio talk show as a virtual synonym for *rabbinisch*, "rabbinical." It could be argued that Professor Whitlaw was sentimental about Immanuel Kant. Professor Whitlaw's relationship to Immanuel Kant and the history of Western philosophy is a little like my relationship to Annette and the history of my personal relationships, or else, somehow, like its negation: I think of my dwindling feelings for Annette—my faint acknowledgment of empty disaster, of remembered feelings rather than feelings—as an anticipation of or follow-up to dwindling feelings for other people, as a measuring stick of remoteness. In Paris, when I was sitting across from Annette, and she was driving me up the wall, after having done nothing wrong but becoming the person she had always promised to be (essentially self-regarding, self-loving, an appreciator of her own jokes; the possessor of a miserable suburban childhood and pleasant suburban adolescence, uneasily and devotedly provincial, a Methodist from Minnesota; a distributor, who understands her experiences as both exemplary and ordinary, obligingly bitter, an ideologue; a success; lost to me), I felt very far away from, but acutely aware of, her, as though she were objectively irritating; during my other visit to Paris, there had been a preview of this. I went to Paris a week after graduating from college, intending on traveling through Europe, and my mother had her first mild heart attack the day after I left. I was in Paris for two weeks, and, when I occasionally called home, no one answered, or my father would answer and say that my mother was out shopping (she was in an intensive care unit), until one day, when I got a telegram at my pension telling me that my mother was out of danger and that I should come home; there was the hospital phone number on the telegram; when I called and spoke to my mother, who sounded weak, but still like herself (now, more mild heart attacks later, and after years of enduring other chronic diseases, my mother can sound like someone else, increasingly like no one), I am not sure that I felt anything, except irritation, or I don't know what I felt, though I remember it as nothing (or as a beginning, an emptiness); when it comes to Paris, I remember empty tables and an empty street and sleeping: kinds of nothing,

nothing being a remoteness from everything, as far away as the forgotten dead. Lately I have felt less remote from Professor Whitlaw: I wonder what his shrug meant. I wonder what Germans are thinking when they consider literature that can seem to preclude their existence, or rather, whose existence they tried to preclude, and I think about Kant's distinction between the world-in-itself and the world-of-appearance (as I remember it from Professor Whitlaw's background lectures on Kant's political philosophy, which usually took up so much time that we never actually got around to the political philosophy except in retrospect, at the ends of semesters when most of Professor Whitlaw's suggested paper topics had to do with Kant's political philosophy); I think about the German Romantics' distinction between life-as-lived and life-as-imagined, of the Germans' need for worldly transcendence—of transcendence as an actual destination, having less to do with redemption than logistics, which in Germany has aesthetic, and then political, implications, of people sitting in concert halls, perfectly still, swooning, or in other sorts of halls, screaming, squirming around at the ends of their voices. I wonder about the difference between German Romanticism and the Jews' Messianism (Messianism: which can seem to be about the extreme unlikelihood of transcendence; about a Messiah who never comes): I think it might be the difference between having a dream (or a nightmare) and insomnia; between feeling (even feeling what can seem like nothing) and nothing. The cab I had ordered to move me to Kahula's was late, and I was early: I had finished packing at ten-thirty and the cab was supposed to come between eleven-thirty and midnight; I had decided to give myself all evening to pack; I had decided to move on February 27, the day before the Krügers had told me I had to move, so that I could come back the next day and look around in case I had forgotten anything. A conceit (or a delusion): that I could forget something, that I would need any time at all to pack; that there was something to forget. (What I brought with me from America: three pairs of blue jeans, three pairs of underwear, three pairs of socks, five shirts, a sweater, a pair of hiking boots, a pair of tennis shoes, a jean jacket, an overcoat, and the scarf; on an especially cold day, I might wear an extra pair of socks and a polo shirt under an oxford shirt, as well as the sweater, the jean jacket, and the overcoat, not to mention the scarf. "For me," I told Irmgard, at least I think it was Irmgard, "packing isn't all that different from getting dressed.") I put all my books in blue plastic garbage bags, which is how I used to move my clothes from one college apartment to another (one year I had to use a whole garbage bag for my twelve pairs of Levi's); I did end up wearing most of my clothes, having thrown out the pants that didn't fit, and the shredded shirts, and the socks with holes, and the old underwear, which was both shredded and uncomfortably tight (I was wearing my blue jeans without any underwear, luxuriating in the draft as I brought down the garbage bag filled with old clothes, which I left, unsentimentally, in the reeking nighttime dumpster). The books were heavy—heavier, I imagined, than if they had been written by gentiles—but the German plastic was strong; my tapes, the tape player, and the tennis shoes fit into the empty beer crate I had gotten from Kurt and Sabine's next-door neighbor, and I had finished "packing" just after I had started— in the scheme of things, at the same time as starting. I had washed my clothes before deciding to throw most of them out and was rereading a day-old newspaper from the Laundromat while waiting for the taxicab; both of the stories on the violence-against-foreigners page had needed rereading, had sounded complicated: In the west of Brandenburg, a policeman, who, weeks before, had become something of a national—though not local—hero after revealing a town plot to burn down a newly constructed, still empty, asylum seekers' home (he had gotten additional coverage after going public with signed hate mail and tapes of obscene phone calls), was now confessing that he had been a Stasi informer for years, that he had driven other people from his town to the November 4 demonstration in Alexanderplatz in 1989 only to spy on them; in another article, a *Burschenschafter* from West Germany, who is studying medicine in Göttingen, was arrested along with several East Germans from Sachsen-Anhalt for burning down an asylum seekers' home on New Year's Eve in a village outside Dessau, and just across the state border from the town that the Stasi informer had informed on. The cabdriver knocked on the door at quarter past twelve; he carried down the two bags full of books, and I carried down the beer crate. He was West German, hadn't really known how to get to the Krügers' apartment, or how to get out of Berlin Mitte and into Wedding, where he said he had lived for ten years. He was around forty, I thought, and wanted to know if I was a student (no, I shrugged); officially, he said, he was still a student; he had come to Berlin to avoid the draft and then decided to study law because he couldn't think of anything better to do, though he had grown up near Goslar, in the Harz Mountains, which has some association with the Brothers Grimm, and is not too far from Göttingen, which is also associated with the Brothers Grimm, and with Nobel prizes, and with *Burschenschafter*, and this week, at least, with young, wealthy well-educated West Germans acting like skinheads, who are all assumed to be East German and unemployed: *"Lumpenproletariat?"* chided the newspaper, which was an East Berlin tabloid, under the photo of the *Burschenschafter*, who was dressed in an English Barbour coat and a silk-and-cashmere scarf, which is the sort of outfit Hans-Joachim likes to wear (and the sort of outfit I sometimes thought about wearing when I was earning all that money last year, and which I always think about wearing now that I don't have any money), in response, apparently, to the Bavarian politician who had claimed on a talk show that the violence against foreigners was all being carried out by *"Lumpenproletariat."* The cabdriver and I talked about the kind of people who end up becoming *Burschenschafter*; he said they were all *"Faschos,"* and compared them to members of fraternities in the United States, which he seemed to have learned about from *National Lampoon's Animal House*, which, he said, was one of his favorite movies because John Belushi was in it. I tried to think about my new apartment: I pictured myself in the elevator, going up and up.

The East Berliner and the West Berliner

Andreas was Julien Sorel in *The Red and the Black* (up and up, to a point), or, perhaps, Rastignac in *Le Père Goriot*, looking down on Paris from Père-Lachaise, declaring his war ("Now it's just the two of us," says Rastignac, meaning himself and Paris). Where did Andreas come from? Who were his parents? Were they alive? or dead? or just ill? It didn't matter: All that was left of what had come before was Andreas's momentum away from it. He encircled Berlin, driving around the new federal states, selling electrical appliances; he got up early on Saturday mornings, after having driven thirty or forty hours during the week, and attended workshops in new, American-style shopping malls in the south of East Berlin; he could get rid of his Berlin accent, could joke with *Leipziger* and *Dresdener* and *Schweriner* and *Neubrandenburger* about how provincial, or otherwise uncivilized, Berlin was, speaking in their dialects or parodying his own; he joked with East Berliners about *Wessis* and with West Berliners about *Ossis*; he went jogging, ran up and down grassy hills, having read in the health advice column of the German edition of an American business magazine that it was healthier to run on grass; Andreas had forgotten, or had never learned, that those hills were made out of rubble, piled in heaps after being dug out by women like his then teenaged mother and his widowed grandmother; he had forgotten about his father, who had worked in a post office in Wedding for thirty years, writing poetry during his lunch breaks about the Bohemian forest of his childhood, often getting them published in a Sudeten German refugee newsletter; about his mother, who had also worked at the post office, who had spent her weekends typing her husband's poems; about his mother's sister, who had lived in Prenzlauer Berg before moving out to Marzahn, though she commuted back to Prenzlauer Berg to work in a post office branch, sorting packages like the ones her sister used to send her, though she had never been the person paid to take out the Deutschmarks and the newspapers and leave in the family photographs, the chocolate, the coffee; about

his other grandmother, and her sisters . . . brother who . . .
wives who . . . refugees who . . . soldiers . . . party member(s)
. . . factory workers . . . peasant, with fingers so black with
dirt that his wife liked to joke that he had dug them out of
the ground (Andreas's fingers were always swollen from holding too tightly on to his steering wheel; at night he would
grind his teeth—his bottom molars, his dentist had warned
him, were as flat as a kitchen table—and until ten or eleven in
the morning, his bottom jaw throbbed). Susi was Lot's Wife,
Eurydice: behind, down. She had met Andreas at a chaos man-
agement workshop, where the West German district manager
had sent her after Olaf, upon learning that he would have to
work on Saturdays, became hysterical and ripped up a rain-
coat, and the police had had to come; one of the customers
had had to call the police. Andreas sat next to Susi; she
watched him taking notes, could smell his cologne—actually,
it was his underarm deodorant—recognized a faint odor of
dry cleaning fluid on his suit coat; they had eaten lunch together, walked out to the parking lot together: Susi had given
him her phone number (he hadn't given her his number,
because, he said, he was never at home; he was getting a car
phone though, and would call her, he said, while going 200
kilometers an hour). He never called. Susi sometimes waited
by the silent telephone; it seemed to throb with silence.

The cabdriver parked his cab on a wide stretch of pavement that
looked vast and dark in the moonlight, like an esplanade. I told him
to wait while I went to check the new keys (I had copied a set for
Irmgard but then had given her the original by mistake). On the
way over I had felt exhilarated and regretful, as if I were leaving
Berlin; I felt that moving out of the Krügers' to somewhere else
was a first step—that I was moving forward (or what in retrospect
would turn out to have been forward; forwardness, too, being a
kind of conceit): to the end, I had thought. Onward to the end.
Until the end, too, is passed. (Then I had imagined myself actually
in the apartment, eating, getting bigger and bigger until my body
met the narrow walls.) The elevator stunk of garlic, of cheap cologne, of garbage; there was graffiti in Arabic scratched into the

metal. I saw the note on Kahula's door right away, even before the elevator had finished opening. At the door, I stuck the key in before reading the note, which was written mostly in long official German, in words that take up three or four lines of narrow print; the key turned, unlocked the door, but the door wouldn't open, it had been nailed shut. The apartment, which I had conceded as a first step, as temporary (like an airplane's cabin, or, as I rode up in the elevator, like an elevator, or even like a prison cell: confining but temporary—assuming that every kind of confinement has to end sometime, even if that ending has to be called death), had collapsed, "died," become a locked door; I fingered the nail heads, could smell the empty air from the other side, seeping out. (Now, of course, it is the twenty-eighth, virtually the first; I am in the Krügers' ruined kitchen, listening to Neil Young, running my fingers over the pages of some book, acting as if this were a leap year, believing, with perfect faith, in the twenty-ninth of February; or disbelieving, and half-wondering if what is happening to me has a name, whether I could describe myself as "having been Februaried.") I think of the picture window as still waiting for me behind Kahula's door (sealed, the cabdriver told me, by the immigration authorities); I think of its views of negation: of East and West Berlin, otherwise boroughless, accompanying and precluding each other, with me, above, looking out, an eye for each; or of Berlin itself, its two parts mysteriously indistinguishable, undivided, historyless, as dark as the apartment with the blinds drawn. A Messiah's function is temporal, or antitemporal: he redeems by ending history, by removing the need to measure time, which is perhaps what Kafka had in mind when he wrote that the Messiah will come "only on the day after his arrival"; or perhaps he was writing about sleep (Kafka, in addition to being a German-speaking Jew in a Czech-speaking Austrian provincial capital, or consequently, or more importantly, was an insomniac), which, to an insomniac, always comes too late, with each waking moment promising—and then going back on the promise—that sleep will come, that a day could actually be over with; or what he had in mind when he wrote "A Little Fable," in which the cat is a Messiah, or an anti-Messiah, providing one kind of ending at the expense of another. I fingered the nails of the door while the taxi waited below, its meter ticking onward, pounding, like a heart (pettily, I considered, on the way back to the Krügers', like a clock), its snout burrowing into the darkened concrete.

PART II

[Greifenhagener Strasse]

Today.

Today I might think about Professor Whitlaw's shrug and about
the clothes chute in my parents' house in Milwaukee. And, perhaps, about the bent light that came through the window. And
about my driver's license, which I got exactly fifteen years ago
today. (Even if those things turn out to be preludes, eventually
about other things.) I shall think: I remember at the same speed
as I walk. Or (as homily): a step (or steps) forward, a thought
backward.

A form of fleeing.

Moving through an abandoned present.
A smaller journey within a larger.
The promise of a detour.
    An invocation.

The new apartment is not like the old one. It is empty, except
for a small kitchen table and a couch covered with an old sheet to
protect it from the dust, and the dust itself, which seems to be in
layers, and is perhaps mostly powdery remnants of paint coats,
along with bits of rubble blowing in with the early spring wind.
For the last two, three, four years (Herr Huberman was not precise),
Autonomen were living here. I can still read a graffito, WIR SIND EIN
DUMMES VOLK, fading between the paint layers. The apartment
actually has the same number of rooms as the Krügers' but is

smaller, deep in Prenzlauer Berg, a back house apartment (unlike the Krügers' apartment—Hans-Joachim once explained to me—which was a "side house" apartment that happened to be built in the back), an authentic tenement. Herr Huberman, a plumber and, somehow, an acquaintance of Burt Kaminsky's, is the legal tenant; he said I could stay as long as I wanted; then the workmen came and started drilling holes in the kitchen—in the floor, in the ceiling, through the wall to the bathroom—and said something about the new owner's son moving in, which Herr Huberman claims to know nothing about. The bathroom used to be a closet until Herr Huberman installed the toilet and the shower himself. He must have installed them badly: when the man above me takes a shower, or flushes his toilet, the bathroom floor floods. When I use the toilet, the floor also floods, though it especially floods when I take a shower—the drain is clogged and there is no shower curtain, and the water, after filling up the shallow tub and ringing my calves with soap scum, spills over onto the floor. The bathroom smells like mold and ammonia and, occasionally, like soap. The apartment smells like plaster, like dust, or like the bathroom if I forget to close the bathroom door, which is shorter than I am, sawed off at an angle, like the door to the built-in ironing board in my parents' kitchen.

Sudden patterns.

The virtue of choreography. (The particular chaos of memory; the choreography of remembering.)

I saw the light through the living room window (the bedroom has no window; *ein dummes Volk*, I thought that first morning, with the door closed, in the perfect darkness), as an awakening, and then as a numbing after I remembered where I was.

My mother's room: unelaborate, but mysterious, like . . . once in the fifth grade, when I forgot how to spell the word "if."

Or was it "of"?

. . .

"There are poisons in my body."
Pause.
"My body is filled with poisons."

The baker across the street has been to Miami Beach. As I was moving in, he came out of the bakery and carried my beer crate through the green-tiled hall, into the courtyard (only one courtyard here, partly destroyed in the war; half a courtyard; a room with two walls), up four flights, into the empty, filthy apartment (filthier now that there are workmen every day, drilling, drinking beer and coffee, eating mysterious sausages that remind me of the butterscotch "space sticks" I used to eat at lunch in the 1970s after they had been invented for astronauts, reminding me of Tang). While climbing the stairs, he had talked about his two weeks in Miami Beach; he was still brown. His face looked like a roll, doughy and brown; there was flour caking his fingers, under his nails, disguising his cuticles; eventually he picked his nose.

(German men pick their noses, have long filed fingernails. German women bite off their fingernails then avoid their cuticles when they polish their nails, wear polish down the middle, like a stripe. I can't remember seeing a German woman pick her nose, except Irmgard, who told me that her father also picks his nose and then instinctively sticks his finger in his mouth. "Like a little boy," she said, with a smile on her face.)

I am deteriorating. I don't like to use the shower, the Laundromat is far away. I sleep on the floor with blankets and a pillow that Sabine gave me; I wake up in the middle of the night after drinking too much beer and don't want to walk barefoot through the filthy apartment, don't want to have to use the leaking toilet, and I urinate into empty beer bottles; I pick my nose, flicking the snot into a pile of dust, feeling superior to Irmgard's father, to the baker from across the street (no one to see me).

. . .

Walking through the half courtyard in the cold spring wind, in sticky, sour clothes, my new blue jeans already too tight, feeling cleaner because of the wind.

The hallway in the front house is a kind of museum. It has green, elaborate tiles running down the walls' middle sections, each tile with the same mysterious kind of flower—a tulip, perhaps, or an iris; or something else, vaguely poppylike—with a swollen pistil; a mixture of styles (*Jugendstil* clearly, though also neo-baroque; curvaceous, then cut off, a little bit geometric), but authentic, untouched, unscathed, permanent (the new owner—who is actually the daughter of the man who owned the house before the war—is renovating; a baffled old woman in a front house apartment told me yesterday that the owner had talked to her about the tiles, about renovating the front and back houses around the tiles, painting everything shades of green); I am here as an unapproved-of subletter, illegally, and don't even yet have a key to the front house's front door; Irmgard and I, a few nights after I moved in, climbed over the fence that stands where the back house's back wall obviously had once stood; an old woman watched us climb, though possibly not the old woman who had been talked to about the tiles; we saw the light go on, the nylon lace curtains shift, the sudden face; "I am Herr Huberman's American cousin," I said yesterday, just in case. (Old East German neighbors are becoming notorious for denouncing people like me to new owners, to superintendents, to tabloid newspapers, and to people in shops, to anyone who will listen.) "My wife lives in Hamburg. Sometimes she visits me."

(The bakery, I thought in the hallway, which felt colder than the courtyard, hungry.)

Then the tiles.

The tiles make me think of history, as such.

Americans, when it comes to history, are night-blind; Germans, having gotten used to the darkness, squint their eyes in the light, look ridiculous; Jews are history's insomniacs: around for everything.

Or some other way: the cool green tiles, waist high, above a destroyed, once tiled floor (or still tiled: a floor of shattered tiles); beneath a rebuilt, repainted wall, flanked by destruction; European history: a tapestry tied in knots.

If Professor Whitlaw hadn't.

The laundry chute—though our family always called it a "clothes chute," which may be a local variation, or even an intensely local one, something private, hermetic; I have never talked about the expression with anybody, have mostly heard it, from my mother on Saturday mornings, when she would come into my room, look at the floor, and say "Throw that down the clothes chute this instant," meaning, it would seem, the clothes and the paperback novels and a previous week's Milwaukee *Journal*s, schoolbooks and notebooks; all of it, the mere mess—runs from what had been my bedroom, down past the den, which my mother eventually appropriated for herself, for her sicknesses and phone conversations, and now for her television set, to the basement, which eventually became my sister's bedroom when she was in high school and moved there from her bedroom upstairs (which became oddly empty; then a screened-in porch, with summer furniture that no one ever sat in and a television set that no one ever watched; and is now an empty screened-in porch, with the screens themselves often ripped, like old metal fences), and then became my father's room, where he would pretend to work, watch television. It transported smells and sounds.

Once, more than once, I imagined I could slide down. The knobbed door, painted pale blue to match something or other, is the size of an adult head.

Voices, memorably. And TV noise.

And clothes. Of course. Sometimes, if my mother was doing

laundry, she would shout up to me through the clothes chute, "Throw everything down!" First from the basement, then later, from her room, with her cleaning ladies waiting at the bottom, staring up into the chute. To clean the guest bathroom on the first floor, my mother always instructed the cleaning ladies to pour bleach on the tiles and then wait, later wiping up the bleach with huge towels that had been stolen from hotels in Chicago and New York and Rochester, Minnesota, where the Mayo Clinic is, and then throwing the wet towels down the clothes chute. My room always tasted vaguely of bleach on the days the cleaning ladies came: the smell had seeped upward.

Falling is a sensation and a fact. An outcome. Later, a perspective.

But not a proposition, not an assumption; without assumptions. Except one—that you will land, end up.

I will walk the length of Berlin, I thought in the hallway, but now have to remember it in the bakery, from here, where I am now.

"We used to take you to matinees," my mother said on the telephone, when I called my parents to get the money for the rent, which I begged Herr Huberman to let me pay late. "And you loved movies. We would take you to movies on Saturday night, like our little friend." She was reminiscing about my childhood, sounding like a child herself.

"My legs aren't mine anymore."

I sleep better in this apartment, though on the floor, with the blankets and no mattress and the electric radiator that Peter gave me so I don't have to use the coal oven, in the dry dusty heat, I feel like a dog.

Irmgard didn't actually sleep over that night; she waited until five for the U-Bahn to start running. Neither of us seemed to have bathed. We lay down on the blankets, and the next day, the quilt I use as a mattress was striped with our separate, strong, smells.

"I'm sick."

[Erich-Weinert-Strasse]

In the other direction, where I once walked: 1920s utopian housing project; bombed-out remnants of once unusual balconies; once stripped-down, functional building façades now scaly, layered, like fossils; vista down a side street: columns of clouded stairwell windows, their frames looking bare and fixed, like vertebrae. Then, at the edge, the one rebuilt building: new, just painted as before, with old-fashioned futuristic simplicity, stripes within stripes, yellow-blue window frames, new ochre walls, disquieting (like: a painted Greek statue, a dummy in an Italian street procession, a German puppet, a department store mannequin).

(Canetti, in August 1945: "The things we hear about prewar days sound paleolithic.")

Also: new West German figures painted in the crosswalks, bodies to warn drivers, reassure walkers, but what might remind someone of shadows left behind after an atomic blast.

How are you?

"I told you already. I'm sick. I'm sick like I'm old. I'm sick like I'm a Republican." (My mother's declension.)

A pause (dramatic; imagined).

"I'm sick like I'm a Jew."

Only briefly that way, until I reach the Karl-Friedrich-Schinkel Oberschule, with a neo-baroque façade—columns, chiseled window heads—and a *Landhausstil* (barnlike) roof. An old woman opens a window, sticks out her white head, is lined up, looks like a stone head.

Then back.

Once. Once, since moving into the apartment, I woke up in the middle of the night, thirsty, and thought that a half-filled bottle of urine was the other bottle, still filled with undrunk beer, and I drank it and gagged, spat it out on the wooden floor, painted and repainted white. After I wiped up the saliva and urine with the old-fashioned, newly made, sandpaperlike East German toilet paper, the floor looked scrubbed, and the paper was bright white.

Once in Chicago, in August, at three in the morning, a man on Clark Street—black, crazy, wearing a winter coat and hat, and gloves with the fingers cut off—was stalling on the pavement. People were walking past him, and I stopped to watch. He was pissing in a glass, then he stopped pissing and drank his urine. "Tastes good," he said to no one.

RUDIS RESTE RAMPE
RUDI'S SUPERSCHNÄPPCHEN:
PORZELLANÜBERTÖPFE
BODENVASE
PLASTEÜBERTÖPFE
UNTERSETZER
TEXTILBLUMEN

(centered and in capital letters, like the text of a memorial plaque)

The houses on this street have exaggerated gables that look like flaps of tailskin on raw chickens. There are traces of paint on the houses—ochre, greenish blue, Della Robbia blue, cream—that look faded, bonded but delicate, like a fresco, like a cave drawing. The buildings up here seem older than the ones on the Alte Schönhauser Strasse (though in fact are newer), less repaired; petrified, then curdled; crumbly, as if their brick and sandstone walls were made of cheap concrete.

Once I stuck my hand out the living room window, grabbed delicatedly at a hunk of decades-old sandy mortar between the scarred century-old bricks, as though it were a piece of flesh, then wondered if I could tear it off; then it fell off, bits blowing back into the apartment.

This morning, looking out the window: A woman's hand out a window across the courtyard, shaking blue towel in wind.

What I have recently heard: the bombed cobblestone streets in East Berlin were repaved after the war with rubble; that the streets, as it were, are paved with houses.

On the wide, differentiated sidewalks (there are three or four lanes; kinds of cobblestones, uneven, almost hilly, multicolored, like a stone beach, surrounded by pentagonal concrete, or rectangular concrete, perfectly flat, but loosening, mealy), the outside lane is lined with dog shit. During and just after the war, the streets were cleared by piling the rubble on the edges of sidewalks, like snow.

Late, late winter; early spring. Old leaves blown into piles by the wind, firecracker carcasses from New Year's Eve, posters from the film festival in February (which I forgot about this year, went to studiously last year, circling all the movies in the twenty-mark bilingual "Official Guide to the Berlin Film Festival" about Jews, Germans, Jews and Germans, and some of the movies about homosexuals, a few new Hollywood movies), a few of last fall's leaves still clinging to trees, bare trees; sudden too warm sunshine.

[Schönhauser Allee]

Here the underground is aboveground, like in Chicago.

The station nearby: glass and iron, stained from coal smoke and leaded gasoline (a satanic church; Crystal Palace darkness).

The U-Bahn station up here is nothing like Otto Wagner's old

Stadtbahn stations in Vienna, and not like Hector Guimard's Métro stations in Paris—has no signature.

Parisian arcades.

Viennese alleyways.

Berlin avenues, wider than the Parisian boulevards they were meant to imitate; up here, still lined with old East German neon, walled-in.

DEUTSCHE BANK

(advertising its loan department)

"If you want your money to grow big and strong . . ." (photo of a tree; German oak, I think).

"If it's love at first sight . . ." (photo of a German house, with gables).

Girl on roller blades. It is early (like in that Joni Mitchell song "Morning Morgantown," which I remember my sister listening to over and over again, when the basement was still her bedroom; it came up through the clothes chute; later I listened to it upstairs, in my bedroom, my father yelling up to tell me to turn the music down, that my mother was sleeping, though before I heard his voice, above his voice, I could hear my mother's phone conversation, her television set; I rarely listen to it here), between rush hour and later when all the stores are open. She seems to be running away to school.

CONNIE'S CONTAINER
Cnallhart Calkuliert

HERUMATIC HANDÄHMASCHINE
"WELLA" HAIR-BODY-SHAMPOO
MOULINEX DAMPFBÜGELEISER

SPORTHAUS OLYMPIA!
STARK REDUZIERT!

New businesses are going broke; the East German S-Bahn station, with its green S, so different from the West German S-Bahn stations and their green *S*s. In Vienna, which now, instead of its old Stadtbahn, has an S-Bahn and an U-Bahn (like any provincial German city, which Vienna first began to resemble after the *Anschluss*), the S-Bahn trains sometimes use an old Runic "S" as an insignia, like the S on an SS uniform.

(S-Bahn trains in Vienna looking like Warsaw Pact tanks in Prague: scrawled upon).

A row of store names across the street:

BURGER KING

FOTO LABOR

CHRISTEL'S BIERSTUBEN

MCPAPER

OBST UND GEMÜSE

DROGERIE

BLUME 2000

HERRENMODE

MODERNE KÜCHE

The East German neon on the last two: typical, superannuated; poignant; remote. And, for me, now, familiar, not mysterious, though jarring, like the light, which, at its early spring angle, is like a peripheral lightbulb.

Newspaper headlines—outside the *Drogerie*, the tobacco shop, the S-Bahn station—on billboards colored red and black, or black and yellow, or red and yellow, like rows of hacked-up German flags.

The papers, probably, are no longer full of stories about the East German pole vaulter whose father, after defecting to West Germany in the middle 1980s, began working for the Stasi, nor about the track coach in West Germany who knew about it and was being blackmailed not to tell, nor about the local sports official who continues to deny, evidence to the contrary, that he hadn't been working for the Stasi and, in any case, hadn't been the one who had been blackmailing the West German coach, whom he admits telephoning several times a day in the summer of 1988.

The papers (conceivably) are full of track meets, pictures of the unusually early spring in Lower Saxony (the track coach and sports official are from Lower Saxony, which Germans, when they are trying to speak in English, always pronounce as "Lower *Saxonia*," sounding foreign and old-fashioned, like East Indians), stories about the union officials from Lower Saxony and North Rhine–Westphalia who were working for the Stasi, a story about the latest Bundestag member who has been revealed as having worked for the Stasi, underneath a photograph of his modified Bauhaus-style office building in Bonn, where all of the offices have a partial view of the Rhine River.

(In the new apartment, I have been going on newspaper binges, leaving them spread out afterward over the living room, like the lining of a cage, or like my childhood bedroom; most of my books are still in the garbage bags, lined up like guests on the sheet-covered couch; the radio reception, especially from the windowless bedroom, is terrible.)

Ahead: the East German television tower (which looks, in photographs, and from closer up, absurd, like a nuclear silo topped with a stainless-steel globe topped with a peppermint stick, but which, from this distance, looks old-fashioned, almost whimsical, with a 1950s science-fiction purposefulness); perfectly ahead— a baroque vista.

KAISER'S DRUGSTORE

"We don't want to live in a ghost town"

WINTER PULLIS REDUZIERT

REPS RAUS BULLEN RAUS

There is a tanning salon where there used to be a porno shop, and the trailer bank, which must have opened in the summer the currencies were unified, has closed. I walked down this street the week I moved to Berlin, in the fall, and remember noticing the temporariness of the bank and the (then) newness of the porno shop. The fall here, unlike the spring, is windless, doesn't confuse in that sense, like the falls and springs in Wisconsin, which are briefly, overwhelmingly similar—in their mildness and in their ability to give way quickly to something else, in their sudden extremeness, are blurred, rather than layered.

Cities, now, confuse me, remind me of other cities.

"Kaiser" (in Germany): the title of the German emperors as well as a vaguely Jewish surname (before); now, the name of a ubiquitous chain of grocery stores and discount drug outlets.

(Don't forget to buy plastic bath shoes to wear in the apartment, in the shower. Black feet from walking across the dirty white floors, or whitish gray feet from walking across the floor when my feet are wet.)

As for Kaiser's: Did the people in the town outside Ravensbrück concentration camp get theirs?

People from elsewhere objected to the building of a grocery store on the grounds of a concentration camp, then the people from the nearby town began their protest: WE WANT OUR KAISER'S! WE DON'T WANT TO LIVE IN A GHOST TOWN! That was just after I got here, and now I don't know if they got their Kaiser's or not, although I can't imagine that at least most of them don't realize that they already live in a ghost town.

The Kaiser's on the Pappelallee: where I buy my groceries (with money left over from the money my parents sent me), though I often misread Pappelallee, named after the poplar trees that no longer line it, as "Peopleallee." That particular Kaiser's reminds me of grocery stores at home in Milwaukee, which are smaller than the ones in Los Angeles and larger and cleaner than the ones in New York and not too much unlike the ones in Chicago, at least in parts of Chicago.

("Bring in the groceries," someone would shout up through the clothes chute, and I would pretend not to hear, as though they had been shouting through concrete.)

Cooking with pans bought across the street at Rudis Reste

Rampe, instead of with the old East German enamel pans in the Krügers' kitchen; having to put the dishes and the food into cupboards at night, which it never occurred to me to do until the evening after the workmen started drilling, and everything was covered with a sort of beige dust (concrete mixed with wood).

Political philosophy, coming down to a quip.

Kant's political ideas, as advanced in Professor Whitlaw's occasional lectures on the subject, could be summed up in the following line, which I remember utterly, almost rhythmically, as though it were a song lyric: "Act so as to treat every rational being, whether in yourself or in another, never as a means only but always also as an end." (Professor Whitlaw's students, of course, tended to treat him as an easy B+.) Nietzsche's thoughts on politics, which, according to Professor Whitlaw, and consequently according to each of my term papers on the subject, actually had to do with aesthetics, with what kind of government inspires significant works of art, came down to: "All great ages of culture are ages of political decline." "One thing leads to another" is something my mother used to say, and which, considering when she would say it, ramifies, has implications regarding free will and just deserts: people should be able to do what they want seeing as they will get what they deserve. Annette thinks that no one gets what they deserve, or, rather, that she doesn't get what she deserves; when she isn't being amused or amusing, she is feeling condescended to, humiliated; she once told me that she doesn't see any difference between the life of the woman narrator in *The Yellow Wallpaper* and that of a prisoner in a gulag, compares the way her women's studies department is run to a gulag, would, I think, be amused and humiliated to have her political ideas summed up as: "The blind leading the bound." I feel cleaner in the wind, which is an aesthetic observation with temporal implications, amounts to a theory of postponement (of eventually bathing), of a particular present, though not of a present tense (nothing seems of the moment; the moment deserves nothing; I deserve to feel something in the springtime, with the wind blowing across my face, deserve to be elsewhere, if only in my mind, to remember). My mother is still a registered Republican ("I'm sick like I'm a Republican. I'm sick like I'm a Jew."), like her gentile neighbors, but unlike her Jewish friends on the other side of town, what moving out to Brookfield has led to. Annette talks about voting for Jesse Jackson and Jerry Brown, expresses sympathy for losers, though in real life failure makes her nervous, except for a failed private life, for loneliness; in her romance novels, the heroines usually end up alone, only vaguely triumphant, reading in bed. (When I left her in Paris, she was stone-faced, seemed suddenly older and withered, like Yul Brynner's pharaoh at the end of *The Ten Commandments*.) Once I didn't vote on the advice of my sister, the tax attorney, who told me that not voting is a good way to avoid paying state income tax. Here in Berlin, I have no rights and imagine that I have no obligations, am, in fact, now that I am no longer teaching, legally a tourist. Tourists bring their own, de facto political philosophy with them, which comes down to: "Ignorance is always an excuse."

DISCOUNT DEN (during and after).

In college, I bought my records at Discount Den, which, when I first arrived, was at the University Square Mall, though later, when they turned Madison's main street, State Street, into a pedestrian mall, Discount Den moved there; but by the time it moved, I was already gone. Across the street from where Discount Den is now, there is a private dorm, popular among Jewish students from suburbs, rather like the one across the street, at a diagonal to Discount Den, where I lived my freshman year, and where Annette, improbably, also lived, working at the front desk to reduce her rent (Annette, who grew up in a lower-middle-class suburb of Minneapolis, near the airport, away from Jews, has the black wiry hair of a Jew, is usually assumed to be a Jew, which she seems to take as a compliment). During my freshman year, the other dorm, the one now directly across the street from Discount

Den, was a halfway house for mentally ill adults and recovering drug addicts and alcoholics; I remember them smoking on the sidewalks, seeming to increase in number at the ends of exam weeks; I remember them going to vote one fall, ten of them, holding hands, marching in a line, with American flags and REAGAN-BUSH straw hats left over from the last election. Later the halfway house was sold, or lost its funding, or simply closed. Two years ago, I was in Madison just before coming here, and there was my old dorm, now in duplicate, and the Discount Den, where I bought Neil Young's three-album *Decade* on two cassettes for my trip to Germany, and I suddenly remembered, as I now remember once again, the old, fat retarded man waking me up each morning with a hacking cough, standing out on the sidewalk, even in the middle of winter, in bedroom slippers, with his robe slipping open, showing his skirtlike underwear, and, it was said, his penis.

Here in Berlin, treating time as horizontal, as though epochs were like boroughs.

Treating people as a means to an end, as a detour.

I have passed the Gethsemane Church, which is said to have been a center of dissidence in East Germany, where, it is also said, there wasn't any real dissidence. Germans are fond of maxims, as they are of abbreviations and of exact change; some people extract political views (or a political fate) from the following: *"Was darf nicht sein kann nicht sein"* and *"Wer die Wahl hat hat die Qual."* (What is not allowed to be can't be, and Whoever has the choice has the torment. Awkward in English, tellingly succinct in German.) My mother and father would translate the first, as well as the second, as meaning, essentially, "You can't afford something if you haven't got the money." Annette wouldn't have much use for the first, but would find the second illuminating—obviously and comfortably true, having something to do with shopping. (Annette's first three novels had the same suburban heroine, and

I told her once that they could be reissued together as *The Shopping Mall Trilogy*.)

In order to remember the wind: I must think of my parents as benefactors and then as strangers, think of Annette as a stranger. (I think of Annette as a friend I haven't chosen, too fresh to be a memory, exactly; I think of my parents as having treated me as an adult when I was a child and treating me as a child now that I am an adult, bullying me with their confusions.)

Whoever is not allowed to be: isn't.

Professor Whitlaw eating, getting soup on his book, which is placed to his right, like a napkin. I am a senior in college. We are talking about my graduate school application (I had forgotten this, until now, until this new Chinese restaurant, which looks so much like the other new Chinese restaurants I have passed already, except for the neon sign next door advertising the old East German state ice cream, crowned with window-sized neon snowflakes).

We always had cleaning ladies. My mother's mother, who, in spite of the Depression and her husband's salary as an auto mechanic also always did. My mother's mother's cleaning ladies, according to my mother, were black; she doesn't remember any of their names. Our cleaning ladies, when I was very small, were black, and I don't remember any of their names. They came once a week, I think. Later, when I was in junior high school, my mother had Mexican cleaning ladies, whom she said weren't very clean, and then, while I was in high school, a Polish family who came with industrial cleaning equipment, and whom I remember as not being very clean; I remember the sound of their *film-noir* vacuum cleaner on the days I was home from school, their accents, their body odor. Now my mother needs a nurse and a cook, as well as a cleaning lady, and has a housewife from Brookfield whose husband is unemployed come over and do everything while she sleeps in front of the television set. I have never seen her; I only know her by name—Edie—and how she answers the phone—"La

Vine residence, Edie speaking"—or accepts collect calls—"Yes. I will," as if she were on the witness stand—in her underwater Milwaukee accent. My mother says that Edie is "sweet" but can never remember where anything is, once calling her a *"goyisheh kopp,"* but then promptly admitting that without her and my father she would have to go into a nursing home. That was a lucid moment. Usually, she pretends that she has just walked in the door, that she is about to cook dinner.

BISTRO

RINDERGOULASH

RINDERROULADE

KOHLROULADE

BRATWURST

KASSLERBRATEN

HACKBRATEN

SAUERBRATEN

SCHWEINEBRATEN

SCHWEINLEBER

(plates of bones)

Avoiding concentration camps, cemeteries.

Concentration camps I haven't been to near cities I have visited: Dachau, Theresienstadt, Auschwitz, Treblinka, Bergen-Belsen, Sachsenhausen; although I have planned to visit Sachsenhausen, which is just outside Berlin, in Oranienburg (I could take the S-Bahn from the Schönhauser Allee S-Bahn station), the day before I leave Berlin for good.

Or: I can't avoid them. All of Berlin is a Jewish cemetery, like all of Europe.

[Eberswalder Strasse]

Ahead: the last U-Bahn station aboveground, and a star of intersecting streets, and, eventually, a Jewish cemetery.

The U-Bahn station's iron has been painted green, its track on either side has also been painted green, its overpass advertising West Berlin newspapers is, also, green.

(The station itself: cleaner, with scoured glass, a little magical; a greenhouse, a pavilion; too large, making the streets seem narrower; signed with Berlin's onetime massivity.)

The intersecting streets themselves are usual—broad and comforting (massive); old-fashioned (the Wilhelminian bigness; the East German neon; other things, surviving from other periods, that I don't recognize), photographable, black-and-white, with the greenness colored in. An afterthought: three streets intersecting, Star of David–like.

And the cemetery.

[DIESER JÜDISCHER FRIEDHOF WURDE
1827
SEINER BESTIMMUNG ÜBERGEBEN
IN DER ZEIT VON
1933–1945
WURDE ER VON DEN FASCHISTEN
ZERSTÖRT
DER NACHWELT SOLL ER ALS
MAHNUNG ERHALTEN BLEIBEN]

After the station, just where the green tracks go underground.

[felled tombstones]

. . .

Sharp left at Dimitroffstrasse, instead of walking straight and eventually past the cemetery, and then down the broader avenue, which becomes tree lined, parklike, where the U-Bahn tracks have disappeared.

Walter Benjamin learned about Berlin, where he grew up, elsewhere—in Paris, in Moscow, wandering through other cities, through their crowds.

Cities, then, meant crowds (the city, to Canetti, was a kind of inflationary crowd; Benjamin compares getting lost in Paris to getting lost in a forest, finding his way around Paris to finding his way through a labyrinth); now, they mean absent crowds, people in suburbs and no longer in cities, are deflationary ("dead," my mother said, when I asked her how Milwaukee was).

I learned about Milwaukee, I now realize, in Los Angeles—on its freeways, in its shopping malls and parking complexes, in its traffic jams (a traffic jam: an inflationary parking lot; a felled forest; a drawing of a labyrinth); in Los Angeles not having a car is like not being sane; a car registration form is like a certificate of sanity; bus stops are like madhouses.

An old stretch of Milwaukee's downtown was enclosed, turned into a shopping mall: the Grand Avenue Mall. It looks like every other shopping mall that I have ever been in, except for the murals on the second floor, which show turn-of-the-century Milwaukee: German-looking men, with handlebar moustaches, drinking beer. I think of the men now as looking German.

Near the baseball stadium, west of downtown: a vast cemetery with a Jewish section.

I don't think Milwaukee has separate Jewish cemeteries, but Jewish sections within cemeteries, unlike Berlin, unlike Prague, but like Vienna. I got to know Berlin, the scale of its inner destruction (of its conceit that it has anything in common with the city it was "before" some imprecise date—before 1914, 1918, 1933, 194-whatever, 1945; 1961, 1989; imprecise but somehow also exact: obvious), the ways in which a city can be absent from itself, in

Vienna, which I visited last summer and which I have so often
read about in Berlin and where everything is decked out in some
kind of temporal drag, like a folk fair commemorating epochs instead of nationalities. My mother's parents are buried in the Jewish
cemetery (or the Jewish part of the cemetery) west of downtown,
and it is where my parents have already bought their cemetery
plots. An interstate freeway was built in the early 1960s just after
I was born, connecting Milwaukee with Madison, running right
through Brookfield (I could almost hear the rush-hour traffic from
my bedroom window), creating a kind of boom there, although by
then my parents had already built their house, with its now ar-
chaic, and somehow timeless, 1950s conveniences (patio, breakfast
nook, garage attached to the house); the freeway also cuts through
the cemetery, which I would have to drive past if I wanted to go
to the Grand Avenue Mall. Now no one goes to the Grand Avenue
Mall except, it is generally assumed, gangs; there are shoot-outs at
the Grand Avenue Mall, afterschool stabbings. My mother doesn't
go, she said (she certainly couldn't go alone, can no longer drive,
is afraid of passing out at the wheel), thought that I was joking
when I asked her. "It's like a ghost town," my mother said, about
the Grand Avenue Mall in particular and about downtown in general, sounding like her old self. When I was a baby, my father
would take her dancing downtown on Saturday nights; I believe,
at some point, she wanted to be a movie star.

My mother likes crowds: crowded restaurants and crowded theaters; when I was a little older (eight, nine, ten), on Sundays, talking on the telephone, she would describe the theater and the
restaurant that she and my father had taken me to as "peppy," or
as "dead." My father told me that my mother used to look like
Ann Sheridan. (My father spent his childhood, adulthood, and
early middle age in movie theaters, claims to have seen a movie
every day for ten years and two on Sundays in the 1930s, using
money from his paper route at the third- and fourth-run movie
houses, now torn down, remote—as remote from their neighborhoods as Berlin's medieval Slavic settlements are from its present
concrete blocks—but vivid in his own mind, even though he can't

reminisce with my mother, who went to movies downtown, on dates with Jewish boys, to palacelike first-run movie houses that, today, are second- or third-run movie houses—"all-black," my mother would say, like the cast of Pearl Bailey's *Hello, Dolly!*, which came to Milwaukee but which my parents didn't want to see—or have been converted to something else, seem unlikely as much as untended, like those single, two-story, ruined baroque buildings in Berlin Mitte surrounded by five-story, neo-baroque ruined buildings.)

And: she must have liked extremes, in expressing herself that way.

(My father: lived in extremes, in Depression-era foster homes, in orphanages, and then in pre-oil-crisis suburban comfort; always suburban-looking, with his cardigan sweaters and top-of-the-line GM cars, except when he eats, when he lowers his head to the table, slurps and spills, hurries up, like in a movie when the ex-con, having his first meal in the real world, slurps and spills his soup at the diner, eats with his arms tight to his body, pushed in by absent arms on either side, is given away. My mother, in the past few years, especially, though sometimes before, spits out her food in restaurants—bits of grizzle, mysterious bits of whatever, bad-tasting bits—as if she were at home, blaming her strict diet and not her temperament, lining her plate with wads.)

Was Grand Avenue actually a street?

(Before there was a Grand Avenue Mall: Walking down Wisconsin Avenue to Gimbel's, where the ground floor smelled of sausages, walking over the rickety metal bridge that crosses the Milwaukee River, holding my mother's hand, as if we were both afraid of falling in. And crowds. Crowds. Shaking the bridge with their feet.)

Berlin, at ten-thirty, on a Friday morning in what is, in fact, early spring, but what could have felt late last night like late winter, what promises to feel like early summer and then, in the evening, by comparison, might feel like fall: empty, crowdless, though with sudden pockets of fullness (here where Dimitroffstrasse meets Schönhauser Allee; back there, at the Schönhauser Allee S-Bahn station; but not between, as if people were walking in small circles, or were standing still).

BERLINER MORGENPOST Zeitung der Weltstadt BERLINER MORGEN-POST Zeitung der Weltstadt BERLINER MORGENPOST Zeitung der Weltstadt BERLINER MORGENPOST in a single line along the overpass.

The bare trees on the Schönhauser Allee, on the verge of blooming, look like posts.

The bare vines lining the doors of courtyards look like metal fences.

And now: suddenly cloudy, colder, but subtly; imagined, vague, a remembered winter; but no coal smoke, and still the fine, whiter light, a lighter grayness.

Renamed streets; an aboveground underground station.

Part of Dimitroffstrasse has been renamed: on the other side of the tracks, it is called Eberswalder Strasse, and the U-Bahn station is now called Eberswalder Strasse, though I think *Autonomen* still occasionally cross out the "Eberswalder" and write in "Dimitroff." It used to be called Danziger Strasse, which, now, would be inappropriate, irredentist; its new name feels both appropriate (most of the streets behind that side of Schönhauser Allee are named after towns which, like Eberswalde, are in Brandenburg) and inappropriate (sudden, temporary-seeming; when the first "Eberswalder Strasse" sign went up at the U-Bahn station, some *Autonomen*, or people who got called *Autonomen*, set it on fire.) Dimitroffstrasse is named after Georgi Dimitroff, the Bulgarian who headed up the Berlin branch of Comintern before the Nazis came to power and who was put on trial for setting the Reichstag on fire; I can't remember exactly how he distinguished himself in court, but I remember reading what was later said of Dimitroff: "There is only one man left in Germany, and he is a Bulgarian," remembering that, too (or perhaps not remembering it exactly; misremembering it), like a song lyric. Back in Bulgaria, after the war, he was apparently a ruthless Stalinist, and there got to be Dimitroff streets all over Eastern Europe.

When I got here: the Eberswalder Strasse U-Bahn station was still called Dimitroffstrasse, though the Eberswalder Strasse part of Dimitroffstrasse had already been changed to Eberswalder Strasse (noticing these changed names is like moving while standing still, a dizziness), and the *Autonomen* had already had their first big post-reunification riot, after which they had painted over many of Prenzlauer Berg's street names in protest, as if that night's contingent of West German riot police had been an invading army (there are still many painted-over street signs in Prenzlauer Berg, which confuse tourists, and which sometimes still confuse me; in Prague, in 1968, the Czechs painted over the Czech street names, or perhaps actually took the signs down, though the street names themselves, until some point in the nineteenth century, would have all been only in German, having gone bilingual after, I believe, a riot; nearly all the street names where my parents live confuse, sound the same—silly, or perhaps, pastoral—as if they, too, were periodically renamed, or were interchangeable, arbitrary). In Dresden, the Dimitroff Bridge has been changed back to the Augustus Bridge (Augustus was the name of the Saxon king who bankrupted Saxony to turn Dresden into the "Florence of the Elbe"). I learned about Los Angeles in Dresden, or at least thought about it: the very center of the Old Town, which had also been the very center of the firestorm, looks like a parking lot, and the nearby Swiss-built pre-1989 hard-currency hotel could pass for an office building on Wilshire Boulevard. Once I walked around there in the middle of the night, near the hotel, past the Frauenkirche (the church that was left in ruins and is now being rebuilt; in the ruins, they keep finding corpses of people who had crowded into the church to pray during the air raids, and newspapers run articles with computer projections of what the church is going to look like next to photographs of human bones on tarmac), and I saw a man standing in front of the church, weeping. I asked him if he was all right. He said he hadn't been to Dresden in fifty years, that he used to come all the time, that he remembered the church. He had a funny accent, which turned out to be East Prussian; he had been born in Königsberg; it was the middle of the night. A ghost.

" 'Of' he was all right," I think now, as though I were myself as a child.

That metal bridge in Milwaukee: unremarkable; much smaller now, as one's schools are said to be; not much longer than a car.

ATTRAKTIVE MODE FÜR DEN HERRN   MASKULIN

Butcher shops, Turkish kebab stands, Turkish kebab stands pretending to be Italian pizza stands [construction sites], flower shops, bookshops, torn-up streetcar tracks.

GRILLHAXEN

GEGRILLTER SCHWEINEBAUCH

WARME BLUT U. LEBERWURST

BOULETTEN

EISBEIN

KASSLERBRATEN

PUTENSCHNITZEL

CORDONBLEU

(Germans like to eat lunch in butcher shops, or just hang out there. Once, in a small town in Brandenburg, near where Kurt's aunt and uncle raise asparagus and potatoes, I walked through empty streets with Kurt and Sabine and Sabine's children, wondering where all the people were. We decided to stop by the butcher shop to buy Hackfleisch—[as] literally [as possible]: "hacked flesh"—for dinner, and found the town, in line, out the door of the butcher shop; even after they had finished shopping, people lingered, holding their meat—which had been put in clear plastic bags that then looked like bags of blood—straight up in the air, like scales of justice.)

In my mother's room: newish furniture, occasionally bought at a discount from her brother—who still sells furniture at a discount mart near the airport, who lives in Shorewood, near Jews (actually, near mostly old, sometimes poor, Jews, or else especially rich exclusive Jews in mansions along Lake Michigan), but whom my mother describes, increasingly, as "*goyish.*" I remember a particular plaid sofa, with short yarn knots for fringe (now there is a newer sofa, bought the summer before I came here, darker, almost brown, and rougher, tweedy—"You know, classy a little bit," said my mother on the telephone, calling me up in Chicago to tell me about it, with what I now remember as a Yiddish inflection but which perhaps also sounds like a working-class Berlin inflection translated literally into English). Two always new recliners, which my parents seem to buy every other year the way people used to buy cars; the old ones go into the basement, or upstairs into my parents' room, a few times they went to my sister's college apartments, once, I believe, to a cleaning lady; but never to me, never into my room: I had—still have, I suppose I could say (or: "the room still has")—an old (it must have been from the 1920s) gold reading chair that had belonged to my grandmother; last year, my mother told me, they bought two black leather recliners ("recliner": what do other people say? La-Z-Boy? chaise longue? in my mind, I see them as detached airplane seats), which my mother ordered over the telephone. And the snack tables: when I was a child, clear plastic with little colored diamonds, then rather fancy-looking mahogany ones, lined with tiles that looked like bathroom tiles. My mother now does everything off her snack tables (though she still has her own desk in the basement, which had been my father's old desk at his office): she puts her two telephones on snack tables, as well as her lunch and dinner plates, and her notepads, which she uses during her rather mysterious "business" calls: she calls department stores and a special butcher shop to order boned turkey breasts, and calls up doctors and pharmacists and insurance companies, and then calls her friends, but no longer my uncle's second wife, and I think, seldom, my sister, to tell them what the doctors and the pharmacists and the filing clerks and the other friends said (though, increasingly, she rests her cable guide over the telephones, places her "changer" on top of the notepads; if she falls asleep while watching TV, the "changer" sometimes falls between the couch cushions, provoking gradual, but predictable, panic.) A closet, divided in two; on one side for clothes, with the door to the clothes chute against the wall; on the other side: telephone books, artifacts from my father's office (old pencil boxes, calendar holders).

What else?

Not a lot of clutter: my mother has always liked to throw things out, or to instruct people to throw things out. (My father likes physically throwing things out, the act of it, taking things to the garbage: something to do with growing up in foster homes, perhaps, or being in the army. I remember him fighting with my mother about the expense of the cleaning ladies, who rode out on the bus—addresses in my part of Milwaukee run to the tens of thousands, like in Los Angeles—from the neighborhood my father grew up in. I can almost remember a black woman in our kitchen, at the breakfast nook, eating a peanut-butter-and-jelly sandwich.) And now, of course, all her medicines, which she keeps in a plastic basket that looks like a little laundry basket.

How she talked about what she talked about: this is what was mysterious, what I would listen to through the clothes chute; there were always subtle changes, or distinct exaggerations, as she repeated what whoever had said and what she had then said in response, like someone playing "I've Got a Secret" with themselves, like a monologue version of *Rashomon*. (My father's office, in the basement, was more elaborate, less mysterious, but comforting; eventually I liked doing my homework there, sometimes at my mother's desk or sitting in one of the old recliners, the way some people do their homework at the kitchen table. What he talked about with his clients was of no interest to me.)

My mother's favorite color: blue; the color of the carpet in the living room, the dining room, and the stairwell, which I used to slide down in my underwear, getting carpet burns on my wrists and knees and stomach; the major color in the carpet in my mother's room; the color of the walls and carpet in my room.

Berlin's favorite color: green; green trees, green tiles, above-ground underground tracks painted green; and the color, in Milwaukee, of "The Green Sheet," the pale green supplement of the *Milwaukee Journal* that ran the comics and Dear Abby and Earl Wilson's column and miscellaneous articles about movie stars; spots of pale green all over the house: my father always bought three copies of the *Journal*, one for each of us. And the color of the carpet in my parents' bedroom.

I remember lying on the floor in my mother's room, feeling the carpet underneath my body and twirling the couch's yarn knots around my fingers, like hair.

Folk fairs. Food.

Last fall, in Munich with Irmgard, at the Oktoberfest grounds, alone (Irmgard: somewhere else, with the philologist, with the viola player, speaking German). It was late at night, and there was vomit everywhere; crowds of drunk people dressed up in Bavarian outfits, marching through vomit; in the beer halls, people eating meat and drinking beer out of liter steins, waitresses carrying away plates of bones, cow and pig carcasses outside tents, the cow rib cages too big to fit in the dumpsters, looking like dumpsters themselves. And thoughts of Los Angeles (where—although I often forget this—I moved after having been promised a job as a reader at a studio, having to work on the game show and at another studio in a continuous meantime; never having any money, buying groceries at a gas station in Burbank that had an especially large food section next to the motor oil and windshield wipers, so I could put them on my gasoline credit card, until the credit card got taken away), of movies: that Oktoberfest, like the Albert Hall in *The Man Who Knew Too Much*, would make a good setting for the end of a thriller. In Los Angeles, I lived in Hollywood itself, and, when I had money, went grocery shopping at the Ralph's on Sunset Boulevard.

(Remembering Los Angeles: all the grocery stores in Los Angeles are called Ralph's or else have one-syllable men's names that sound like "Ralph," and all look the same.)

Milwaukee's Folk Fair, which I was always begging my parents to take me to: I went, but I don't actually remember going; I remember driving past—it was always held at the old Arena downtown, during the week of Thanksgiving—on my way to the dentist on the Friday after Thanksgiving, when I always got my teeth cleaned, passing the marquee. (I haven't had my teeth cleaned in almost two years, since the summer I quit my job as a paralegal and lost my dental insurance: I run my tongue over my teeth, which, no matter how much I brush them, still feel furry, over my puffy—middle-aged—gums.) My parents took me to adult things: to a touring Broadway production of *Man of La Mancha*, to eleven o'clock showings of movies like *The Garden of the Finzi-Continis* and *Cabaret* and *The Godfather* (but not to *Midnight Cowboy*); in the summer, to the Melody Top, to summer stock productions of *How to Succeed in Business Without Really Trying* and *Fiddler on the Roof* and anything by Stephen Sondheim, then, afterward, to Karl Ratzsch's downtown, to the Strauss waltzes and a midnight supper of what were called "German pancakes" and turn out to have been eminently Viennese *Kaiserschmarrn*. We would get home at two in the morning, too late to get up for Sunday school. Later, I went skiing on Saturdays and Sundays, ordered pizza, watched TV. By that time, my mother was already noticeably more something (older, sicker); she wasn't allowed to eat any of the pizza.

I think I must have gone to the Folk Fair with my Sunday school class. At my temple, on a Sunday between Thanksgiving and Christmas, the eighth-grade class ran a folk fair in the hall where the Bar Mitzvahs and wedding receptions were held (it was presumptuous, apparently, to have them at hotels, the way Jews in Chicago did) and used the money they earned to plant trees in Israel. I didn't know anybody from my Sunday school class, except my cousins, who by that time had already stopped going because my uncle couldn't afford the temple dues; I missed the day that groups of friends from suburban high schools on the other side of town had chosen which countries they wanted to do; I would have to do something on my own, decided my Sunday school teacher, and he assigned me—or perhaps I chose—Austria, which apparently no one else had wanted. I sold Maxwell House Café Vienna out of a Thermos my parents bought for me at the newly opened —and for Milwaukee, at that time, exotic—Kmart on Blue Mound Road.

In most of Germany: hot dog–like sausages are called *Wiener,* though in Vienna they are called *Frankfurter,* which, in most of Germany, are all-beef sausages, except in Frankfurt, where they are made out of beef and pork. People in Berlin are famous throughout the rest of Germany for eating—and actually do eat—*Currywurst* and *Bouletten.* A *Currywurst* comes with or without *Darm,* a word meaning both "intestine" and "sausage casing," and, by definition, is covered with ketchup and curry powder. A *Boulette* is some ancestor of the hamburger; its French-sounding name is meant to invoke the Huguenots finding refuge in the duchy of Brandenburg in the seventeenth century and, ironically, invokes its awfulness (*Bouletten* are pretty much meat-laced bread crumbs fried in lard), about which people can get sentimental, invoking nineteenth-century Berlin factory-worker steadfastness (as opposed to late-twentieth-century Berlin factory-worker Turkishness; many of Berlin's "real" factory workers—"real" meaning German, or eventually German after having been Polish—moved, along with most of its factories, to West Germany decades ago), in the hope that something from "before" has survived. The German word *Gericht* means "meal" as well as "court of law." I get cravings for *Bouletten* and *Currywurst* when I walk by butcher shops, though have often gotten sick after eating a *Currywurst* (which is also deep-fried; more or less a hot dog cooked inside a potato chip, with the intestine itself—I always eat them *mit Darm*—getting hard, cracking open), and have often found bits of bone, or what seem like bone, in my *Bouletten*.

"*Eine Wiener, bitte.*" (Lazily said, heard, and stared at.)

[while eating] Dimitroffstrasse has no façades; blown up during the war, completely sandblasted off after the war.
The houses look merely scoured.
Or: new gray satellite dishes look like stucco.

On the ripped-up stretch of streetcar tracks, the dug-up pieces of dirt look like blocks of cement.

(Eating too fast, a section of sausage in my mouth, horizontal, pushing at my cheeks; then the knot of casing left over, rolling it around with my tongue, over the ridges of the top of my mouth, then spitting it out on to the street; no one really, except the construction workers, to see me.)

The stairwells leading down to New York's subway stations: designated mouths.

My mother used to be thought of as a hypochondriac and is now more or less an invalid.
What's wrong with my mother:

Angina
Arteriosclerosis
Arthritis
Diabetes
Emphysema
High Blood Pressure
Kidney Disease (neuropathy, edema; pain and swelling; push a finger in her foot and the waterlogged flesh gives way, turns into a finger-sized hole; she has to have her

toenails professionally cut so she doesn't get gangrene, and has to have her teeth cleaned twice a week: gum disease, too).

Something prophetic about all that hypochondria, "sibylitic." Or just willful.

She can't go up stairs (because of all the water in her legs, the loss of strength in her arms); she needs electric stairs, she told me the other day on the phone, which would cost around $1500. (My parents sent me $750, which I said I would need until the summer term at the new school started, though of course there is no "new school," and it probably wouldn't have a summer term; "just like that movie job," I could imagine my father telling my mother later.) She is in her room much of the time, and wouldn't call for my father down the clothes chute, as she used to do; she would use the telephone, call him on the other line. My parents have an aversion to certain kinds of new things: for years they didn't have a VCR, claimed, in spite of their numerous television sets, not to understand what one was for, until my sister gave them one for Christmas (we have always exchanged Christmas presents, though, unlike my grandfather, didn't have a tree, had instead, on occasion, Hanukkah decorations, bought at a store on the other side of town, that looked more or less like Christmas decorations, with blue-and-white Hanukkah bushes topped with Jewish stars; on Christmas Eve, now, instead of going out to a Chinese restaurant, my parents get take-out Chinese), which they never use, waiting around for a cable channel to show their favorite movies, which they watch the way I listen to music (my mother's favorite movie: *Orchestra Wives* with the Glenn Miller Orchestra and Ann Rutherford, Andy Hardy's girlfriend, whom my mother thinks she used to look like; my father likes movies from the thirties and forties with Jewish movie stars—Paul Muni, Edward G. Robinson, John Garfield); they still have dial telephones: three lines—three phones—in every room (not to mention call-waiting), which used to ring arrhythmically, competing against the television sets and the phone conversations in other rooms. (Now: they don't plug in one of the lines, there are fewer phone calls; real silence.)

And there is something old-fashioned (or perhaps just resolute) about the newspapers, about the fact that they seem to get their news from newspapers. Though when I was home, before coming here, my father would buy one newspaper, which sat on the dining room table, unread, while he slept in the basement, and my mother slept in her room, which they both persist in calling "the den."

When I was a cub scout, my mother was also my den mother, in a way. She came up with the idea of redistributing the labor among many den mothers (in Brookfield, until then, there had been apparently one den mother per den), of subcontracting, as it were, which meant that she decided what the den would do at their afterschool meetings, which usually involved going some-where other than the den mother's basement, and then she would call up the McDonald's or the pizza parlor or the bowling alley, and the other mothers would take turns driving us there, staying with us, and picking us up. She was always much older than the other den mothers, one of whom had actually been a senior in high school when my sister was a freshman; she was as old as people's grandmothers, Jewish (exotic, or possibly invisible: only visible as someone gentile and younger). She was always a few steps ahead of the grade school, who, on two occasions, arranged trips (to a different McDonald's and to the same pizza parlor) months after my mother had already sent us there.

At the pizza parlor (I can see a man—although he must have been a high school student—twirling the pizza dough over his head), at the McDonald's, did the boys in my class who had al-ready been there with their cub scout den act bored? already adept? (we had to take turns, both times, saucing pizzas, salting french fries). Did they pretend that they hadn't already been there? I don't remember: I remember an open can of tomato paste with a ladle sticking straight up.

I am walking away from Eberswalder Strasse.
In Eberswalde last week: skinheads burned down a Turkish ke-

bab stand, then beat up the Turk who owned it, while two off-duty policemen were watching from across the street.

In heading down Dimitroffstrasse, I am avoiding Brandenburg altogether, I am heading toward Mecklenburg, to a part of town where the streets are named after towns in Mecklenburg. Mecklenburg is north of Brandenburg, though I am, in fact, walking south, as I walked north, before, down Erich-Weinert-Strasse. My mother has mostly talked on the phone to Jewish housewives on the other side of town, though, lately, seems to be talking to gentile housewives nearby, or perhaps just to Edie, who talks about people I went to high school with—what their jobs are, which my mother tells me, estimating how much money they must be making, which my father might then repeat, when he gets on the phone after listening to my mother talking to me, getting the names wrong and jacking up the salaries. (My father always gets names wrong, calls Annette "Annie," and once "Alma"; calls the few clients he still has, many of whom originally came from Pakistan and all seem to be related, like southern Jews, by what he thinks of as comical versions of their real names.) I have been calling them collect from an old East German pay phone on the Humannplatz.

Failure: not always a road outward, or down (though mostly that); also a meandering.

Last week, with Kurt, walking with Sabine's daughter, through the part of Prenzlauer Berg where the streets are named after towns in Alsace-Lorraine, talking about trips: he remembers coming in from his village in Brandenburg in the 1950s, before the wall went up, to West Berlin, with his mother for the afternoon; then he remembers coming in during the 1960s, around West Berlin, on overnight trips with his school, to the opera and to museums; he told me about the first time he kissed a girl, which happened during one of those trips. If he were here now, I would tell him that, in America, schools send their pupils to places like McDonald's to learn how hamburgers are made, and, for a laugh, might describe those trips as *"ideologisch."*

. . .

Ideologisch (ideological—which, after considering the German translation, sounds in English for the first time as sounding like "logical idea"): every few months, all the cub scout dens would get together at meetings called "packs," which always had themes, having to do with American history, say, or with fire prevention, or with cars, and the dens were supposed to give presentations of some sort; our den, improbably, though fairly often, would lip-synch to songs from Broadway shows, to "You're a Grand Old Flag" from *George M.*, to—especially improbably—"Side by Side by Side" from *Company*, which was my mother's favorite Stephen Sondheim musical because it was Sondheim at his most "sophisticated." Stephen Sondheim, the Helmsley Palace Hotel, and Cold Duck on New Year's Eve were—and perhaps still are—my mother's idea of sophistication; the opposite of sophistication—my uncle, his second wife, anyone and anything having to do with my father before he met my mother, Wisconsin in general—would have been described by my mother as "plebeian," "plebeian" and "sophisticated" being the sorts of words my mother often used before she got old (and which she might have first picked up at late-thirties forensic tournaments) and sick, and began using words like "classy" and "goyish," and conceding to my father's, or perhaps to her mother's, Yiddish.

At a pack commemorating the 125th anniversary of Wisconsin's admission to the union, everyone in our den had to read prepared speeches—background descriptions of Wisconsin's state bird, of its state animal, etc.—and there was a speech left over, meaning that someone would get to read two. We were in our basement, where we always prepared for a pack, and my mother assigned the extra speech to Peter Schulz, whose professor father had actually written the speeches, and I became enraged, went upstairs to my room, and, while everyone waited in the basement, threw a tantrum, which, conceivably, could be heard through the clothes chute. My mother's solution was that I would read two speeches and Peter Schulz would read two speeches and someone else whom

I can't remember wouldn't read any but, instead, would hold the Wisconsin state flag.

Something logical in the way that turned out, and with what, or who, gets forgotten.

Clothing stores, along with the butcher shops and flower shops and bookstores; bird-faced mannequins; stores repeating themselves, like coefficients in a geometric series. And the construction sites, which are hard to notice, which aren't yet anything.

Learning how to drive.

I learned in high school, during first period, badly. I remember my drivers' ed teacher teaching us how men were supposed to get into cars (foot first) and how women were supposed to get into cars (hip first). I found this confusing; now I often get into cars strangely, sometimes hands first, as if I were crawling in.

I did not pass my driver's test the first time, in January, but the third time, in March, today, the thirtieth, fifteen years ago, just in time for the Junior-Senior Prom in April. I asked the girl who sat in front of me in chemistry class, a senior who was taking chemistry a year late and a cheerleader who had resolved not to go to prom that year. I remember calling her from my uncle's house on the other side of town. When I went to pick her up, she introduced me to her mother as the only boy at Brookfield South High School who wore Ralph Lauren shirts. She decided to wear a tux, which she bought and had tailored, and we got our picture in the senior slide show, looking (I myself joked at the time) like the top of a gay wedding cake.

(In Chicago, there is a warehouse district that has been renovated and turned into an avenue of mini-malls with art galleries and restaurant-sized breweries and bookstores. "It's like a SoHo for cars" Annette said when I took her there; she was in for some sort of women's studies conference. Annette grew up in Minnesota, then went to college in Wisconsin, and graduate school in Ohio and lives in Vermont; she occasionally goes to Europe; as if she

were following a line, reading a map. I learned about Chicago
while going home to Milwaukee, and my mother would be quite
sick, on her couch, with her head where her feet should have
been.)

Off a side street: a row of repaired houses, painted in the colors
of a spectrum—cream to yellow, yellow to green, green to blue.
Looking like paint swatches, like some variation of a geometric
series.

The East German workmen in the new apartment, like the East
German workmen in the old apartment, each have one pierced
ear, like American—and then West German—homosexuals did ten
years ago, many of whom now dress like East German factory
workers might have five years ago (leather and denim, work boots)
or the way American homosexuals did twenty years ago, and the
way most homosexuals now dress in the countries I have been in.

Irmgard doesn't want to be a banker, she said, sounding excited,
and she doesn't want to be an art historian: she wants to be a
painter, then told me that she used to finger-paint when she was
a child. Until Hans-Joachim gets out of the hospital, she has the
apartment to herself, has bought paints and an easel; when I asked
her if she was going to quit her job, she just smiled.

The remark about the Ralph Lauren shirts: coded, in a way that
"rich," where I come from, can be a code word for "Jewish," and
"well-dressed," when I was growing up, was a code word for
"homosexual." In Europe, these days, "fat" is a code word for, or
perhaps just interchangeable with, "American."

I can imagine one of the cub scouts going home after my tantrum and telling his parents what happened and the parents saying, or thinking, "Jew" (which is what my mother remembers a
neighbor saying under his breath while my grandfather carried his
neighborhood's first television set into the house). Germans, in a
poll for a national news magazine that was meant to provoke anti-
Semitism, identified *selbstsüchtig* (selfish), along with *geitzig*

(stingy), *übelriechend* (smelly), *reich* (rich), and *mehrsprachig* (poly-glot) as unfavorable words (*ungünstige Wörter*) associated with Jews.

A used-bookstore window:
Something by Goethe, with *"Jahre* 1810" written on a tag where a price might have been.
A single volume of Robert Musil's *Der Mann ohne Eigenschaften* from the East German 1950s (or '60s or '70s or '80s).
A collected works of Thomas Mann in a used, 1980s West German paperback edition, as long as an outstretched arm.
Alfred Döblin's *Die neue Urwald* in a Weimar-era edition ("The New Primeval Forest," with a cityscape collage on the jacket).
A 1927 Hamburg shipping schedule.
A 1935 Reichsbahn train schedule.
Jean Paul (whom I have never read—I can't find any of his books in translation, can only find the German editions printed in the old-fashioned, hard-to-read, almost Runic-like, Gothic type—but have wanted to read him because of Gershom Scholem, who took his collected works with him to what, in his memoir, he invariably calls "Eretz Yis-roel," and because of a quote I once read in an English translation of an Italian Germanist's intellectual history of the Danube River in which Jean Paul is quoted as having described the traveler as "like an invalid, poised between two worlds." I had never heard of Jean Paul before I came to Germany and started reading these books in English translation; he also vaguely reminds me of an old, now closed, more classy than sophisticated, French restaurant in downtown Milwaukee, which I thought might have been called "Jean Paul" though I now remember it was called "Chez Paul") with a marbellized spine, Wilhelmi-nianly opulent, but small, the size of a large hand. I can't even make out the title.
A 1923 20,000,000 Reichsmark note, with a "DM 2,-" price tag.

A 1990 *"Ostmauer"* catalogue of murals that went up in 1990 along the inside of the eastern side of the wall, with the famous caricature of Brezhnev and Erich Honecker French-kissing.

Ludwig Tieck and Karl May, spines facing out, a little ageless, or preserved.

A West German Karl May paperback, with a scene on the cover from the West German TV series.

(My eyes move back and forth, as if my feet were stuck in concrete.)

Kinds of distances.

I never see my students in the street, in Alexanderplatz; I rarely think about them: having taught at the school seems further away in time from now than the day I got here, before I had even seen the school, in the way that the building of the wall—the fact of it—is somehow more recent, more enduring, than the tearing down of the wall. Although I am beginning to feel as if I have always lived in Herr Huberman's apartment, as if I wouldn't really mind running into my students, teaching in Marzahn again—in the way that what happened during the Cold War can now seem remote, but more ordered, medieval; as if everything were long ago by comparison. I haven't seen any I WANT MY WALL BACK graffiti in a while, mostly the illegible hard-to-notice graffiti, the kind that I remember from Los Angeles, that look like pictographs.

Do I wish it were ten or twelve—or even five—years ago?

No. Not really.

I wish it were seven, eight days ago, between the time I paid my rent and the first time the workmen showed up, with their own key, drilling in the kitchen at six-thirty in the morning.

Vacations.

We went to New York and Chicago and stayed in hotels, saw Broadway shows, or touring companies of Broadway shows, took the towels home with us. My father always wanted to go to Las Vegas, and my mother always wanted to go to New York or Chicago: every time they were supposed to go to Las Vegas, my mother got sick. My uncle and his wives (his first wife, reluctantly, his second wife, exuberantly) and my cousins went fishing on lakes in northern Wisconsin, like my grandfather had done (my grandfather and my uncle fought over everything, especially over my grandfather's old motorboat, which he refused to give my uncle even though he had already bought a new one; my uncle refused to go to my grandfather's funeral, went to my grandfather's empty house instead, with a trailer hitch attached to his car, and drove away with the new motorboat). "What do they do up there?" my mother would say. "Sit in an inner tube?" Gradually they stopped going to New York and less often to Chicago, started going to the Mayo Clinic, twice, three times a year, then even more. Sometimes I would go with them: "We're going to Mayo's," my mother would say—she always called it "Mayo's," while my aunt and uncle always called it "the Mayo Clinic" (Annette, who, though she is from Minnesota, has never been to the Mayo Clinic, can't resist, calls it "Hellman's," "that place for sick condiments," or, the summer after college, after my mother had her first heart attack and was out of the hospital and didn't trust any of the cardiologists in Milwaukee and I drove her up and called Annette from the Kahler Hotel, "Rochester"); my aunt and uncle went once, when my aunt had a hysterectomy, and my mother went along, got them "right in" without an appointment, boasting that night to her friends and to me, long-distance. Once I was up there with them during the High Holidays, and there were services that we didn't go to in the Elizabethan Room of the Kahler Hotel, where my parents always stay (most of their towels are from the Kahler Hotel, and so is the one towel I brought with me to Germany: "Kahler," of course, sounds German and is pronounced with a long *a*, as though the *a* had an umlaut: very German). When they first started going, they were always seeing movie stars in the hotel lobby, like Danny Kaye, who my mother said was "carrying a purse"; now my mother talks about how her doctors, or doctors she has seen walking by, have famous patients, are King Hussein's nephrologist, Ronald Reagan's dentist; they go all the time now because of my mother, whose heart is too weak for dialysis, whose body is filling up "with poisons," and because of my father's prostate. He might have to have surgery, my mother said, sounding a little envious (which she usually sounds like when she is talking about other people's illnesses), a little terrified, though she said I shouldn't worry about coming home because of my new job: "We don't want you to interrupt your career. It's nothing; a little this and that. You know Daddy always makes a big deal." In high school I went on weekend ski vacations and, once, after coming back from Little Switzerland, which is a garbage hill not too far from Milwaukee, my father and mother picked me up at the shopping mall parking lot where the bus always dropped us off, because my grandfather had just died; I remember feeling irritated because I had promised two girls that my father— usually my father would pick me up; by that time my mother was already often in bed on her couch—would give them rides home. My grandfather had never really noticed me: he had noticed my sister, the first grandchild, who would visit him in Florida with her high school, and later college, boyfriends and stay with him and his senior citizen center girlfriends (hard to connect: the picture of my mother's mother, who died before my sister was born, and her gentle homely face underneath a 1910s hairstyle, on top of a 1940s dress, with my grandfather, who was rather dapper, brutal) and my cousins, whom he continued to visit even after he and my uncle had stopped speaking; the semester after he died, I took my first German course.

The strangest thing my mother said on the phone the other day at the Humannplatz (actually, she has often said strange things on the phone; she used to call me at the Krügers, in the middle of the night her time, because the pains in her legs were waking her up and she can't take painkillers, or even aspirin, because of her kidneys): when I told her that I had moved into a new neighborhood, she said, "Don't go into bad neighborhoods like you did in New York. Where did Hitler live? Go there a little."

My mother can't sleep, is technically an insomniac; my father, it stands to reason, is impotent.

One ornate house with a cupola; its bay windows are stacked, look inverted, like an externalized spine. (The clothes chute in my parents' house: a hollow spine.)

Across the street, an almost finished house, white bricks piled up, a man taking a picture, a crane (not at all birdlike; twirling, a lasso in slow motion; I would have thought that they moved faster or not at all).

The only people in sight: me; a man with a camera; and the construction worker coming out of the blue porto-toilet.

After the street with the painted houses, sudden color: blue porto-toilet, yellow posters, the pale green—Greensheet color—paint on an old house.

Professor Whitlaw's plans for me: a master's degree in political philosophy at a political science department.

"You could always get an MA in theory," he might have said, although I can't remember the way he talked (in German: to remember is a reflexive verb; people don't remember, as such; they remind themselves, turning "I don't remember" into "I don't remind myself"; especially willful) that day at the Chinese restaurant, in the winter of my last year of college. I would have been wearing a particular down coat, expensive, that is still hanging in dry cleaner's plastic in the front closet in my parents' house. A potential thesis topic might have been "The Politics of Aesthetics: T. S. Eliot, Henri Bergson, and F. H. Bradley" (I needed a thesis topic for fellowship applications). Now I tend to think of T. S. Eliot as anti-Semitic and Henri Bergson as actually Jewish, and the only thing I remember about F. H. Bradley is that his initials were "F. H." They seldom come up in the books I have been reading.

(What comes up unexpectedly when I read: the phone number of St. Mary's Hospital at the Mayo Clinic, where my mother spent a night last year, written inside the cover of the second volume of Elias Canetti's autobiography.)

Professor Whitlaw never wrote me a recommendation for graduate school because I never asked him.

And if Professor Whitlaw had written me a recommendation for graduate school?

If I hadn't seen him at the union that day, almost two years ago? (If he hadn't seen me, and I had seen him?)

Where I would be (if Professor Whitlaw not and not and not . . .): still on a floor, perhaps, but on a futon, and in a different city—graduate school and the trip to Germany being detours, as it were; irrelevant in the end, detours being delusional, not a new—merely different—way forward.

And Professor Whitlaw might not have gotten into his car accident (or might have gotten into it later), which is delusional of me to think, but not illogical. Germans have a special way to say "I forget," derived from the word *drängen*, "to press." *Ich verdränge* means "I forget," but it really means "I won't remember," "I refuse to remember, but I remember, in some sense, anyway." It is especially useful for describing how Germans think about Nazis, and now about Communists, and their crimes: a refusal to be reminded of.

I should try to remind myself of Professor Whitlaw, and then of circumstances within my control.

[Prenzlauer Allee]

I think I told Professor Whitlaw that I didn't want to go to graduate school, that I wanted to move to New York. My parents didn't want me to move to New York: they wanted me to go to law school or to business school (they had wanted me to go to medical school until my senior year of high school, when I didn't do anything and got a D in senior chemistry and an F—later changed to a D— in my final semester of a four-year advanced placement math course); they thought of going to New York as a sort of vacation. I think of having lived in New York and Los Angeles and Chicago and having worked at all those different jobs as a form of "marching through the institutions," which is the phrase used to describe what radical West Germans did in the 1960s, when they worked in party politics and wrote graduate theses before deciding to become or not to become terrorists. I think of having worked on Wall Street and in the Garment District and in Hollywood and in the Loop, and now having no money and almost no clothes and no television set and living within the rattle of an elevated train that doesn't have to take me anywhere as being terrorized by irony.

How skiing is like praying: the mind remembers; the body forgets. When I have been in synagogues as an adult, I always feel awkward, not knowing when to stand, forgetting how to move my mouth convincingly to the Hebrew, which I could do at that summer camp, at the end of each summer, the way people at some other kind of camp might have finally learned to water-ski (there was no waterskiing at the camp, just a large, heavily chlorinated, resortlike swimming pool; some of the campers were taking Hebrew classes in the morning, earning high school credits; there were more rabbis than lifeguards); that first year here in Berlin, I tried to go to services on Rosh Hashanah; I stopped in at the "Jewish Community" House, which is on Fassanenstrasse in West Berlin and is famous for having been photographed on Kristallnacht, in its prewar synagogue version, in flames, with fire trucks on either side protecting the nearby buildings (before that it had been famous for not being built in a courtyard like nearly every other German synagogue until that time, for not being hidden away), and the Russian at the information desk told me where to go for liberal services, but one of us misunderstood the other's German, and I ended up at the Orthodox *shul* on Joachimstaler Strasse, across the street from a shopping mall famous for a deluxe porno theater, and deep inside its building, like a doctor's office; inside: old, old men, speaking Yiddish, a woman, two teenagers: it was like a movie set (or like stepping onto the set of a wrong movie), or like a funeral (like joining a stranger's funeral procession); I looked at the old prayer books, which were from Breslau, printed in the 1920s, sometimes coverless; eventually one of the old men pulled me aside into a hallway and put a *kipah* on my head, said nothing, threw his eyes backward. I walked out in the middle of the service and set the *kipah* down on the top of a bookshelf emptied of its prayer books, then walked down the Kurfürstendamm; it was a Thursday night, the one night stores are allowed to stay open late; it was still warm, and I waited in line at the Häagen-Dazs store, then ate my ice-cream cone while walking, walking.

FLOWERS AND VEGETABLES

Roses	Cabbages
(Red	(White
Yellow	Red
Pink)	Kohlrabi)

No tulips; no strawberries and asparagus, no leeks; later, after spring has irreversibly set in, people will walk around with upside-down leeks in their backpacks, with the green ends sticking out like the bottoms of flower bouquets, and long stalks of rhubarb that they will carry under their arms, like kindling. (The English Communist I met once at the video store: she had defected *to* East Germany in the 1970s, talked about the fruit and vegetable shortages: in winter, there was only cabbage, but then in spring there were strawberries, and, if you knew someone, asparagus, which was grown for export, strictly controlled; she remembers carrying home kilos of strawberries, stuffing herself with strawberries, remembers her ex-husband's cousins showing up in the middle of the night with asparagus wrapped inside newspapers then hidden inside a suitcase. I don't remember the seasons that way, in terms of food: I don't remember what our house was like before we got central air-conditioning, remember my mother sending back a refrigerator with an ice-maker on the door; remember refrigerators filled with fruit all year, remember my mother telling someone to throw out uneaten fruit and my father taking the garbage bags out; the smell of rotting fruit, and the pale blue plastic garbage can next to the television, which rested, because it was in the kitchen, on a white metal stand.)

The only people I have known who have died: my grandfather, Professor Whitlaw. (I found out about Professor Whitlaw from Annette, who had read his obituary in the newspaper; the next week I got his letter in the mail; months after my grandfather died, my mother came home one day with his copy of *Collier's History of the Great War*, which my mother thought that I might like because I read books. I don't remember what I felt. I don't remember my grandfather's funeral; I just remember wearing a brown, three-piece corduroy suit. I seem to have surrounded those memories with nothing, or with brown corduroy.)

A hole in the ground where a tree had recently been: leftover tree roots looking like buried barbed wire.

Kebab stand, butcher shop, shoe store [construction site], Chinese restaurant, construction site.

The TV tower (from another angle, as though the world were rotating around it; as though I had been standing still all this time).

Bakery. (*Mischbrot, Zwiebelbrot, Weissbrot, Roggenschrotbrot, Kartoffelbrot, Nordländerbrot, Malzkornbrot, Leinsaatbrot, Häfersonnebrot, Roggenbrot, Kraftbrot.*)

Beds.
I remember a girl at college whose father was in prison for embezzling money. She never left her apartment, insisted people come to visit her there; she often cooked Jewish food, described herself as *"haimisch"*; she smoked Marlboro Lights and long joints and drank diet sodas, read the same book by Colette over and over

again, was on the dean's list; I don't think she ever went to class; I never saw her anywhere except in her apartment, in her bathrobe. We fooled around once, in her bed, which, I remember, was filled with crumbs, and we both decided the next day that it had been a mistake; the next night I went home—actually, to a dorm room on the other side of campus, where no Jews lived—with a dorm counselor who had the same last name as Annette (Larsen, spelled "on" instead of "en") and was fucked up the ass by a man for the first and second-to-last time and went to the communal toilet in the middle of the night to shit out his come. The day after that, I went home to Milwaukee to have my wisdom teeth out. It was January (ten, twenty degrees below zero; dry blue skies shining off the ice), I recuperated on my mother's couch (she sat on a recliner), with the old wooden shutters drawn to keep out the light, eating rice pudding, watching TV.

I have always left women and then gone back to them (or left men, gone back to them). Something about my childhood perhaps, which gave me the courage (need) to leave home, but not the will (need) to stay anywhere else.

"You were raised to get back into bed in the morning," Annette once said to me, years after the week and a half that we were actually sleeping in the same bed and I was getting up for my eleven o'clock class and she was sleeping in, because she only had afternoon classes and had probably been working at one of her two jobs, or had been studying, until two or three the night before.

A row of TEST THE WEST cigarette ads, lined up in front of a construction site (like the onetime murals on the then half-torn-down Berlin Wall, or like parodies of those murals, which were already parodies, like a negated negation: perhaps, then, the real thing, which would be, I suppose, merely an ad): a blond-haired, contemporary-looking German man offering a West cigarette to a Chinese coolie with a conical hat and horrible (late-nineteenth-century, perhaps) obsequious smile; meant—in its blunt, failed way—to encourage racial tolerance but actually racist, and more

than a little homoerotic; ripped off in different places, with REV-
OLUTION IS NO CRIME written over a stretch of furry white paper,
as though the ads were fortune cookies and REVOLUTION IS NO
CRIME were the fortunes.

Smoking cigarettes now, more than I ever have, mostly in
the apartment, as if there were someone else there smoking along
with me.

Eventually, I have always stopped going to school. In my senior
year of high school, in my last semester, I went to shopping malls
in the afternoons—to Mayfair and to Brookfield Square; to North-
ridge on the other side of town; to Bayshore, near my uncle's
house; once or twice to Southridge on the south side of Milwaukee,
where everyone is Polish (my uncle always calls Polish people
"Polacks"; most of his customers, and most of the people he works
with, are "Polacks"; he calls black people "niggers" and some of
my mother's Jewish friends, who occasionally invite him to their
children's weddings, "a bunch of kikes"; my sister and I are assumed to despise him, although my mother claims that he has the
same "personality"—my mother's word—as her father, whom my
sister always adored). I stopped going to class my senior year of
college, got a D in Special Topics: Film History of the 1930s for
low attendance. I missed the last week I was supposed to teach in
Marzahn, simply didn't show up, rode the S-Bahn all the way
through East Berlin instead, through Biesdorf, Kaulsdorf, Mahls-
dorf, through Hoppegarten and Neuenhagen, after which the
buildings just stop, become sand.

I stopped going to graduate school before I started.

Professor Whitlaw's shrug.

I imagine it now as a puppet's shrug, shoulders being twitched
upward.

Or: not a shrug, but a slouch; an enacted sigh. (All those abandoned jobs, unsent graduate school applications; not showing up
for his classes at the end, not showing up for a lunch date years
before; all remembered.)

Or: involuntary. What else to do? I was there again before him, didn't need to be remembered, effacing myself.

My father worked all the time (as an accountant for an office supply company downtown, whose former factory is now part of Milwaukee's version of a loft district, and at home, for clients he had on the side), like West German fathers in the 1960s, but unlike East German fathers in the 1960s. (East Germans often have happy childhood memories, won't learn to hate their childhoods in retrospect; West Germans seem to have had unhappy childhoods, for which they occasionally learn to accept there may be another, impersonal—historical—reason.)

Or: my father took me everywhere, to baseball games, to the state fair, to swimming pools, to tennis lessons, to playgrounds to teach me how to play baseball or how to kick a football; into the bathroom, to watch him shave, while I pretended to shave along, scraping his Old Spice shaving cream off my face with the child's shaving kit he had bought for me at the Winkie's—which at one time were all owned by a man actually named Mr. Winkie—on 96th Street; later we would often go out for dinner alone, without my mother, because she had been too tired to cook, too tired to go along.

In the daytime, she would be less tired; while I was still going to grade school, on days when she would let me stay home from school, she would take me out to lunch, or to downtown department stores, or, a little more reluctantly, to shopping malls wwhich were still new then and which she would compare unfavorably to downtown Milwaukee before the war, when she and her mother would take the streetcar down Wisconsin Avenue and her mother wore gloves; going through my mother's desk one day, I once found her dead mother's Schuster's charge card, its paper all worn and velvety, creased over what looked like tin; the charge "plate," as it must have been called, might now look East German to me, oddly old; or just old, like the name "Schuster's," which, even then, after having been bought by Gimbel's, was closed down and forgotten, like Gimbel's is now), into the dressing rooms with her, while she tried on clothes, took me to the other side of town, to expensive clothing stores in Whitefish Bay and bought me the kinds of shirts in different colors—button-down shirts in three colors; several colors of the old-fashioned alligator shirts that came from France and had ribbon on the shirttails—that people at my Sunday school, but not at my grade school, wore; later the Ralph Lauren shirts, which I would often have to pick out on my own, put on her charge accounts while she sat waiting in a restaurant in the mall, resting, sipping Diet Pepsi; after I got my driver's license, she would just hand me the charge cards while lying down on the couch and I would come home, show her what I had bought, and she would ask for the charge cards back, moving her fingers together, which is what she does now when she is looking for her TV "changer."

In high school, wandering around shopping malls, past the stores and the restaurants, I was like a high school student wandering around a grade school, already a ghost. Now I tend to get vertigo in shopping malls: they remind me of airports. Walter Benjamin, in "Paris, Capital of the Nineteenth Century," saw the construction of the Paris arcades as anticipating the construction of its train stations; my visits to shopping malls anticipated my visits to airports—fleeing to and from Milwaukee, to and from New York and Los Angeles; even when I lived in Chicago, where, before my parents gave me my mother's old car after she couldn't drive anymore, I would use a bus to go back and forth to Milwaukee that picked me up and dropped me off at airports. I am afraid of flying—of the physical discomfort that comes over me when I am in an airplane and it is too late to change my mind and get off— and of not flying, of staying in the same place; flying, to me: all regret, no relief; I think of the tunnels that connect airplanes to airports as vacuums; I think of airports as looking like vacuum cleaners—streamlined and shapeless. And yet: I remember when I was a child, before I had ever been on a plane, begging my parents to take me to the airport to watch the planes take off and land; I remember the first time we flew to New York, and my mother insisted that my father and I wear ties—or neckties, as they would have still been called—on the airplane.

Berlin used to be famous for its arcades, many of which, if they were in the West, were rebuilt after the war, or rather, they were built to look like, or ended up looking like, shopping malls but still called themselves arcades. The Europa Center, underneath the Daimler-Benz tower, was built to look—and actually does look—like an American shopping mall. The arcades that perhaps accidentally look like shopping malls (though which always still look like arcades from the street: suddenly tunnellike, mysterious, beckoning) seem, once inside, to be the opposite of mysterious: blank, like something that has been forgotten, or never known.

In fact: Milwaukee's airport has been remodeled, and its terminal is now meant to resemble a shopping mall.

FATHER'S ROOM	MOTHER'S ROOM
elaborate but unmysterious, like a woman's body	unelaborate, mysterious, like a man's body

Except for those Saturday nights: always alone with one or the other of my parents, like a best friend, like a date.

My father's hands: fleshy, round, and large, like a woman's ass.

My mother's back: broader at the top, with a trace of line down the middle, like a man's chest.

"Daddy never hit me," my mother said the other day. She was talking about my father, of course, although she also used to call her father "Daddy."

My grandfather loved his German food, his *Sulze* and his *Kassler Ripchen*; he was an auto mechanic, lived on Milwaukee's West Side (his neighbors' names: Schulz, Becker, Zweifelhofer), ate, lived, and worked without Jews. Once my mother, who was the only Jewish girl at her high school, brought home a gentile boy, and my grandfather punched her in the face, broke a tooth. (There were four other Jews in my high school class, three of whom had a name derived from Levi; we treated one another as rumors, except in the attendance office the days after Rosh Hashanah and Yom Kippur, waiting for our readmittance passes, when we were more like co-conspirators, or perhaps double agents.) He smoked cigars and cig-arettes, drank beer and some kind of schnapps; he loved wars, loved fighting for America in the First World War; next to the picture of his dead brother Samuel he kept a picture of himself in a trench behind a machine gun, which is now in an old Gimbel's box upstairs in my parents' attic along with pictures of my mother in halter-top evening gowns and of my father in an army uniform standing under a palm tree (my cousin Amy has the picture of Samuel); in the Second World War, he volunteered, but the draft board turned him down, and he involved himself in the black mar-ket, filling up my mother's bedroom—she once told me, with a mixture of dread and awe, the way Germans in the nineteenth century would talk about Napoleon—with gasoline and steaks. He and my uncle fought the way my mother and my sister fight (my mother was old when I was born, and her mother was old when my uncle was born; my sister lives a few streets away from my mother and sees her about once a month, meets my father, I think, for lunch downtown). My grandfather was choosy about German restaurants, wouldn't go to Rotenhahn's in particular, which, con-sequently, we could never go to either (Rotenhahn's was the fa-mous one; I remember contestants on 1970s game shows winning trips to Milwaukee, and dinner for two at Rotenhahn's; now, be-cause of Jeffrey Dahmer and all the other murderers, a trip to Mil-waukee might seem like a booby prize, like a punishment) because, according to my mother, the German-American Bund used to meet there in the 1930s and because my grandfather got food poisoning there once in what, from my mother's description, must have been the 1950s, though my uncle, whenever my mother repeated the story, would contradict her, claim that my grandfather never went to Rotenhahn's because he was too cheap. (Now my mother and my uncle fight about my uncle's second wife, who won't drive all the way across town to visit my mother, and about my uncle's first wife, whom he doesn't even talk to anymore, because she won't drive across town to visit my mother and take her to the grocery store the way my mother used to drive across town and take her to the grocery store while my uncle was at work because they were too "poor"—my mother's, and my aunt's, word—to afford more than one car; my sister talks to me like a child, in baby talk). The day Germany officially unified, in 1990, I was in Milwaukee visiting my parents, and a German restaurant I had never heard of celebrated by rolling back its prices to October 3, 1945; on the evening news (they were packed with people—Polish-looking people, I remember thinking—paying $1.25 for plates of sauerbraten), the owner told the camera that he had chosen 1945 because that was the last time Germany had been one country and because that was the oldest October 3 menu he could find in his basement.

"I have a new thing. I chew bubble gum. Daddy brings me gum."

I am hungry, am back at the bakery.

Waist-high, Spreequell plastic-blow-up mineral water bottles, next to the bakery, in front of the grocery store; also: a blackboard advertising sausages from Eberswalde. And people: women with plastic shopping bags, old men with crutches and plastic shopping bags.

An endless Prenzlauer Allee, repeating its stores, and Jablonskistrasse, soon, with the Laundromat where I did my laundry after the Krügers disconnected their washing machine, with the bench in front of it—a place to sit and eat *Baumkuchen*, a temporary return.

A familiar graffito on the guardrail of the streetcar tracks—"DER ERSTE SCHWULE IN SCHWERIN VON FASCHOS ERMORDET"—from last year, when skinheads gay-bashed to death someone in Schwerin.

(Schwerin: in Mecklenburg, weirdly appropriate because of the street names. Though, actually, Prenzlau is in Brandenburg; at least, I think it is, might be. Perhaps it was in Mecklenburg before the wall came down but ended up in Brandenburg after the new *Länder* were created, or the other way around; or perhaps it has been divided in two, à la Berlin.)

I have never talked with my parents about sleeping with men —or about sleeping with women, for that matter. Once, when I was living in New York, and about to quit a job as a secretary to a literary scout who represented foreign publishers in America and who lined his office at any given time with book jackets of the same book in nine languages—like a geometric series, I had probably thought (in those four years—well, three and a half, not counting the semester I failed—of advanced placement mathematics, I learned adult-seeming, college things like calculus and logic, and I still doodle mathematical symbols in margins, on place mats; pi signs, summation signs, integrals, certain equations that I have memorized like song lyrics, or, perhaps, the other way around)—I went home in April, during the tax season when my father was always too busy to drive my mother to the Mayo Clinic, and she insisted I have a physical, then insisted I have an AIDS test (I had already had two in New York, once after a friend I had slept with in college had had one and was negative, and once, later, when I was living with the social worker, whose voice cracked when she told me that she didn't care one way or the other). After I told her I was negative, my mother said "Thank God," which is what she said after I finally passed my driver's test.

Sometimes my father will ask me when I am getting married (introduced with a "Hey! Boychik?"), predictably telling me that when he was my age he was already married, with a child and a mortgage. And my mother will say quickly—almost, I have considered, triumphantly—that I may never get married, that that's my business, and then add that she always liked the social worker who "looked like a little doll, with all those blonde curls." Annette met the social worker once, was offended at something she said, later often forgot her name.

Is there a spiritual version of an AIDS test, a way of learning what is, or is not, in store for that part of you?

[Jablonskistrasse]

In Prenzlau this week: skinheads burnt down an asylum seekers' home, and the asylum seekers ran out in time, into a forest, but got lost, didn't all show up until days later.

Or maybe last week.

In my advanced placement math class: the same ten students every year, except for the one who ended up in a mental institution; four of them went to MIT, two of them, including the other Jew, went to Harvard, one went to Cal Tech, one went to the University of Wisconsin–Green Bay, where my sister's husband went for a year before transferring to Madison and which he likes to call "a high school with ashtrays"; one got married and works as a checkout girl in a grocery store in Brookfield (many of the other counselors at my summer camp went to Brandeis, except for the southern Jews, who went to LSU, the University of Mississippi, the University of Alabama, disappearing into Jewish fraternities and sororities); I went to Madison—where, not too long after I graduated, the local Jewish fraternity got national publicity after staging a minstrel show and was fined or banned or has in any case disappeared—which felt like another world at the time but was, in some sense, merely down the road, then elsewhere.

Baumkuchen crumbs everywhere, falling off the bench planks, onto the single lane of concrete: not much wind here, on this side of the street, and cool in spite of the white light, which is far away and shimmering: a distant—abstract—scalding. A man walking past looks at me too long, a middle-aged cruiser. Or accuser.

(Runes/ruins. Doodling ruins. The intersecting streets at the Eberswalder Strasse U-Bahn station might look, from a certain distance, like a Star of David doodled by a city planner, a scrawl.)

Towns near concentration camps from where gay men I have met come from: Oświęcim (on German maps, always left in Polish), Dachau.

They were both defensive. "Where are you from?" Pause. "Near Kraków." "Oh?" "Well, I am from Oświęcim—Auschwitz. It's a lovely town with sixty thousand inhabitants." Pause. "Really?" He spoke Englishy English: "Simply because one is from Auschwitz everyone assumes one is from a concentration camp." He slapped his hand on the outside of his wrist, shook it; I thought of Primo Levi writing in *The Drowned and the Saved* how men at Auschwitz were tattooed on the outside of their wrists and women on the inside. (Later, back in Berlin, I also thought of that part of *The Drowned and the Saved* where Primo Levi goes on to remind his readers that tattoos are forbidden by the Torah when I saw a photograph of the man who owns Kaiserschnitt in *Zitty*, the Berlin equivalent of *New York* magazine, naked, and faceless, with a chain connecting the ring through his pierced foreskin with the ring through his pierced nipple; his name was in the caption, but I recognized him from his tattoos; he usually walks around Kaiserschnitt without a shirt on.) The man from Dachau had a pierced nipple and was the only person I have met who has read all three volumes of Elias Canetti's autobiography, which I myself have just finished, and which ends, like Maria Riva's book, with his mother's funeral. (I met a friend of the man from Auschwitz—we were in a sort of gay bar, though a "Polish gay bar" sounds like a joke, like a name for a place where straight people would go to pick someone up—off Novy Swiat, where all the houses have been rebuilt with one storey less than they had before the war, who said I was the only other man he had ever met who had heard of Stephen Sondheim; he kept leaving notes at my hotel, inviting me to his apartment for "Scotch whiskey and music records." Many of the Americans at the hotel had just taken, or were planning on taking, the hotel's overnight trip to Auschwitz, which was advertised in the lobby with a handwritten poster that read: "See Auschwitz: The biggest concentration camp of them all!") The man from Dachau came over to the Krügers' and said the apartment looked like his grandmother's apartment in Dachau. "Really?" I said. "You're from Dachau? You were born there?" He showed me his passport, said that Dachau was a thousand years old, that there had only been a concentration camp there for twelve of those years, and there was another pause, as though he were giving me time to do the arithmetic. We slept in the same bed, though by that time I was already impotent (at that time, actually, especially impotent; I remember staring down at him as he was trying to give me a blow job and thinking that my cock looked like part of his nose); the next day, after he left, I found a crab louse in the hair on my back.

Trying not to arrange those things in any order, or only in two different orders—temporal (Auschwitz and everything before and after it) and personal (things that happened in some sense to me, that I am remembering).

[Prenzlauer Allee]

I only think I avoid Jewish cemeteries, have actually been to two of them often. (Or: I think I have been to them often, have actually avoided them; after I actually do go to the cemeteries, the rest of Berlin seems less like a cemetery, more like a European city.)

The Jewish cemetery I avoided today: smaller, like a cemetery. The Jewish cemetery a borough away, in Weissensee (the largest Jewish cemetery in Europe, according to the old man with the *kipah* and the hearing aid whom I always have to leave ten marks with as a deposit on the *kipah* they make me wear; Germans I have talked to who have been to the cemetery in Weissensee—the cemeteries attract tourists, sell postcards and CDs of liturgical music—always talk about wearing the *kipah* with a smile, fondly, as though it were a party hat): larger, more formal (I have never had to wear a *kipah* at the cemetery on the Schönhauser Allee, cannot remember wearing one when going to the cemetery in Milwaukee to put geraniums on my grandmother's grave, cannot, as it happens, remember putting geraniums on, or even visiting, my grandfather's grave, which is, of course, next to my grandmother's; after going to cemeteries here, I always wash my hands, which my mother always did after visiting her mother's grave, which is Jewish custom, I guess, and my mother's favorite pastime; she washes her hands after reading the mail; my father never washes his hands, even after going to the bathroom, has never been sick a day in his life, as far as I can remember, until now—"I'm fine," he said, after I asked him when he was going to have his prostate removed, about his pre-cancer, which, it turns out, is a slow-growing malignancy; he sounded like the social worker talking about my AIDS test, his voice cracking open; after the cemetery on the Schönhauser Allee, I wash my hands at the nearby German restaurant that turns into a leather bar at night; after my last visit to the cemetery in Weissensee, I washed my hands at the new Chinese restaurant on Puccini Strasse; all the streets near the cemetery are named after non-Jewish, Jewish, and baptized Jewish composers; the people actually buried in the cemetery seem to have been especially assimilated, avoided Hebrew on their *Jugendstil* and Art Deco tombstones, preferred quotations from the Bible translated into German, or from German poetry, except for the tombstones erected after the war in memory of the people who died in the camps, where the inscriptions are written in Hebrew, and German is avoided except where necessary—GEBOR. IN DANZIG, ERMORDET IN THERESIENSTADT); so large that you forget where you are, like a necropolis rather than a cemetery; people who are trying to find particular graves, who aren't just strolling around like I do, walk with maps: the cemetery is divided from A-1 to Z-1 through A-5 to Z-5 (like the Mayo Clinic, where each medical specialization is given a numbered floor and then a lettered wing); there are tens of thousands of graves; thoroughfares between the blocks of graves look like streets; the gravestones facing the "streets" are better kept than the ones inside, which are smaller, overgrown, almost plowed under (the difference between the outer and inner gravestones: like the difference between the front and back house apartments in Prenzlauer Berg); you only realize how decrepit the Jewish cemeteries are (or perhaps I should, once again, think "overgrown," the way an overgrown field once again becomes a forest) after you have seen a German cemetery, which are immaculately cared for (the graves are always outlined in ivy, or with flower beds), like formal gardens, or like parks: there are a number of trees, often evergreens.

German cemeteries: like inhabited forests.

On a train (from Cracow—which is so old that, because of accumulated dirt, the streets have risen, turning ground floors of buildings into basements—to Warsaw), talking to a perfectly amiable American college student, thirteen years younger, dressed as I might have been dressed (to compare: the way American college students dress, which, in Europe, if health were like pedigree, would seem aristocratic, heraldic, to the name Princesse de Guermantes in Proust, whom I occasionally try to read by picking out paragraphs, pages, in no particular order, like picking out clothes from a closet—one name, countless women; one outfit, countless bodies; of time disappearing as it accumulates, of youth being passed on like a title), in fact, as I still dress, making me something of an imposter, or a ghost (to consider: a Paris full of women calling themselves the "Princesse de Guermantes"), who said he had just been to Auschwitz. He said it looked like a park. "Well," I said. "It has to look like something. It can't *look* like a concentration camp, can it?" (Actually, in the photographs and movies I have seen, Auschwitz always looks like a concentration camp—negating; or like an image of negation, like a spirit that needs to be photographed in a mirror).

Places I haven't been: Auschwitz (Oświęcim), Kaliningrad (Königsberg), Lemberg (Lwów, etc.).

In the photographs and films I have seen of Kaliningrad, the city looks a place that had once been a death camp for buildings —buried foundations find their way upward; north German red bricks still under the ground smell, I imagine, or perhaps no longer smell, but are still dug up by local farmers, like bones.

Lemberg apparently looks like Lemberg (baroque and *Jugendstil*, petit-Viennese), but taken over by Ukrainians, who would have been the charwomen and janitors when Lemberg was Lemberg: like a palace after the Revolution.

Berliner factory workers	Viennese "upper ten thousand"
Berlin's (Jewish) bourgeoisie	(titled baptized Jews)
	Emperor Franz Joseph (who, in spite of his palaces, lived a famously simple life, never read books, wouldn't have indoor plumbing installed in his palaces; workerlike, peasantlike)

Primo Levi's books, in their various translations, always refer to concentration camps as *"Lagers"*—in the original German. Germans call many kinds of things *"Lagers."* Travel agencies (which I have not been noticing, which are everywhere, between the butcher shops and the kebab stands, between the kebab stands and the construction sites, because I can't afford to go anywhere, except onward, now, by foot, using my memory as a travel agency) advertise *"Kinderferienlager"* where East German parents can send their children while they take vacations in the Sudtirol, in the Salzkammergut, at Lake Balaton in Hungary, which Germans always call the Plattensee.

What would it be like to think of Primo Levi every time I saw the word *Lager*?

What would it be like to think of concentration camps every time I spoke German?

Often, when I was taking German in high school and college, I remembered my father's Yiddish words, which seemed to make learning German easier; now, thinking about Yiddish, here, when I speak German, takes my breath away, silences me.

(*Luftmensch* is Yiddish—and German, although no German I have asked recognizes the word—for "air person," for, actually, Galician Jews in Vienna who had nothing, seemed to survive on air instead of food and water. To save money, I have been surviving on lentils and cabbage and potatoes, like a German peasant, and, extravagantly, on new kinds—every kind—of German pastry and German sausage and German beer, like an American tourist.)

The last time I was at the cemetery in Weissensee, I had to speak German with Jews from Paris who were in Berlin visiting the husband's parents' graves and had gotten lost, needed help with their map; I thought that the woman, who turned out to be an Egyptian Jew, looked remarkably like one of my mother's best friends, Lana Hurowitz (my mother's friends all seem to have ridiculously Jewish first names, or seemed to have been named after movie stars; names on the tombstones in Weissensee are ridiculously—poignantly, tragically—German: Hedwig, Heinrich, Erich; once I found the tombstone of a Berthold Marcus, who I thought had been a relative of Peter's, and who, along with his wife and two sons and daughter-in-law, had all died in Auschwitz, but who turned out to be no relation: It had been his grandfather's sister, Peter explained, whose whole family had died in the camps; he likes to put up posters of *Night and Fog* and of Marcel Ophuls films in the window of his video shop; "I like to remind the Germans," he says, in his German accent).

Trying not to think about Nazis all the time: like (or not like) trying not to have an erection. (Trying not to think about Nazis in Germany: like trying not to think about sex in a porno theater. Why go in at all?)

Trying to think about Nazis without thinking about concentration camps.

Trying to think about Nazis, as opposed to thinking about Communists: Nazism seems more hard-core than communism, which had more time—took longer—to go about its destruction.

Trying to think about Kaliningrad (Königsberg, always afterward, like a maiden name): like trying to think about Germans and Russians as well as Nazis and Communists, at the same time: an aphasia, another—more internal—kind of negation.

Berlin: a capital of dead ideas; a card catalogue for a library that no longer exists; intricate, somehow superfluous; symbolic capital of the twentieth century, or else just capital of twentieth-century symbols.

(Kaliningrad: on the Baltic, must smell of the sea.)

Trying to think about kinds of death.

My grandfather's hands?
Professor Whitlaw's hands?

Annette's back.
Younger, in the dark, smelling like soap, a bedspread with roses on it. (Thinking, now, about having sex with Annette: incestuous.)

(My grandfather was fat and strong, like a German peasant; he worked with his hands, must have had strong, stained—with tobacco and motor oil—fingers; I remember him at dinner, in a restaurant, eating spareribs with his hands gripped all the way around the bones, as if he were holding onto a violin bow, onto a cock.)

(Professor Whitlaw, whom I feel as if I have avoided thinking about today, looked like a cartoon character, round, like Elmer Fudd, with soft doughy hands and sausagy fingers; no picture along with his obituary in the paper, though one in my alumni newsletter, which my parents forwarded to me here in Berlin, that made him look shockingly young. Murderer, I thought.)

Now, more than ever, I have my grandfather's face, which was always round (his nose was long and narrow, like my nose), but also feel as if I have Professor Whitlaw's body. And dirty, doughy hands.

Straight ahead. Karl-Liebknecht-Strasse, Unter den Linden, Strasse des 17 Juni (Charlottenburger Chausee), Bismarckstrasse (Adolf-Hitler-Strasse): all one street, now; an elongated Prenzlauer Allee (before: several streets; before Albert Speer widened the Charlottenburger Chausee and moved the Franco-Prussian War victory column to line up with the Brandenburg Gate, creating his famous—infamous—East-West Axis; before the Communists didn't rebuild the narrow streets between Unter den Linden and Prenzlauer Allee, or rather rebuilt one broad street, for parades).

Trying not to walk straight ahead: only natural for some people.

Actually, I have been to Sachsenhausen, in Frankfurt, where the classiest part of town is called Sachsenhausen (I went there one weekend last summer so I could ride on one of the new high-speed German trains, which turned out to have seats lined up in rows and overhead storage compartments, were designed to resemble airplane cabins). To get to Sachsenhausen from the train station, which is on the other side of the Main River, you can walk over a pedestrian bridge designed by Albert Speer, who is the son of the other Albert Speer, also an architect. (No one I have talked to—Germans, I mean—seems to find this ironic; Germans don't really find anything ironic, only find things contradictory, which can seem like a more violent—the most violent—kind of irony.) Speer's bridge, built out of steel pylons, is meant, in the language of an architectural guidebook, to be a "late-twentieth-century counterpart" to Frankfurt's other pedestrian bridge, which was built out of iron in the middle of the nineteenth century and vaguely resembles the archway of an arcade, and which will also get you to Sachsenhausen.

I avoided walking over Albert Speer's bridge—I didn't know what it would mean—but then walked over it anyway on Sunday afternoon because I was late for my train, only remembering, while I was walking, that I was in a hurry; later I thought about not remembering while I was walking, about merely walking, which I considered to be a form of *Verdrängenheit*; like walking through a place where the Berlin Wall had once stood and not thinking about it, which is what people now do all the time, as though the tearing down of the wall had been the rebuilding of an absence, as though walking through where it once stood wasn't extraordinary, heroic, a defying of history, like visiting the Underworld had once been a defying of Death.

(Being a tourist at a concentration camp—strolling around its grounds—seems like it might be a defilement of life; violently contradictory.)

I am walking slower, remembering faster.

Or forgetting faster, walking faster. I am already at the Immanuelkirchstrasse, in yet another crowd.

Crowded restaurants
Crowded movie theaters
(Orphanages, foster homes, army barracks)
Dances (casinos)
Waiting rooms

A child among adults.
A Jew among gentiles (a German-speaker among Jews).
A homosexual among heterosexuals.
A heterosexual among homosexuals.
An American in Europe.

Cemeteries.

A visitor in a cemetery.

[crowds—or a crowd—of one, dispersing]

I learned about sex and Nazis from books: from *The Nazi Olympics*, which must have come out in time for the Munich Olympics, with peekaboo photos of athletes that probably came from the Leni Riefenstahl films (I remember a shot of Helene Mayer, the Jewish fencer allowed to compete for Germany, accepting her silver medal with a *Sieg Heil*, remember her clingy dress, remember thinking that she was Jewish, the sort of girl that I should marry; and I remember the male athletes, posed and exotic-looking, though they must have looked like the people I went to school with, who tended to look, or at least were, German); from *Everything You've Always Wanted to Know About Sex* *But Were Afraid to Ask*, which my parents had hidden in drawers—in my father's underwear drawer, in a drawer of my mother's, which, improbably, contained long white gloves with pearl buttons—often next to old condoms and tubes of K-Y Jelly (I used to blow up the condoms, try to figure out how to open the unopened tubes of K-Y Jelly, which I once did with a needle from my mother's ignored sewing box, squeezing out the mysterious contents in thin, fine streams), which my mother had needed (I once overheard her say on the telephone) since going through menopause just after I was born (the condoms—by the time I got to them—like the charge plate: decades old); from *Hawaii* and *The Winds of War* and *Exodus*, from *QBVII*, which I had already read in time for the miniseries (my mother would let me pick out paperback books at Winkie's, while she was buying dental floss and lightbulbs and ballpoint pens), from *Once Is Not Enough* and *The Exorcist*, which my cousins and I found at my uncle's house in his tackle box, from *Valley of the Dolls*, which was lying around our house and which is the only book I remember seeing my parents read. And with my cousins: I remember the last year my uncle's family still went to temple, on the afternoon after a special Sunday school session when all the grades had to go to the sanctuary to listen to a lecture about the Holocaust (in preparation, one imagines, for the miniseries), and, afterward, back at my uncle's house, my cousins and I quizzed each other about concentration camps—their names, how many Jews the teachers said had died there—as we would also quiz each other about state capitals, about how to spell long words; I remember my cousin Amy sleeping over at our house (I was twelve; she was

thirteen, a kind of baby-sitter), on a Saturday night: we slept upstairs in my parents' bedroom where the twin beds were occasionally pushed together; in the middle of the night we sat up with
our legs in the small alley between the beds and I stroked her neck
and shoulders, had the biggest hard-on I have ever had—may ever
have; I remember making my younger cousin Tony look at gay
porno magazines, at pictures of huge cocks, in the lobby of the
motel with the swimming pool where our families always went on
the Fourth of July. All my cousins are married, live near their father
and real mother, call their stepmother by her first name, divide
holidays between their mother and their father and stepmother
(they rarely invite my parents; my mother complains about salt in
the food, about the pains in her legs, about how no one calls her
or comes to visit her, and they don't invite my sister, who is older
than they are and who drives up in a Saab, makes more money
than they do). My sister had two miscarriages, and once, my
mother told me, an abortion. After reading an article about impotence in an *Illustrierte*, I tied a string around my cock before
going to sleep to find out if I was having erections during the night
(I was). I remember going to one of my cousins' sons' *brises*, when
my mother's legs had first started swelling up: "Look at my legs!"
she kept saying, hiking up her skirt, like the father in "The Judgment" mocking Georg Bendemann about his fiancée *("Weil sie die
Röcke gehoben hat . . . so und so und so gehoben hat . . .")*. I have
never seen a La Vine at any of the Jewish cemeteries I have visited
(in Berlin, in Vienna, in Prague, in Warsaw, in Frankfurt, in Hamburg, elsewhere), and I have never seen one in Milwaukee, where,
like elsewhere, there are probably many Levines and at least some
Lurianskys. My father has some cousins still named Luriansky
whom he doesn't speak to (the "kikes"), who once wanted money
for maintaining some graves—perhaps his parents' graves; I don't
know, although I remember my mother fighting with my father
about some graves, about not spending money on them.

My parents' bedroom, now: my mother sleeps on her couch to
avoid going up the stairs; my father sleeps in my room because he

has to get up so many times during the night to urinate and doesn't want to wake up my mother in case she has decided to attempt the stairs and sleep in her own bed; derelict.

Once, in New York, while cat-sitting for someone, watching *Shoah*, or something like it, on public television, lying on a couch, falling asleep, waking up, falling back asleep, waking up, each time, with an erection, while people on television were talking about concentration camps.

Noon. The sun is like a head.

(A pleasant memory: a summer day in Milwaukee, driving over to my uncle's house with bikes in the trunk, then riding the bikes up Lake Drive, to Doctors Park, with my parents, my uncle and his first wife, my cousins, meeting my sister and her boyfriend there, grilling out, sitting on a rocky beach, surrounded by pine trees, looking out at blue, flat Lake Michigan, which can seem to go on forever; Baltic-like).

The summer before college, while I was working as a camp counselor: my mother threw all my books away (I can see the empty bedroom when I got home, and the door of the clothes chute looking larger, the size of a wall); she had her cleaning lady throw all the books in my room down the clothes chute, into the basement, then had her put them into garbage bags, which my father (presumably) carried out and left in the driveway (like, perhaps, the cradles and strollers and tricycles of the last—the very last—child). I don't remember being angry, or even irritated: I was in a hurry to go away to college, to grow up, and wouldn't need —I assumed—*The Nazi Olympics, QBVII*, the rest.

I have never had a Walkman, have, usually, objected to them with a vehemence that, in Europe, would pass for political conviction: I used to think that people—when they are walking, when they are riding on the subway—should pay attention to what they are seeing; though now I wouldn't mind having one, to give the wide, scoured street a soundtrack.

Also, through the clothes chute: listening to my sister and her boyfriend having sex, and the sounds are so vivid in my head, that I can smell something, moist and tinny; the clothes chute is lined with what looks like tin; there are echoes: I remember flicking the tin with my index finger, remember the sound, which is what you hear when you watch a movie about the radio, and someone is re-creating a thunderstorm.

Tram stop.

People, waiting, in the colored clothes of Marzahn, in the colorless clothes of Prenzlauer Berg, as varied (or unvarying) as the repeating rows of stores, their faces as unvaried as the buildings: open-windowed, expressionless; scoured inside.

Trains.

I picture myself on a train, in an empty compartment, stretched out, like on a recliner in my mother's room, listening to something familiar on a Walkman. And I picture the trains from *Shoah*, the train tracks, remembering—as if an object can remember—the taking of people to their deaths.

Two platforms, separated by a high wire, pulling, fleeing.

Inner and outer lives, while walking; glances, paths; the city and myself.

Immanuelkirchstrasse.

Where Felice Bauer lived when she first met Franz Kafka, and where Kafka began sending his letters, after some confusion—one might even say, a willful confusion; a dithering—about the actual street address. (Kurt once met someone who lived in what had been Felice Bauer's building, who may indeed have lived in what had been Felice Bauer's apartment; he can't remember.) When Kafka came to Berlin to celebrate—but, as it turned out, to break off—his engagement with Felice Bauer (who by this time had already moved to Charlottenburg, to what was then thought of—as if in advance—as West Berlin; to Wilmersdorferstrasse, not too far from Peter and Svetlana's video store, which, on its calling cards, lists "Wilmersdorferstrasse" as its U-Bahn stop), he sat on a park bench on Unter den Linden (although I don't think anybody really knows which bench). Between Felice Bauer's house and Unter den Linden (between near where I am standing now and near where I will probably pass by later), there was something called the Jüdisches Volksheim, on the Dragonerstrasse (now Max-Beer-Strasse), in the Scheunenviertel (barn quarter), which was the poorest—and, for a time (between the First World War, when German troops "liberated" parts of Poland from Russian control, to just before the Second World War, when the last of the Jews living there were deported in cattle cars), commonly thought of as the most Jewish—section of Berlin (besides Grunewald, which was the richest, as well as the other most-commonly-thought-of-as-Jewish, section of Berlin), though now most people use "Scheunenviertel" to describe several, somewhat distinct, sections of Berlin—anywhere from the Oranienburger Strasse (and the rebuilt synagogue and the prostitutes) to the cemetery on the Schönhauser Allee, to the rather isolated synagogue behind Prenzlauer Berg's Water Tower (the round-shaped, onetime dormitory for workers at a pumping station, and now an unusual apartment building and the most recognizable symbol of Prenzlauer Berg, of Berlin's onetime factory workers, though if Berlin had gotten the Olympics, the Water Tower was scheduled to become a luxury hotel, to become a symbol of Berlin's property developers, who tend to come from out of town, of carpetbaggers), here, down the street from the Immanuel Church itself, a connect-the-dots of anything having to do with Jews. The Jüdisches Volksheim had been set up during the First World War by assimilated Jews who were interested in Judaism—dabblers, not religious, not zionist; they liked to sit around and recite Franz Werfel's poetry, ran a kindergarten for Jewish refugee children; Gershom Scholem visited one day—he was still Gerhard then—and who should be there, sitting on the floor, with her skirt wrapped "aesthetically" around her knees, but Felice Bauer; Scholem, who was still a teenager (and about to read

Kafka for the first time, independent of his meeting with Felice, who was just another girl inside her draped skirt), provoked an argument, insisting that everyone read original texts, learn Hebrew, and Felice Bauer wrote about the argument to Kafka, who agreed with Scholem; fifty years later, Scholem read Kafka's opinions of himself in the letters to Felice, although the publisher had identified "Scholem" as Shalom Aleichem, who was, Scholem admits, more famous than Gershom Scholem but already dead at the time of the argument; Scholem himself, in *From Berlin to Jerusalem*, gets the Jüdisches Volksheim's address wrong, locating it on the Grenadierstrasse, the Scheunenviertel's most famous street; the Krügers' apartment on the Alte Schönhauser Strasse is in the real Scheunenviertel (what had been the Scheunenviertel and what now feels like a kind of pause, a concrete version of a park, between Alexanderplatz and Prenzlauer Berg; most of its buildings—with old Hebrew lettering clinging to them like lint— were torn down or utterly rebuilt in the eighties, years before I got there), one street away from the Max-Beer-Strasse, and I would often walk by the concrete-lined building that had once housed the Jüdisches Volksheim, or rather, would avoid it, look away, walk down another street, as if I didn't know its real address; Max-Beer-Strasse also sometimes made me think of Max Baer, Jr., who played Jethro on "The Beverly Hillbillies," of the TV set in my bedroom, of watching cartoons and game shows and old sitcoms all morning instead of going to school; if, today, I continue walking straight ahead, I can avoid—exactly—the Scheunenviertel and the Jüdisches Volksheim, and the Krügers' apartment house, which I haven't walked by since the day I moved out. Canetti, who wrote a whole book about Kafka's letters to Felice (called: *Kafka's Other Trial*), makes much of the fact that Kafka broke off the engagement in July 1914, just in time for the First World War. Canetti lived in Berlin for a few months in 1928 and ate in still famous, completely-torn-down restaurants near the Potsdamer Platz with people like Bertolt Brecht (and even, on occasion, with Karl Kraus, though he shows up in the section on Berlin in Canetti's autobiography as an anticlimax—you almost forget that he's there.* Actually Canetti spent much of his time in Berlin with a blasé Hungarian poetess with a Jewish-sounding last name who, it seemed to Canetti, flirted with men in order to tell nasty stories about them afterward; he also spent time with Issac Babel, who liked to stand around Aschinger's restaurant in Alexanderplatz, silently watching workers eat their pea soup; Aschinger's: the famous restaurant once near Alexanderplatz, across from the onetime central police station, though now in West Berlin, on the Kurfürstendamm, and pretty much for tourists and almost across the street from the apartment house where Canetti had stayed in 1928 (I have the address underlined but have never knowingly

---

* Canetti—implicitly, in his autobiography, and somewhat explicitly, elsewhere, in an essay—makes a distinction between the Vienna of Karl Kraus, in which everything was forbidden, made taboo by Kraus's scorn, and the Berlin of Bertolt Brecht, in which everything was permitted, indeed encouraged, in which Brecht—who, when Canetti knew him, was about to make his transition from class-conscious Marxism—could enter a jingle contest for a car company and then drive around in the car he had won, bragging. I might make a distinction between the "eastern Berlin" (as an American newspaper's style book would demand it be written) of Christa Wolf (unofficial co-worker code name: "Margarethe," which many German literary journalists liked to condemn with references to, and, if space allowed, quotations from, Paul Celan's "Todesfuge"), in which Wolf can claim and not be believed that she had "forgotten" about having worked for the Stasi thirty years before, and the eastern Berlin of Heiner Müller (unofficial co-worker code name, among others: "Heiner"), in which Müller can claim, and not be believed, that he had been "naïve" in thinking that he could talk for hundreds of hours to Stasi agents in the seventies and eighties without actually being used as an informer; between Christa Wolf comparing a year spent in Los Angeles, after her reputation fell along with the Berlin Wall, to German Jews in exile there in the 1930s and '40s, and getting listened to, telling her onetime audiences, who seem to have gone back to her in the way that they have gone back to Spee (the revamped East German state laundry detergent), that what Germans have to be proud of (she was quoting her grandson, who had also been to California) was their bread, and Heiner Müller —whom people have never really left because, although he doesn't exactly write plays anymore, he is considered the greatest playwright writing in the German language—showing up at a reopened U-Bahn station, part of which had been turned into an art gallery, where, in the old tunnel which people need to walk through to change lines, advertisements from the day the wall went up and the station was sealed shut had been taken down and replaced with phonetic spellings of names of cities (of Berlin, of New York, of Kinshasa) with his own bottle of whiskey, which he drank out of with a straw.

walked by, though I have probably walked by often; although the house itself may have been blown up and not rebuilt, wouldn't mean anything, or, rather, *would* mean, like so much else here, nothing), and which must have then seemed part of another world entirely. (Aschinger's always reminds me of my grandfather, whose last name, Ascher, sounds—and, to me at least, especially looks— similar; I don't know if Herr Aschinger was a Jew, or, if he was, whether—and how—his restaurant was aryanized in the 1930s.) Joseph Roth, the Galician-born Jew who was the German lan- guage's most famous journalist between the wars, and who often came to Berlin in the 1920s, occasionally to write about Jews ("No *Ostjude* willingly goes to Berlin. Who in the whole world willingly goes to Berlin?") is nowadays much more famous for his novels; in his last novel, a pre–World War I Viennese aristocrat claims that he is no longer an anti-Semite because his servants, having learned their anti-Semitism from aristocrats, are anti-Semites (I have been thinking of Roth because of those heterosexual workmen in the apartment with their pierced ears, giggling at Abba music on the radio); Roth spent the 1930s in Paris in a kind of irredentist stupor—he was plotting a revival of the Hapsburg monarchy—as well as an alcoholic one, drinking himself to death in time for the start of the Second World War, which makes me think of Paul Celan's very late poems, and of his drowning himself nearby; Ce- lan has a very late poem with the line: *"(Betrink dich / und nenn sie Paris.)"* Get drunk and call it Paris; he has another very late poem with the following stanza: "the menorah poem from Berlin, / (Unasylumed, un- / archived, un- / welfare-attended? A- / live?),", which I recently found and memorized (knowing it now almost automatically, too automatically, like a poem from grade school, like "The Highwayman") first in the translator's English, then in Celan's "German."* I could walk by the place where Gershom Scholem's childhood home used to stand, which is now, I believe,

---

* After having strongly identified with Celan's "Berlin" poem, I identi- fied strongly with Christa Wolf in Cali- fornia identifying strongly with Jewish refugees.

some sort of small park, thickly surrounded with new concrete apartment blocks. (Actually, I have ridden by in taxis innumerable times, never remembering to notice that particular stretch of new concrete apartment blocks surrounding that particular small park.) In Scholem's book about Walter Benjamin, I have underlined the address in Grunewald of Benjamin's parents' house, which was on a corner of a street now renamed, for some reason, Richard-Strauss-Strasse (Richard Strauss was Reichsmusikkammerpräsident under Adolf Hitler, until he was caught trying to collaborate one too many times with Stefan Zweig, who was a Viennese Jew; Strauss wrote a hymn for the 1936 Berlin Olympics, though who likes to remember that during one of his earlier—or even later—compositions?). Kafka, in the 1920s, when he was living in Berlin with Dora Dymant and on the verge of dying of tuberculosis, lived in Grunewaldstrasse 13, in Steglitz (which was famous in the 1920s for attracting as residents an unusually large number of civil servants—which is what Germans call people like postal clerks and high school teachers—and, a little later, for its unusually large percentage of Nazi voters), though I used to think he lived in Grunewaldstrasse 13 in Schöneberg; I have walked down Grune-waldstrasse in Schöneberg, looking up admiringly at number 13, at the neo-baroque splendor, and thought that the building—which looked, as buildings almost never do in Berlin, unbombed and unrestored, accidentally intact, like the opposite of an accident—had more to do with Kafka (whose papers were famously saved by Max Brod, not destroyed, as Kafka had famously wished, surviving, one might argue, accidentally, if disobeying someone's last wishes can be described as accidental) than the buildings in Prague that I had tracked down with the German-English-French-Italian guide I bought at Prague's Old-New Synagogue; now I walk down that street and think that my mistake has more to do with Kafka than if he had actually lived there; or I walk down the street and forget about Kafka entirely, hurry past, don't really want to have to think again about Kafka, as if I were merely on my way somewhere. I may walk past that house today; I like to think of myself as walking all the way there—through the Brandenburg Gate,* past the ruins of the Fascist Italian embassy, down the Potsdamer Strasse.† Or I think of myself as walking all the way to Steglitz and the real Grunewaldstrasse, where Kafka really lived, dying. But that wouldn't be a stroll, that would be more like a pilgrimage.

Here, past the Immanuelkirchstrasse: no people, and no shops, cross streets named after Strasbourg (Strassburg), Mulhouse (Mühlhausen), Metz (Metz), and the view, which reveals an incline, letting Prenzlauer Berg (*Berg* means "mountain") live up to its name. In the distance: Alexanderplatz; or, specifically: the pale blue, remodeled, renamed, onetime Interhotel, the faded green of an old office building, a Toshiba sign and a Sanyo sign (the East German skyscrapers surrounding the Alexanderplatz, with their new neon signs, make me think of a carnival, of people putting their faces through outlandish backdrops and getting their pictures taken; or

---

* Berlin's Brandenburg Gate was the old entrance for people coming from and going to the city of Brandenburg, which was famous for having been the first capital of Brandenburg, for having been "depopulated" in the language of an architecture guidebook I have, during the Thirty Years War, and for having had the largest mental institution and largest prison in East Germany. (Hospitals in Germany—I would have passed one in Marzahn, if I had taken a streetcar instead of the S-Bahn to school; I have been twice to the hospital, though I thought I would go more often, to see Hans-Joachim, who has pneumonia— look campuslike, like liberal arts colleges. The prison in Brandenburg, which I drove by once with Hans-Joachim, looked like a prison: like an American hospital or an American high school, like a suburban synagogue, like an airport; populated, in spite of appearances to the contrary.) Recently outside the

city of Brandenburg, a Soviet Army barracks was attacked with Molotov cocktails, sprayed with swastikas; the soldiers, in a subsequent cartoon in a West German satirical magazine, under the caption *"Aktion Barbarossa,"* were shown fleeing in tanks.

† In Potsdam, one day last week, although it seems like weeks ago because of all the attention (the news articles have turned seamlessly into reflective essays): the Jewish Cemetery that had been restored with a great deal of publicity a year or so ago was attacked during the night; tombstones were "daubed" (as an English newspaper I read described it) with swastikas, and a large bonfire was set, which people living nearby must have seen but didn't bother to report to the fire department, which is what most of the articles have been about, Jewish cemeteries themselves getting desecrated more often than newspapers can keep track of.

of plastic nose-and-glasses), and the Kaufhof department store (founded by Heinrich Tietz and called Kaufhof before and after aryanization, though it hadn't been in Berlin before the war because Tietz's brother Hermann had his own department stores here, called Hermann Tietz—which eventually took over Wertheim and the KaDeWe—before it was aryanized to Hertie; there is a Hertie now in Alexanderplatz which stands, more or less, where Hermann Tietz's department store used to stand, and the Kaufhof, which had been a fairly nameless socialist department store before the wall fell, stands, I believe, where Israel's department store used to stand, though it's always hard to tell with Alexanderplatz because of the square's two main buildings, which, in addition to being blown up by the Allies and then rebuilt by the Communists, were built at the very end of the 1920s with a drastic modernism that, in real life, makes them look as outsized as a pair of Nazi ministries, as bleak as a cluster of socialist apartment blocks, though in photographs they still look expressionist, of their own place and time, quaintly severe; underneath the Alexanderplatz, the green tiles from the 1920s renovation have been, in many places, painted back on, with the white grout as fake as painted-on stocking seams) with its forest green, West German S-Bahn–like "KAUFHOF" sign (as green as the Berlin police wagons with their Hollywood Gestapo sirens), pushing its way out from behind the Toshiba sign, collagelike, like a still from the Weimar classic *Berlin: Symphony of a Great City*, in which the city itself is the hero, or antihero.

There seems to be a bridge here, between where I am standing (which had once been the Prenzlauer Gate, used by people who were on their way to or from Prenzlau centuries ago; lately I have been reading a bilingual Central European architecture guide that I bought for thirty-five of my remaining hundred and fifty dollars, reading it with studentlike curiosity, the way my father used to read Earl Wilson's column in "The Green Sheet"):

The bridge in Milwaukee, whose name I can't remember.

The Brooklyn Bridge, which I used to walk across to get to work, when I temped on Wall Street and lived in Cobble Hill, or, on a few occasions, when I lived in Fort Greene, had no job, was saving on subway fare.

Bridges and overpasses in Los Angeles and Chicago that I never noticed.

The Charles Bridge, the Elizabeth Bridges (in Vienna, in Budapest), the Poniatowski Bridge, the Augustus (Dimitroff, né Augustus) Bridge . . . Albert Speer's bridge.

Le Pont Alexandre III.

And before me, out of sight: Schinkel's rebuilt Palace Bridge, at the start of Unter den Linden, after Prenzlauer Allee ends, or begins, at what had been the old city wall and turns into Karl-Liebknecht-Strasse, which bends through what had been medieval alleys, turns into Unter den Linden, near the East German Palast der Republik, where East Germany's version of a Parliament convened, and the once temporary, increasingly permanent, trompe l'oeil façade of the old Hohenzollern Palace painted onto canvas and then reflecting jokelike (and realistically: wall-like) off the Palast der Republik's sunglasses façade (some people are loudly advocating tearing down the Palast der Republik and rebuilding the Hohenzollern Palace, or at least its façade, are practicing a sort of architectural irredentism, though their cause suffered a setback when one of the most famous, and the most eloquent, advocates was caught giving money to Franz Schönhuber's Republikaner Party), and the old hard-currency Palast Hotel, with its sunglasses façade, which has been bought by the Radisson hotel chain who have opened up a TGIFridays, right across the street from the old neo-baroque Hohenzollern cathedral, built at the turn of the century and immediately thought of as bombastic, as a sort of imperial temper tantrum: that way, just ahead, but out of sight, now that what would feel like a straight line has been revealed as something else, a swirl.

And this bridge, before me, which doesn't exist, which has no name, but beckons, as though it could be crossed.

.   .   .

Ways out, into safety.
The safeness of elsewhere.

Summer, summer light—almost translucent; an egg white with
a bit of yolk, with traces of something [windless].

Beds, masturbation.
At night I would lie in bed, listening to the television in my
parents' room, with my legs up, and masturbate, rubbing the come
into my stomach, then I would drop my knees and a draft would
move out from under the covers, run the smell of come across my
face (the other day: my legs up, in the dark windowless room, and
then my legs down, with a draft smelling vaguely of urine—of my
own, familiar, urine; unlike the bathroom, which smells, to some
extent, of other people's urine, like a public toilet). When I was
about eleven, my mother had the cleaning lady put plastic sheets
on my bed (for wet dreams, I later figured out, so I didn't ruin the
mattress) that might have been leftover from when my sister was
living there and she and my mother were menstruating (now, I
am fairly sure, there are plastic sheets on both beds in my parents'
room, and on the bed in my room; beds in drag as adolescents'
beds). I was fat until I was eleven, when I grew six inches in one
year and started shaving a false-eyelash-like moustache with my
father's razors and, a few times, with my mother's Lady Gillette,
at her insistence (she said the moustache looked "hoody")—I
would do it at her makeup desk, in front of her makeup mirror,
with the lightbulbs she had had to special-order at Winkie's. We
always had to exchange valentines at school, and, until I was
eleven, I would always get valentines with elephants and hippos
on them; when I was twelve, in the sixth grade, which was the last
year the school made people exchange valentines, I got giraffes
and apes instead. Now I am fat again—holding my elbows close
to my hips, the bones rub against the flesh, as if I could rest my
elbows there, like on a gun holster—with the body of a lesbian.

Once at the Mayo Clinic alone, my mother was apparently courted by a middle-aged lesbian who was about to have a colostomy; I think she and my mother would eat together in the Diet Kitchen of the Kahler cafeteria. "She's plenty tough," my mother said, with admiration (envy), and what sounded like fear. (My mother was the German and the lesbian got to be Napoleon.) "She's going right in for that colostomy. Do you know what life is like after a colostomy?"

My mother was always somewhat fat, but got thinner just before she had to start injecting herself with insulin; just before I left she looked too thin and bloated at the same time; my father was always thin, lanky, like I became, but, my mother tells me, has lately grown alarmingly fat, eats sweet rolls at his desk, where he still works on a few of his accounts—because they need the money, my mother tells me; because he likes to, my mother has also told me. (Imagining my mother at a spa, forestalling, and my father at his desk, at his adding machine, until he drops.) My sister was always rather fat, except between the time she graduated from law school and the time just after she got married; now she is quite fat, fatter than my mother ever was. When my sister was thin, and we were all out for dinner somewhere, and my sister would reach for a roll, my mother would look at her, or my sister would think that my mother was looking at her, and they would start to fight: my mother would tell my sister that she would never get a husband if she got fat again, then told her that she if she got fat again she would end up with diabetes and heart attacks. My sister likes to get up in the middle of the night, her husband let slip out, go into the bedroom she uses as a study (which has some books and a desk, a television set, a couch), and eat in front of the television. Her husband, who was on the cross-country team in high school and whom I think of as bone thin, as thinner (and much healthier) than Peter Marcus, was in fact fatter the last time I saw him; I was shocked, actually, when he got out of his car and had to hold on to the car door for support, seeming enfeebled with fat. (My uncle is fat and strong, like his father; at grill-outs, he would eat the rings of fat off other people's steaks, gnaw on bones.)

I feel, actually, like a shorter, thinner man; the outside inside me.

I can picture Unter den Linden: the baroque palaces; the opera house; Schinkel's royal guardhouse, described in my architecture guide as "the most monumental building on the avenue," once dedicated to German soldiers who died in the First World War, then rededicated after the Second World War to "the victims of fascism and militarism" oor thereabouts) and constantly guarded by an East German People's Army contingent who goose-stepped back and forth in front of an eternal flame, and recently re-rededicated as the "Central Memorial of the German Federal Republic"—with a reproduction of a Käthe Kollwitz sculpture replacing the flame—to the victims of "war and tyranny," which, in its plaque's stanzalike paragraphs, can seem to include Nazis and their victims, and Communists and their victims, everyone, and, therefore, it has been argued, no one (the government's choice of Käthe Kollwitz, who was a particularly pious socialist along with being a socially conscious Lutheran, and who got streets named after her in East Germany that no one is demanding be changed to something else, was considered a public relations coup, while the choice of the actual sculpture, which is of a mother and her dead son, unmistakably a pietà, was, because of subsequent objections by Jews, some of whom boycotted the commemorative ceremony, considered a public relations disaster, or worse), and which is given—like the synagogues in East (and West) Berlin, like the West Berlin gallery now displaying Gypsy musical instruments, like the Jewish day school in West Berlin—ordinary twenty-four-hour police protection, unlike the Treuhandanstalt building, which is patrolled against random *Autonomen* violence, or against passersby who just want to spit on it, by its own security force; the baroque imperial library and the vast square next door, now a parking lot, where the SA and the *Burschenschafter* burnt books in 1933; the old Prussian Staatsbibliothek, where Walter Benjamin, among others, spent a lot of time and where Hans-Joachim told me men have sex in the toilet on the first—in the European sense—floor (books and sex: Benjamin also spent a lot of time at the Bibliothèque Nationale in Paris, which has often been surrounded by famous—or perhaps, infamous—brothels); the park benches, one of which was, or has replaced what once was, Kafka's bench; Albert Einstein's office; the hole in the ground off Friedrichstrasse where the new Friedrichstadt Arcade is being built (no one knows how to talk about it except as a shopping mall, or else as a series of shopping malls) and which, now, as the largest construction site in Europe, until they break more ground on the Potsdamer Platz, looks preposterously deep, like some downward-pointing skyscraper, like the subterranean passage in Kafka's "The Pit of Babel" (at Christmas, last year: the cranes building the hole in the ground were decorated with Christmas lights that looked irregular in the nighttime sky, almost abstract, like a constellation, like a piece of fallen sky). Unter den Linden is Hans-Joachim's favorite street; he says the buildings converse with one another, that the distance between the Brandenburg Gate and where the Hohenzollern palace had once stood—like the distance between the palace that became the university and Schinkel's guardhouse next door, and the distance between the guardhouse and the palace across the street that has became a restaurant complex (and that housed what passed for a gay bar while the wall was still up)—is the "perfect" distance (he is very much against the rebuilding of the Hohenzollern palace façade and somewhat against the tearing down of the Palast der Republik); he can talk, with asides in three languages, about "architectonic etiquette." He went into the hospital just as TGIFridays was opening, hasn't yet seen the TGIFriday sign, which is now almost as conspicuous as the Thyssen sign, which runs along the top of the Palast der Republik, above the reflection of the trompe l'oeil façade of the Hohenzollern palace, because a Thyssen subsidiary helped pay for what simply gets called "the exhibition" and is trying to help raise the money for the façade's actual rebuilding; Thyssen is a famous name in Germany—for steel making, for art collecting, and, for a while, for supporting Adolf Hitler, whose rise to power was lavishly financed by Thyssen's one-time owner, "Fritz" Thyssen.

Also in my head: Vienna's Ringstrasse (Ring Street: oxymoronic, like Austria's official name, which, translated into English, means the "Republic of the Eastern Empire," though not wrong, like " 'Unter' den Linden," where the linden trees look small and sick, and the buildings seem to tower over them, and tall West German tourists, gazing upward, look like John Singer Sargent heiresses moving their heads through the pasted-on-looking leaves; in Brookfield, in the new subdivisions, the new trees always grow faster than people expect, eventually throw the new houses out of proportion with one another, often grow in wrongly, through sewers and poorly laid foundations, sometimes have to be cut down), where the enormous buildings were not built along any axis, seem unrelated to one another, don't converse (or converse with silence), which feels absolutely empty (you don't notice the buildings until you're standing in front of them, in their shadows; until you have to notice them too much), like: a freeway, a vacuum, a wall-less tunnel; a desert. I can't picture the neo-gothic and neo-Renaissance, and neo-baroque buildings themselves (can't even recall their photographs in my architecture guidebook); Hitler could: as an Upper Austrian *Luftmensch* during his time in Vienna, he had nothing better to do than wander up and down the Ringstrasse, memorizing the architecture; years later, he could make detailed sketches of the Burgtheater and the Opera House and the Rathaus, along with his other favorite buildings, like the Paris Opera, from memory. (I seem to do the opposite—sketch their absences.)

Kerwin, whose house I have walked by without noticing, without caring, is going to Vienna (he says), and asked me if I knew of a cheap place to stay. I tried to find Professor Whitlaw's list because the only thing on the list that actually existed turned out to be a cheap pension off the Ringstrasse (Vienna: finished off, embalmed, dead forever; Berlin: dead things pieced back together into something lifelike, Dr. Frankenstein as city planner); but I can't find the list, may have thrown it out, or perhaps it has evanesced, was covered and devoured in the new apartment, has turned to dust.

A memory: looking out a window in Brooklyn at a newly arrived car that someone had stolen and was about to strip; it was early spring, and I went to Prospect Park, and when I came back two hours later the car was missing its tires; after I took a long bath, its four doors, along with its hood and trunk doors, were missing; I woke up in the middle of the night and looked out the window, and the only thing left was the car frame and bits of broken glass; the next day it was raining, the car frame was gone, and the rain had washed away the glass.

I did not learn about my mother from my father, nor about my father from my mother; I learned about them separately, as though I belonged to two different families. In some sense, I have never learned about my sister. I learned about my cousins in retrospect, in college, from the friends I made there (though at college I was never friends with my cousins, all of whom were at Madison while I was; they joined Jewish sororities or lived near the engineering campus, watched television, studied too much, embarrassed me whenever I ran into them, the way people in high school are embarrassed when they run into their parents at a shopping mall). I learned about forgetting from Annette, whose voice holds no memory of the time we spent together; I learned that people can forget each other, or remember each other in different ways, become ghosts for each other.

I have walked too far: the imaginary bridge has disappeared, become an ordinary crosswalk.

I am about to walk through one of the old Berlin Walls (but am lingering, am still outside the "city"), past the cemetery where the Nazi "martyr" Horst Wessel was once buried (cemeteries in Berlin were usually meant to be outside the city walls, but the city was always growing too fast, knocking down its walls and incorporating the land around its cemeteries, reclaiming its dead) and where Hitler, a few days before seizing power in 1933, took a photo opportunity at a commemorative ceremony; and past the Wilhelm-Pieck-Haus, which had been the East German equivalent of the White House, and which, now, with its leftover East German plaques and new West German government sign [OTTO GROTEWOHL/VORSITZENDER DES ZK DER SED/UND/ERSTER MINISTERPRÄSIDENT DER DDR/ARBEI-TETE/VON 1946–1958 IN DIESEM HAUS WILHELM PIECK/VORSITZ-ENDER DES ZK DER SED/UND/ERSTER PRÄSIDENT DER DDR/ARBEITETE/VON 1946–1956 IN DIESEM HAUS *Stiftung Archiv der Parteien und/ Massenorganization der DDR/in Bundesarchiv*] talks to itself.

Last summer, when I walked by the cemetery where Horst Wessel was buried, the heavy smell of pine trees always reminded me of summers at the Jewish summer camp, where the cabins were surrounded by pine trees.

I don't want to be here this summer.

The television tower is too tall to be a part of the view, is busy talking to (actually, ignoring) the fifteenth-century Marienkirche, which is now technically the oldest church in Berlin; the nearby, onetime fourteenth-century Nicolaikirche, which had been the oldest church in Berlin until it was flattened during the war, was rebuilt quite late, in the 1980s, may in fact be the newest church in Berlin, and though it was rebuilt with nineteenth-century-looking red bricks, it looks, at a distance, as if it were built out of poured concrete; the Marienkirche looks primitive, as if it were built out of piled-up stones: a house built out of pieces of houses, a sand castle built at a rocky beach.

Where to go, ending up.

(Not wanting to go to Auschwitz, not knowing what it might mean; afraid of no-ing what it means.)

Wanting to go home, or beyond home.

Milwaukee (Brookfield).

Kaliningrad [Königsberg].

I learned about Professor Whitlaw through my grandfather—
they both, now, look alike, like Elmer Fudd, cartoonlike, both
German.

My mother has never been unkind to me, by which I mean: she
never said anything unkind to me when I was unhappy, was never
cruel (she says irritating—but not exactly unkind—things to many
people, provokes unkindness; fights between my mother and my
sister end with my mother in tears, and with my sister triumphant,
gorgonlike, hailing down waiters to order hot fudge sundaes), except once, when Annette broke up with me and I called my parents
in tears (I thought of it, even at the time, as some sort of last
chance; and so it was, like dropping the accounting class: an end-
in-itself), and she told me to stop crying because men didn't cry
(I was twenty). My father's criticisms are, really, more playful than
vicious, and predictable; comforting in that sense (it amused me
—soothed me, somehow—to imagine him reminding my mother
of the movie studio job). I like my parents, liked the filling up and
emptying of the refrigerator—the local, inner seasons of our house.
And I liked the noise of the televisions and the ringing telephones
and competing telephone conversations, which, after all, where I
come from (and, increasingly, where so many people come from),
is what life sounds like.

Imagining myself.
In Kaliningrad: laying a wreath on Kant's—on Professor Whitlaw's—grave. I can see it in my head (buying the wreath, walking
up to the memorial plaque, bending down . . .), in panels, like a
somber cartoon.
In Milwaukee: stocking and cleaning out the refrigerator, going
to the drugstore for my parents, dropping by my sister's, baby-
sitting for my cousins, running into people from high school at a
shopping mall, watching television; familiar, full of shallow
pleasures—a bath up to the knees, an anointing of myself with the
familiar.

. . .

Familiar.

Family liar.

Famished. (Starving for half-truths.)

The sky in Kaliningrad—in Königsberg, in East Prussia—is legendary; people who go back after half a century find everything else unrecognizable (I remember reading), except the sky.

The sky in Berlin, today: clearer, but still something else; sooty, though most people have probably stopped heating with coal; still familiar.

Back in Milwaukee, the sky might look familiar, or it might look smaller; I only remember what it looks like in my parents' backyard, which is always smaller than I remember, as small as a parking space; or else much larger, as large as the world.

A Jew who won't leave Germany.

An American taking the long way home.

A Jew about to leave Germany

An American on his way home.

American soldiers leaving Berlin (after people find out that I am American and not a student, and they ask, always in English, if I'm "in the military," I am always offended): ceremonially, with German-American friendship festivals that show up the next day in color on the front pages of conservative West Berlin broadsheets, the American beer logos waving over everybody's heads, like winged lions, like double-headed eagles (but not like swastikas, only somewhat like hammer and sickles).

(Going East and West at the same time. Chicago-style stuffed pizza parlors in Wroclaw; concentration camp guards in suburban Milwaukee, or other kinds of murderers with—when they're white—German-sounding last names.)

. . .

Stalling, not wanting to walk across the street.

When I first got here: wanting to walk through the Brandenburg Gate (like Napoleon, like Hitler; like Tom Brokaw; like visiting Scandinavian royalty on the local TV news, answering reporters' questions in German, which is considered polite, or refusing, answering in English, which, if their countries had been occupied during the war, can seem politely defiant; like visiting Japanese royalty walking gracefully through the columns, which, for the occasion, have been draped with rising-sun flags).

I can picture the market at the Brandenburg Gate: the Turks selling Warsaw Pact souvenirs and, still, pieces of concrete that they say were part of the Berlin Wall; fat Russian women selling matryoshka dolls and amber necklaces; the same dark Turkish and round Russian faces; the same watches and hats; the same doll; only the pieces of amber look different, actually similarly different, like markets themselves (to compare: the market at the Brandenburg Gate with the market in Jerusalem, inside the Temple).

Something decisive about my stalling, like Christ not entering Jerusalem.

All alone here, except for the dog shit (actually, kinds of dog shit, from various seasons, from concrete gray to greenish brown; graded by time).

Germans and their dogs.

Germans seem to prefer dogs that look like other kinds of animals: their German shepherds look as sleek as lizards; their Yorkshire terriers look like pigs.

Germans distinguish between kinds of blond hair. Whenever I am supposed to meet Hans-Joachim at a café and he doesn't show up and I want to leave him a note with the waiter telling him that I have already left, I have to describe him as having "dark" blond hair. Older Germans have blond hair that turns gray—a yellowish, grayish white; the color, perhaps, of the sky now (ashes mixed with egg yolk), and of unrepentance. (A trip to Kaliningrad, like a trip to Milwaukee—penitential.)

The difference between a Berliner *Mietskaserne*, with its back houses and series of courtyards leading back for what can look like forever, and a Russian matryoshka doll, leading inward, to smaller versions of itself: one ends with a fire wall; the other also ends, but seems as if it might only end with a model of a heart (though actually it ends with nothing, with mere air; a model of heartlessness).

The difference between the various hospital rooms that my mother has been in, and Hans-Joachim's hospital room.

My mother's rooms were always private; she was choosy about visitors, wouldn't let people in, or wouldn't even let people know she was in the hospital (the vanity of the modest), instructed everyone who visited to wash their hands (like in a cemetery). Hans-Joachim's room: shared, for a while, with a chain-smoking drug addict who, the second time I was there, had disappeared (to another wing entirely, according to Hans-Joachim, who said all the gay men had made him nervous), his bed stripped and folded up; Hans-Joachim, now that he is much better, has told everyone that he is in the hospital, invites them to visit, keeps them waiting; the first time I waited for half an hour and the second time I waited for almost two hours. Somehow, even though I had lived in New York and Los Angeles, I had avoided all of this, never had a friend who had gotten sick; the AIDS wing of the hospital, which has its own building, looks like the old building in Madison that houses the political science department, like a college campus taken over by dying students (many of the nurses were men who looked like gay men, and most of the gay men who were sick had begun to resemble one another: the same youthfulness, preserved, and withering). On the wall there were posters of photographs by Herb Ritts and Bruce Weber, which you might see on the wall of a gym, or on the living room wall of a certain kind of gay man in his thirties or forties, or perhaps on the bedroom wall of a teenage girl, and posters of Tom of Finland cartoons (Tom of Finland drew preposterously, if rather affectionately, exaggerated cowboys and bikers and policemen fucking each other, sucking each other off, French-kissing, or just wooing; he perfected his style, I learned from a documentary at last year's Berlin Film Festival, as a teenager in German-occupied Finland, sketching Wehrmacht soldiers and SS officers, who have only rarely shown up in his subsequent cartoons, though after you see his early cartoons, the cowboys and bikers and policemen all look like the Wehrmacht soldiers and SS officers) that you would probably only find in a gay bar, or perhaps in a porno shop; there were people coming and going with food from the Feinschmecker Etage at the KaDeWe; both times, I bought books: by Joseph Roth, the first time, and by Christopher Isherwood and Julian Green the second time; Hans-Joachim, when I called him from the Humannplatz, said he wanted a book by Christopher Isherwood in English and by Julian Green in French; I bought them in West Berlin, at the gay bookstore, where I lingered, paging through Christopher Isherwood in German and Julian Green in English; afterward I lingered at Savignyplatz, which is the part of West Berlin that feels the most like the rest of Western Europe, sitting in a café and watching people for what seemed like hours drink their Italian coffee and page through Spanish fashion magazines and English rock magazines, sing along with the 1930s *chansons* that the bartender played all afternoon, order baguettes, greet one another, feeling myself in another world.

The hospital rooms: they might have smelled alike.

(The uriny smell of a subway staircase in New York; of a European, coffee-and-cigarette, red-wine-yeasty-beer, rotten-tooth smile.

Mouthsful of death.)

I can't remember the hospital room smell—from years ago and from last week. The spot near the Humannplatz, where the old

East German phone booth is, smells, almost, of springtime, of wet earth.

Beyond the Brandenburg Gate: the Tiergarten—where all the prewar, often centuries-old, trees that hadn't been incinerated in the bombings were cut down for firewood—now has trees that can't be more than forty, forty-five, years old, or a little younger; middle-aged trees.

Andreas and the Former Volkhochschule *Teacher; the Patient and the Dentist; a Husband and His Wife; a Woman and a Man; the Architect and an Architectural Historian*

Poor Andreas! Business was bad: Everyone in Schwedt and Prenzlau and Brandenburg and Neubrandenburg and Frank-furt-an-der-Oder already seemed to have bought their appli-ances (people in Frankfurt-an-der-Oder were buying theirs in Poland, eating caviar in their cars as they waited to go back through customs); he had begun to hear about East Germans (actually about one in particular, who had been a clerk at the distribution center in Greifenhagen—Gryfino—just over the Polish border), with their Young Pioneer contacts and their grade school Russian, making deals themselves, in Poland, in Russia, in Byelorussia, even in the Ukraine, where people were waiting in line all day to buy lard. Andreas thought about Uwe whatever-his-name-was, and saw distribution cen-ters spreading out over the steppes, about selling appliances all the way from Berlin to the Ural Mountains; during traffic jams, he looked in the back of his book of German road maps, studying the road map of Europe, and saw roads and money, money instead of rivers and mountain ranges and lakes, instead of cities; he saw coffeemakers and irons and towel warmers, made for a tenth or less of what it cost in West Germany and sold, even in the Ukraine, at a 100, 200 percent markup; "I can't stand up straight," he said to him-self, imagining the borders of East Germany as a waist-high ceiling, and Uwe, somewhere in the Ukraine, with a bullet-proof limousine, wearing a custom-made suit. "I can't breathe." He decided that he had to learn Russian and went to the *Volkshochschule* near his office in Tempelhof to sign up for a summer course, wanting to sign up for an advanced course, figuring he would teach himself a little bit every day before June when the term started; "You'll have to take a test, Herr Hildebrandt," the secretary told him, handing him a paper booklet with Cyrillic lettering all over it. "A test? Right now? I don't have time for a test. I have a meeting, all the way in Oberschöneweide. In an hour. Do you know what the traffic is like? Berlin isn't a city; it's a construction site!" "Well if you can't take the test we can't let you in the class. That's how we do things here in Tempelhof. Take a class in the East; I hear they're not so fussy." (Andreas imagined the cotton-wad walls of an East Berlin *Volkshochschule*, the smell, say, of a nearby *Currywurst* stand, the women in the class, with their hennaed hair, their terrible accents.) "Can't I talk to someone about this. To the teacher, or to the *Fachbereichslei-terin*, or to . . ." The secretary, without looking up, wrote down something on a piece of paper and rolled over to the counter in her office chair. "You can talk to her, but you'll still have to take the test," she said. "You can talk as much as you want." Later, in his car, stalled near the Potsdamer Platz, Andreas picked up his phone and called the number, written beneath the name "Frau Julia Kraus." (Andreas had once known a girl named Julia, in school, but had forgotten her; he had once pulled her hair, then, years later, had danced with her at a youth club, got a hard-on when he touched the curve of her hip.) A young woman answered the phone. "*Bei* Kraus," she said; there was classical music play-ing in the background. "I would like to speak to Frau Julia Kraus, please. This is Andreas Hildebrandt speaking." "This is Frau Kraus." "Frau Kraus, I have just had a small disagree-ment with the secretary at the *Volkshochschule*. It seems that I have to take a test in order to gain admittance to your ad-vanced Russian class. Now I am not a housewife or a pen-sioner who takes one of these classes just because I am sick of watching nonsense on television or looking out the win-dow waiting for someone to drop their green bottles into the brown bottle recycling bin. I work. I drive all over East Germany, three, four days a week. I can't tell my colleagues that I have to take some sort of test just so the bureaucrats at the *Volkshochschule* have an excuse for getting paid. I am paying for this course, and do you think I would waste my money if I didn't think I was up to the so-called standards of the *Volkshochschule* Tempelhof?" There was silence, a breathing in and out. "Are you still there, Frau Kraus?" She had hung up. He dialed back, and she didn't answer; he let the phone ring fifteen times, then hung up and decided to call her from Oberschöneweide. She's probably from the East, he thought, not yet being able to match up boroughs with their new telephone exchanges, all uppity because now she gets to teach housewives and old women in Tempelhof instead of in goddamned Marzahn. He honked his horn. "Is this a city or a construction site?" he said to no one, to everyone. Julia, after having let the phone ring (she hadn't taught at the *Volkshochschule* for two—no, three!—years, but was still getting calls during registration weeks), imagined herself elsewhere: she was on her way to the dentist. She imagined herself in a small house, in the country, or riding a bicycle down a road lined with plum trees; she could smell the grass, feel it between her toes. Well, not exactly to the dentist; she was meeting her dentist, for dinner, in Charlottenburg. I am fucking my dentist, she thought, trying to feel younger, less pathetic. (She was thirty-four, with a lapsing Ph.D. candidacy in Russian, living in an apartment that she had once squatted, for which she was now paying—until January, when the rent went up again—fifteen marks per square meter.) Which is better than fucking my professor. (She had, briefly, lived with her Russian professor—a Jew from Moscow who had moved to Paris years ago, leaving his German wife behind; Julia had sometimes seen her at the university cafeteria, reading over her salads.) Julia considered the dentist: his aging, earnest face; his large hands; his terrible teeth. (She had fallen in love with his teeth, she had decided; a dentist with terrible teeth, she would think, over and over, admiring the imperfection of the world.) She saw him in his office, above the Europa Center. (Oh, how she hated the Europa Center! It was like crawling into a television set, like going shopping at an airport. She hated the flat, empty view from his office.) She was thinking, rather hazily, of their last dinner, when they had talked about going away somewhere while his wife visited her mother in Wiesbaden. He took vacations in Pomerania—in Poland, she had corrected him—to see the village where his father had grown up, complained about the Poles, actually used that awful expression "Polish housekeeping" to describe how run-down everything was. A married dentist. A Christian Democrat. She was guessing; they had never talked about politics, but she had noticed the newspapers in his office, and his genuine alarm when she first told him that she lived in Kreuzberg; she hadn't told him that she was thinking of moving to the East, to Prenzlauer Berg, after her rent went up again. (She had often gone over to the East before the wall fell, had spent long evenings in an apartment somewhere in Prenzlauer Berg, drinking vodka and listening to singing Russians who wept as they sang; now she never went; the ruins and the construction sites depressed her; the ripped-up streets cut holes in her bike tires; she couldn't stand the stares, the feeling of being a tourist in her own city.) A Christian Democrat, who probably votes. A husband with a bad marriage. A father who never sees his child. She thought about his bad teeth, the smell of his breath. He's forty-three, with the face of a student and the mouth of an old man. She felt older now that the weather was turning warmer; another spring, she thought, and another and another. She turned up the music: it was a Haydn string quartet, and it sounded like a dirge. Her dentist, meanwhile, was still in his office, on the phone with his wife, arguing about the tickets to the Philharmonic, which he had paid good money for so why shouldn't she use them even if he couldn't? She was going on and on, as she often did; he thought about her body, about running his hands up and down her body, so familiar and warm, and then he thought about Julia's body, which was thinner, almost brittle; he loved the way she would lie on top of his back while he was trying to sleep, her hair falling over his face; I love women too much, he thought. That's my problem! He thought of the woman who had come in today to start a root canal; she must have been over forty, but there was still something about her, wasn't there? He thought about her legs, saw, again, her squirming into place in the chair, the way her skirt had risen just above her knees, and the way her legs spread apart, almost imperceptibly, as if he were merely imagining it, then how he let his leg move, how his knee had touched her leg, his pant crease catching briefly—pausing—on the roughness of her stocking. His wife went on, and he looked out the window at Berlin, at what he had seen five days a week for years, but today, in the bright sunshine, the vastness frightened him; he swallowed consciously, almost studiously, as if he had been tasting his own saliva, and began listening to his wife, Anna, who had been talking—to herself, she knew—about their son, Philip, smoking cigarettes in the house. Philip was fifteen, smoking with his friends, but she thought that he shouldn't smoke in the house, that this would be the way to break him of the habit. (She, of course, smoked; her husband smoked; everyone they knew smoked, but when Anna thought about her son smoking her eyes filled with tears.) Today, she had watched children in the park; they seem so nervous, she had thought. So helpless. She had thought about herself at the Philharmonic, about having to go there alone like last time and giving away her husband's ticket again to a stranger in line at the box office, when a little girl seemed to have come out of nowhere and asked for help: she had lost her shoe. *"Meine Schuhe!"* she was crying, over and over; her hair was white, like an old woman's (she thought of her mother, saying, over and over, *alles falsch gemacht, alles falsch gemacht,* her hair, her skin, the color of old sheets, and the dry cool touch of her hands). "Have you lost your little shoe," Anna said. "Shall I help you find your shoe?" Anna got up and looked around with theatrical concern. "Where could it be?" she said. She bent down. "You shouldn't take off your shoes on a day like this. It's practically still winter!" The little girl was crying; Anna noticed a hole in her sock. The kindergarten teacher came up holding the shoe, was polite, nervous herself, and took the little girl's hand, seemed to drag her away. She was still talking, pausing over her son's name, couldn't remember what she had wanted to say. "We'll speak later," her husband said, as if she were a child herself; she saw his frown, the lines around his mouth, felt the flesh on his hips, on his back, and saw him, too, as an old woman; bitter, she thought. Everyone, she thought. Lost and crying; then old, and bitter; and she spoke her sigh. The man in line at the box office had been attractive—homosexual, of course, smelling of cologne and cigarettes, and handsome, certainly, but there had been something strange about him; she had thought of a pickle, of youth preserved in vinegar. He had talked and talked, which had soothed her, while they were waiting for the concert to start, and later, during the intermission, in line for a drink. He had talked about the music (it was an all-Tchaikovsky program; " 'If the devil wrote music,' " he had said, quoting Julian Green—whom he described as "an American Protestant who spent his life in Paris in drag as a French Catholic"—" 'it would be Tchaikovsky, seductive, skillful, and vulgar' "). And he had talked about architecture, about the Philharmonic itself, and its recurring use of pentagons—"Look," he had said, "how the audience is divided up into five asymmetrical pentagons"— and about his own new office building in Prenzlauer Berg, and its use of cylinders. He had wanted to please her: fifth row for the Berlin Philharmonic; these were 125-mark seats! T. often showed up at concerts alone, waiting to meet someone (not, of course, a housewife from Zehlendorf, with her funny little shoes and a hat like a helmet, although he had found the hat rather charming; heard his mild pedantry as charming, even a little flirtatious, was careful not to let her know that he was homosexual, careful to let her know that he was an architect), except when he admitted that he had already met everyone, that there was no one left to meet, only to meet again: to see. In the afternoons, lately, he gave in to the part of himself that he used to like—respect, in fact—and went to the Staatsbibliothek on Unter den Linden on his way back from the construction site (another "office block with stores on the ground level," too expensive for the neighborhood, with white sandstone that had looked like poured concrete in the merciless spring light, and a ridiculous upright cylinder in the middle that he had meant as comment on the gabled buildings on either side but which had ended up looking like a turret; a concrete fortress, he said to himself today), and had sex in the bathroom on the first floor, or, more likely, just waited around, listening to other men having sex. It amused him to stand in front of the toilet stalls, watching the doors furtively open and then slam, or open widely, dangerously, and there would be a construction worker, or a student, or a librarian, or a businessman, jerking off, with his pants around his shoes, his tongue hanging out of his mouth: it reminded him of Judith in *Bluebeard's Castle* (a favorite opera), or rather, like a parody of Judith, and of "Der Preis Ist Heis," which he had watched last year, when he hadn't done anything except lie in bed all day. Afterward, he felt nothing, empty (an emptiness that he had once respected as the opposite of sentimentality—as anti-Romantic, as an extreme objectivity; as something distinct, outlined with something else—but that now seemed indistinct, ordinary, merely another part of him, the part he hated). He drove past the Staatsbibliothek on his way to dinner, remembering the smell of the soap in the bottom of the urinals (forgetting the smells of piss, of shit, of unwashed cocks), but changed his mind and decided not to go in, as if he were late. He was having dinner with a man he barely knew, an art historian named Johannes something-or-other, whom he had met through Hans-Georg, who, it turned out, didn't know Johannes very well; he was an art historian who had just moved to Berlin. Or was he an architect? T. couldn't remember, but there had been something, hadn't there? A look in his eyes? He must be five, ten years younger than I am, thought T. And only occasionally queer, or worse—officially "bisexual." And he is snobby, from Hamburg, which I always like; he had said something nasty about Berlin right away, something about the bad restaurants, that everyone says; he'll have expensive, new-looking shoes. (T. thought about his own shoes, expensive, old-looking; wretched.) He is a meritocrat and an aristocrat, thought T. with admiration and secret dread: if he can't despise someone as a fool, he despises them as a slob. (T. was a solipsist and a nihilist; he saw the emptiness in himself as the center of everything, was that kind of Romantic.) T. parked his car on Kollwitzstrasse and walked through the Kollwitzplatz, which, because of its intactness, always cheered him up, even though it was terribly laid out, and they really shouldn't have turned half of it into a playground; then he approached the Water Tower, which he also admired—or, he thought, looking up at its round, ridiculous [cylindrical] shape, I admire the way it dominates the neighborhood. It's gotten colder, he thought. On his way over, he had wondered if the restaurant had already set up tables outside; he had loved sitting outside in Berlin, years ago, while the wall was up, and people stayed out all night; he could remember coming home at eight, nine in the morning, with a bag of fresh rolls, and a pleasant throbbing from drugs and too much *Weizenbier*; although that seemed like another life; now, at thirty-eight, he fell asleep in front of the television set and read travel brochures. He walked down Knaackstrasse, in the shadow of the Water Tower, and into the new Russian restaurant, which he had read about in *Zitty* but had never been to, and ordered a mineral water. Johannes was sitting at a table in the small mauve room next to the bar, out of sight, reading a newspaper, and T., after having looked around in vain from the bar, drank his water, then another, began to talk to the bartender, whom he eventually recognized, and they talked about Kreuzberg in the early 1980s, how wonderful it had been (the bartender had been "bought" as a political prisoner in the early 1980s, and was now back in the East; he looks fifty years old, T. thought, and he might be younger than I am!). T. went to the bathroom and watched himself in the mirror, while Johannes was taking his second look around the restaurant: he had waited fifteen minutes, which was his limit, and he left. Johannes had a lot to do: he was editing a series of guidebooks about the architecture of Eastern Europe, as well as teaching and writing articles; he was curating an exhibition. He knew something about T.'s work from an architectural weekly and was eager to meet other architects in Berlin (Johannes was technically an art historian, though now he was making a name for himself as a historian of architecture; he was especially known for a Feuilleton piece he had written attacking Hans Scharoun, the man who had designed the Philharmonic. Scharoun had conceived of the Philharmonic—with its collapsed version of a domed roof and its fairly inscrutable, if vaguely mystical, seating arrangement—as a visual representation of Martin Heidegger's ideas, though Johannes claimed that Scharoun's notions were such a vulgarization of Heidegger that the building really was, ultimately, fascistic, and he compared the Philharmonic to some of the buildings Albert Speer had planned for Berlin, most persuasively to the House of Tourism, which had once stood near the Potsdamer Platz—virtually across the street from where the Philharmonic now stood—and which Johannes had spent so much time considering that he had become, somewhat secretly, an admirer. Soon he would go on a nationally televised talk show to talk more about Speer—yes, that article had been quite controversial!—on which he would express his outer disgust, his inner respect), but fifteen minutes had, and would always be, his limit. Johannes, quite consciously, could despise human frailty (T., in his way, had been right!): when traveling, for instance, he worried about appropriateness, mastering bits of Polish and Czech and even Slovakian and now Ukrainian (a whole section of one volume was to be devoted to Lemberg), about fending off sympathy from too kind strangers, about not seeming frail himself; while visiting Katowice, where he had admired the unusual local mixture of Prussian-style historicism with Viennese *Jugendstil* wwith *Sezessionismus*, he corrected himself, which was the Austro-Hungarian term for *Jugendstil*), he had made the brief trip to Auschwitz, planning it beforehand and bringing with him CDs of Bartók's string quartets and Schubert's "Der Tod und das Mädchen" and a copy of Paul Celan's "Todesfuge," which he had reread in his dreadful—and almost comically expensive—Cracow hotel room ("Death is a master from Germany his eyes are blue . . . your golden hair Margarethe / your ashen hair Sulamith," etc.), having read it already, years before, in grade school. But did he, one wonders, think about the color of his own eyes (which were blue)? or about the color of his own hair (which was blond, though prematurely gray; ashen)? Tonight, after leaving the restaurant, he thought about the Cyrillic letters he had been trying to learn that morning, but which, in the cold night air, seemed to have vanished from his head, and he thought about his girl-friend back in Hamburg, who couldn't—or said she couldn't—get away next weekend and make the trip with him to Lemberg. He saw himself in the breakfast room of a dreadful hotel, eating alone, writing things down in a new, empty leather-bound notebook.

Unter den Linden is where they start a *Lichterkette* whenever anybody actually gets killed in a skinhead attack—the "chain of light" protests, which are meant to be antiracist, and anti-anti-Semitic, and *Ausländerfreundlich*, and almost spontaneous (a city brought together on short notice), but which end up looking staged, Busby Berkeley–like, *Totentanz*-like (Schnitzler-like), Riefenstahl-like. People carry around what really could be torches—they seem like cat-o'-nine-tails dipped in paraffin—or flashlights, or cigarette lighters, or else spontaneous lanterns made with candles stuck in plastic cups left over from the mulled wine or potato salad that people always buy while waiting around for the exact moment when everyone is supposed to hold the hands of the people on either side of them *and* their *Licht* at the same time, forming a chain through the Brandenburg Gate, down Speer's broadened avenue, sometimes all the way to Bismarck-strasse, where Speer's original streetlights are maintained and, if necessary (I assume) replaced, and which look Art Deco, faintly glamorous, like something from a Fred Astaire and Ginger Rogers movie, or from an UFA movie.

(East German gay men, like West German gay men, all seem to get a kick out of Zarah Leander, the tenor-voiced, bushy-eyebrowed "Nazi siren" who is said to have taken Marlene Dietrich's place in the thirties and early forties, until she decided the Germans were going to lose the war and went back to her native Sweden; there are Zarah Leander drag queens and Zarah Leander CDs played in gay bars, and, as it happens, in a hospital room down the hall from Hans-Joachim's; Zarah Leander movies—unlike other UFA movies and unlike Dietrich movies—actually get shown on prime-time television; I think if the devil were a movie star, he would be Zarah Leander.)

Totentanz: dance of death. There is one, in fact, in the Marien-kirche. Perfectly horizontal, wrapping itself around the walls of a small rear chapel: a row of figures (peasants, burghers, knights, cardinals, etc.) in their medieval clothes, holding hands with death; the church was bombed during the war, and the fresco was damaged, and, now, until the restoration is finished, many of the death figures (skeletons wearing shrouds) are partly, or completely, absent (have to be looked at on a small cartoonish model, or read about, or just imagined, assumed), and the *Totentanz* is more like a crowd breaking up, like, perhaps, people half a millennium ago on their way home from a *Lichterkette*; strangely singular, like buildings on the Ringstrasse, like crowds of one, like corpses.

In fact, of course, death is everywhere here—in the foreground and in the middle ground; in the background. (I know this, what I don't know is: which is the foreground, and which is the background; which is the middle ground; like trying to decipher a tense from all the verbs at the end of a German sentence.) (Buildings, mothers, foreign cemeteries, nearby faces, fathers, winter trees and bushes, a taste in the mouth.)

Remote but plainly intricate: kinds of death.

I am sitting in my mother's room, during the winter vacation of my freshman year; I am sitting on the floor, watching television in the middle of the night, leaning against the foot of the plaid couch, and I smell something sweet and horrible—a trace of urine on a cushion, and what I would now recognize as the urine of a diabetic, as my mother's urine—and unfamiliar, a whiff transformed into a glimpse of what I now think of as death.

"I just want to die," my mother actually said the other night on the telephone (à la Petronius à la T. S. Eliot, as Maria Riva might have had Marlene Dietrich put it), taking me outside myself (or sending me deeper inside), shocking me (like the first time I saw Hans-Joachim in the fake hospital bed in his apartment, then later, in the hospital, when I saw him in his real hospital bed, underneath his oxygen mask), breaking my heart.

Thinking about the absence of death in Berlin's local *Totentanz* can make me feel almost invincible, that what might be done and what should be done correspond, overlap.

In Kaliningrad: death would be very abstract, symbolic, more remote.

In Milwaukee: death would be too near but still abstract, subconscious.

Models of the end, rather than my own.

In Berlin my own absence has become imaginable, surrounds me, like an idea would seem to surround a feeling, like history [of everyone else] surrounds (precedes, later comments upon) memory [-ies] (mine), or: like my mother in her room, surrounded; intricate and absent (or simply no longer there), like something remembered until it was forgotten, gone unless it comes back again.

At Auschwitz: the visitor has brought himself along, surrounding history with memories that can never become transparent enough; what can he notice—except the buildings (and the vinelike, derelict fences; and the trees)—except himself? And the fact of his heart, pumping, pumping?

One day, last spring, though it really was spring, I walked across Berlin and ended up where I began, or, more precisely, returned to where I had just left. I walked and walked, I ran my hands over the city's body; at the Charlottenburg Palace, after ducking into the *Jugendstil*–Art Deco museum (stocked with French furniture and Austrian place settings and German light fixtures—with swirls and angles of a foreign, destroyed place), I got on a bus, at the Spandauer Damm, and returned, went eastward, to Alexanderplatz, and got off at Spandauer Strasse, in front of the Marienkirche, in the shadow of the television tower, five minutes' walk from the Krügers, and the tiles, once green, now mostly absent, in their hallways.

MILWAUKEE/KALININGRAD

Forward and backward. (Sideward—assuming the Horizontal—from here.)

In all directions (falling, in all directions, like the "we" in Nietzsche's Madman's speech).

Kaliningrad (laying a wreath on . . .)
Milwaukee (stocking and cleaning out . . .)

Two directions.
A form of fleeing. An utter departure.

In Spandau [on another day] four or five teenagers chase a Turk or Serb or Croat down the main street, past Spandau's Rathaus, past its Nicolaikirche, into . . . and out of . . . until they get tired, give up, go home.

Home: an origin; a target.

The sky is effaced by targets, to the east, to the west. On the streetcar, back up the Prenzlauer Allee, without a ticket, without the money really to go anywhere except back where I have just come from, while looking down from the streetcar window at the pavement I have just been walking on, like moving my pillow from the foot back to the head of the bed (detourless), I will think (as if it has already happened, as if it were something I were remembering), Yes!

Yes.
I will have saved myself.

PART III

[April 15]

After the flea market, back in the store in Charlottenburg, Peter said, unpacking videos before I could get the chance, and as if he had never said it before, "You've gone native." He says it whenever he sees me. He says it at the market when he comes by to take a look at our stand and complain that the television set is playing too loudly or too softly or that the contrast hasn't been adjusted properly or that the videos I sell for him aren't displayed in the proper order ("French New Wave movies on the *right!*" he'll say, "with the spines of the boxes facing *out!*" if he comes by early and I am about to set everything up, or, if he comes by later, "with the *face* of the boxes facing out!" if I have the spines facing out; after telling me to put all the Italian neorealist movies on one side, he'll tell me to put a few on the other side, next to the French movies, with the spines facing out unless the spines of the boxes of the French movies are already facing out; he insists I play Holocaust documentaries all day on the VCR with the boxes of the other Holocaust documentaries stacked like books on top of the television set, or next to it, or on a special shelf next to it, with posters of Marcel Ophuls's *The Memory of Justice* and *Hotel Terminus* hanging down in front of the stand, or suspended behind from a clothesline next to this year's art calendars, which he is selling four months into the year, supposedly at a discount, with a handwritten sign reading "DM 39.95" pasted on the corners of the posters, which is how much I am supposed to be charging for the videos, not the posters, which I said was confusing, that people will think that the posters, which Peter at first said I could sell for five marks or just give away if someone bought enough videos, cost DM 39.95, to which he said, "Fine. If that's what these fucking Germans want to pay, who are you to stop them?"; or he'll want the art calendars in front of the posters, as if the two went together, as if we were selling *The Memory of Paul Klee* and *Renoir Terminus*), and he says it when I go by the store during the week to listen to him change his mind about which videos he wants me to take to the market and I have shown up ten or fifteen minutes later than I said I would, as I invariably do (going from the new apartment on the Metzer Strasse all the way to Charlottenburg can take an indefinite period of time, especially when the city is doing track work on the S-Bahn; once, when I read at Alexanderplatz that they had shut down the S-Bahn entirely between Friedrichstrasse and the Tiergarten and people were supposed to get off and take a special bus and I took the U-Bahn instead and was an hour late, he screamed it: "You've gone fucking native!"; "there's track work," I said, telling him about the signs up all over Alexanderplatz, trying to scream back, but not really being able to because the only people I can scream at are my parents and my sister; "And you believe them!" he said, waving his hands next to his ears, as if he were about to grab my head, or his own, and shake it; he seems to be closing his mouth whenever he screams, with bits of food—cheese and liverwurst, usually, though, in the morning, poppyseeds from pastries he holds on to like teacups—cracking off the corners of his mouth and catching on his wiry blond stubble, like dried-up shaving cream), meaning, usually, that I have turned into an East German (he wants to expand into East Berlin and has been shopping around for a storefront, running into what sounds like indifference from realtors, which he likes to interpret as ideologically minded laziness, as "Stalinist," or as "fucking Communist," or as "anti-Semitic"); or into an Eastern European (he has been making trips to Poland and the Czech Republic, hiring business partners whom he always ends up firing, and shopping around for warehouses so he can expand even further eastward, sell Marcel Ophuls documentaries at flea markets in Sverdlovsk, in Vladivostok); or into Svetlana, who walks into the store even later than usual now because she assumes that I am going to be there (even though she herself has usually told me not to bother coming in during the week, that I can decide which videos to take on Saturdays and Sundays, just before the flea market, on my own, before Peter gets up and when she is usually supposed to be out of town), and who, instead of unpacking all the new videos and entering them into the computer while Peter stands over the fax machine waiting for messages from, say, Łódź (which are in Polish, and which, even though he can't read Polish, he flies into a rage after reading; later, after he gets Svetlana to translate them, he flies into another, quieter, but eventually more violent rage, which won't end until he kicks over a box of videos or rips some pastries into pieces; I imagine him ripping up the faxes, which he actually would never do, with his teeth, covering the corners of his mouth with ink, catching bits of paper on his stubble), pushes back the flaps of a nearby, already opened, overflowing cardboard box and sets her ashtray down, then slowly peels an orange with a knife, or sips her black, black coffee, saying, when she has gotten around to noticing me, "What are *you* doing here?" though one day, when I was in the back and she didn't know I was there, and Peter was in front waiting for her, yelling at her for showing up two hours late, she said, "I thought our American would be here. They love to work!"; or into an animal: he calls East Germans and Eastern Europeans (Poles, in particular), "sloths," which, because he has problems with his *th*'s, always ends up sounding like "sluts"; he calls Svetlana "Lana" when he gets angry at her, though I sometimes imagine him calling her a "rancid brat," which is the sort of mistake he might make in English; Svetlana calls him, even when he's not angry, "choleric," to me, and to other "friends," confidentially, as if we hadn't just heard her screaming it at him. After only five days of selling at the market, I have earned enough money to pay for my *Sonderzug* to Kaliningrad next weekend, a student-discount trip back to Milwaukee, a month's membership at a health club, and, if I were inclined, to pay Peter back some of

the money he loaned me for the new apartment that I have sub-
letted indefinitely (Peter, as agreed, let me keep 30 percent of the
daily gross, which turned out be 30 percent of at least 3,000 marks;
today, after the market, he told me that 30 percent of the gross
was unfair to him and that he wants to cut me back to 20 percent
of what he decided was his net profit, which would be about 10
percent of what I have been making; "Sure" I said, "that's fair,"
knowing today was my last day). The rent for the new apartment
is 1,950 marks a month (the woman who officially rents the apartment, or rather her son, who more or less restored it, but badly,
with new versions of old East German wallpaper and linoleum, was
asking five times the official rent, which itself, they told me, dou-
bled last year); at least I can't be evicted from this apartment, like
from the Krügers' apartment, and then from Herr Huberman's
apartment, because I am leaving it myself before anyone will have
the chance. Peter, when I showed him Herr Huberman's note telling me to be out of the apartment in three days because the new
landlord had threatened to call the police, said I should set the
apartment house on fire, that he would help me do it, which was
a joke, of course, though one he repeats too often, like the jokes
he makes about concentration camps and Nazis and the Stasi,
which are more or less variations on Jewish jokes, with cheap Jews
getting gassed or attacked or denounced by beer-drinking, sausage-
eating Germans. When I was picking up his electric radiator last
month and he had first offered me the job at the flea market, I
hadn't really heard him; I was too busy thinking about other
things (about my body, about my handsful of flesh, and about not
having any money, about wondering what I could afford to eat
and eat) but then, on the thirty-first, which was Saturday, the day
Herr Huberman slipped his note under the door, which I couldn't
even read by myself, let alone translate (he has old-fashioned East
German handwriting, which is sometimes even harder to read
than old-fashioned German handwriting), and Kurt and Sabine
were out of town and Irmgard wasn't answering Hans-Joachim's
phone and Hans-Joachim's phone at the hospital was busy for half

an hour and it was raining and I didn't feel like standing around the Humannplatz waiting for him to get off, I took the S-Bahn across Berlin and gave Peter the note; he laughed after he read it and said that I was having the same luck with apartments that he was having with wives, meaning that Svetlana was actually his third wife, which I hadn't known (I had to find out from the Polish woman who cleans up the store and whom Peter sometimes pays in zlotys, or in videos; once—though he later claimed he was only joking—he tried to pay her with Ukrainian coupons), and that they were planning on getting divorced, which I had in fact suspected, but were also planning on still living together and, Peter seemed to imply, still sleeping together, because, Svetlana later told me, of the "store" (though not, I believe, the "business," which is how Peter refers to the store in East Berlin and the various stores and distribution centers and his potential network of contacts in Eastern Europe—all of which he pretends to be working on behind Svetlana's back, or which he flaunts, as if he were doing it all to spite her), which they both can refer to as their "child." Peter, again, offered me the job at the flea market (which is held at Tempelhof airport, though he usually just calls the flea market "the airport," each time offering me "a job at the airport"), and told me about an apartment (he buys illegally imported gasoline from the woman's husband), and then offered me the money for the apartment as an advance and told me I could pay it off by the end of the summer; I didn't tell him about going to Milwaukee, or about going to Kaliningrad: I told him that I wanted to start the next day. He hasn't asked me yet for the money for the apartment, though he did insist I pay him 10 marks for having used his electric radiator for a month; he came to pick up the radiator one day last week at seven in the morning, looking as if he had stayed up all night ("I hope I am not disturbing you," he said, in one of his sudden fits of politeness, when he goes in a single breath from seeming like a street person to seeming like an aristocrat); I was already temporarily up because of the construction noise going on outside, which inspired Peter, as soon as he got in the apartment and noticed how loud it was, to open up one of the person-sized windows (the apartment is in the front house, on the third floor; built originally for civil servant types and then taken over by factory workers, and now decrepit and palatial, except for the East Germanness, which is immaculate, in spite of its sloppiness, and dreary) and screamed out, in English, "Keep quiet, you Nazi-Stasi swine!" then closed the window and looked embarrassed; he insisted on carrying the radiator down the stairs himself, and, after I had closed the door and gotten back into bed, I could hear him on the stairwell, muttering above the construction noise); he asked for the 10 marks today, after I sold more than 3,500 marks' worth of videos. I like the market, even though the setting is strange: Tempelhof was built in the late thirties as the airport for Speer's never built Berlin and looks somewhat like the Luftwaffe building (when Peter first mentioned "airport," I had thought of Tegel, where I had landed when I first arrived, and where I will leave from when I get back from Kaliningrad on the twenty-third, and which looks like an airport), but is even more outsized, with wide arcades lined with blocklike columns (Hans-Joachim said they are "colonnades"), and columnlike windows on the innumerable surrounding office buildings; the stone itself is a uniform brownish gray, like dust-colored marble. The Americans took over Tempelhof, which was in their sector, just after the war and turned it into an air base, used it during the Berlin Airlift (Tempelhof, in spite of the way it looks, makes people think "American" rather than "Nazi"; the terminal is enormous but smaller than one might expect after the football fields of office buildings; Grand Central Station as anticlimax), and now that the Americans are gone, it has been partly taken over by several smaller airlines that fly businessmen to places like Prague and Zagreb and Riga with a matter-of-fact, post-1989 (or pre-1945, though post-1941) efficiency; no one seems to fly to these places on the weekends, and apparently the airport, after being fairly deserted during the week, was entirely deserted on the weekends until they ("they" being the corrupt—and vaguely foreign—father and son who run most of Berlin's flea markets from a closetlike storefront in Kreuzberg: Rumanian, I have been told, but in Berlin for decades, though they have a Hungarian name and could very well be ethnic Hungarians from Rumania, or even Hungarian-speaking Rumanian Jews, which I think would make them Transylvanian, though most people just call them Rumanian; the son, apparently, never shows up at the market, but the father does, walking around in the afternoon, shaking hands with people or nodding at them from under his fedora, looking courtly and despised, like a tyrant) started holding the flea market in the colonnades and then expanding, taking in most of the empty space between the 1930s subway station and the terminal; the only occupants left in the blocks and blocks of fascist office buildings (which is how my architectural guide refers to them, "fascist" having become something of an aesthetic term, good for describing over-the-top Art Deco buildings like the Trocadero in Paris or the train station in Milan or the House of Art in Munich—once known as the House of German Art, at the edge of the English Garden, the public park where men fuck in the bushes—though the columns there are even more outsized than Tempelhof's, almost celestial, like Asgard's, or perhaps infernal, certainly inhuman, or just hallucinatory, as if you can't really see the tops of them; I remember walking around there at night with Irmgard, past the huge columns; we had gone to the museum, which was open until ten that night, after having been up in the mountains during the day and our faces were sunburned) are the chief of police's headquarters and Berlin's local weather bureau, which, I said to Irmgard, excitedly, is *"so German"* (by which I meant: repressive and transcendental, below and above, absent); now that she has quit her job (or rather, admitted to having quit her job, which she actually did weeks ago), I see her all the time; she seems less unhappy but more something else (nervous, actually poor); I buy her coffee and bring her over in a taxicab to the new apartment, where we fuck on the futon I bought (there is now a futon store in Prenzlauer Berg, and a Thai restaurant, and a clothing store for rubber and leather fetishists and competing health food stores and a gelato stand that quietly violates Germany's strict closing laws by selling wine and pasta and pesto and imported Italian cookies until midnight), and afterward I give her the money to take a cab back to Hans-Joachim's, who, though he is officially still in the hospital, visits his own apartment in the afternoons with one or two male nurses. The flea market at Tempelhof is the newest in Berlin; until now I have avoided Berlin's flea markets, which are supposed to be the best in Europe ("a civilization up for sale" according to the special flea market issue of *Zitty*), because of the crowds: I usually hate crowds, have always hated them, even before I read Canetti's *Crowds and Power* and learned about their sinisterness (though actually in Canetti people like being part of a crowd: Canetti thinks that the "crowd instinct" is as fundamental as the sexual instinct; since starting work at the market, where I have been on the edge of a crowd, more an observer of one than a part of one, my sex drive has picked up, or perhaps I should say "resumed": I have erections and orgasms all the time and, even if I have fucked Irmgard the night before, have to duck into bathrooms while running errands or while sitting in a restaurant to jerk off in a stall, or just finger my hard-on through the pockets of my jeans, which—now that I exercise all the time, even on the weekends, after I have spent the day lifting crates full of videos, and the television set and the two VCRs—flop around my tightened thighs like a skirt; I don't eat, or only eat miso I buy at the health food store a few streets away from the new apartment; I found out that I have lost six kilos when I weighed myself tonight at the gym, and my legs, especially, feel all tight and smooth, like an animal's, like haunches; the last time Irmgard and I fucked, she was on her knees—we were fucking doggy-style, which I had thought she used to like—and I took her hands and put them on my thighs, but then she took her hands back and reached out for the bedroom wall and I had to touch my thighs myself; she didn't come at all, or didn't seem to, and I came twice; afterward I gave her thirty marks for the twenty-mark taxi fare), and I suppose I still hate them, though I am often too fascinated to hate them. Everybody goes to the market: West German students in their ironed blue jean jackets and, now that the weather has turned warm, amphibianlike leather-and-rubber sandals; East German families, in their new, old-fashioned-looking, blue jean outfits, only recognizably new because of the bright "American" decals having to do with football teams or motorcycles ("I'm from there!" I said to a man with a Harley-Davidson decal, "Milwaukee! Where Harley-Davidsons are made!" He was already thinking about buying *All Quiet on the Western Front*, which I sold to him along with *Aguirre the Wrath of God* for sixty marks instead of seventy-nine marks and ninety pfennigs, which I am never supposed to do, and which I lied about to Peter, telling him I sold *Aguirre the Wrath of God* for fifty marks; "now you're learning!," he said; he never keeps track of the videos, and I actually saw him stepping on some, and then, later, after he smoked his hashish, which sends him into fits of honesty, throw out perfectly fine videos by mistake because he thought that they were the ones he'd stepped on); they always look dejected and fat, like American army families, who also come, in their jeans and windbreakers, with their doughy empty faces and dwindling cheerfulness (sometimes, when they stopped instinctively to watch the TV and then picked up a video or two and then would ask for something like *Parenthood* or *Lethal Weapon*, I pretended not to speak English, then joked about having pretended, then tried to sell them a Tarkovsky movie, which I told them was a Russian western, that Tarkovsky was the Russian John Ford, but they had never heard of John Ford either and ended up buying nothing, or buying an Alfred Hitchcock movie, which Peter buys pirated copies of and sells for twenty-nine marks, and which I sometimes sold for fifteen marks and once for five marks, with Peter's face in my head, with me screaming at him, "You cheap son of a bitch! You fucking lunatic shithead asshole!"); British army families (though never French army families, and never Russian soldiers), with their poignantly damning accents; Italian tourists, in American imitations of Italian imitations of American clothes; Scandinavian tourists, who look American from a distance and sound English and never buy anything; Polish tourists, who ignore the Poles actually selling things, like the Polish man selling Polish movie and theater posters (which, if they are from before 1989, are famously witty and disturbing, with, say, a man with a nose that looks like a penis, with a crown of thorns around the penis, on the poster for a production of *Hamlet* in Wroclaw, which the Polish man who sells the posters always calls "Breslau" in a nervous, ingratiating way), who is always getting hassled by the blond, butch, private security force that patrol the colonnades in paramilitary uniforms, collecting bribes (the father and son more or less extort money from people who want to have a "good" stand, which means in either set of colonnades near the terminal's main entrance; a "bad" stand is on the concrete stoop near the Berlin Airlift memorial sculpture, just beyond the parking spaces where Gypsies and Russians spread out sheets and sell what looks like garbage until it starts to rain; I was always assigned a stand near the main entrance, which Peter took care of that first morning by slipping one of the security guards a wad of what looked like dollars, but they still harassed me early in the morning and late in the afternoon because I was always late in unpacking and packing; actually they seemed to harass everybody, but especially the many Poles, and the Vietnamese cigarette sellers, and the Angolans, who would just show up and often weren't selling anything; they actually physically kicked Gypsies, one of whom I saw run into the police station and then never saw, or noticed, come back out again; at the end of the day, while the Russians were trying to pack up their wet things—it rained every day that I was there—one of the security guards in particular liked to scream at them and try to fine them hundreds of marks); Russian tourists, with the women in fur coats, even last Sunday, when, until it rained, it must have been over seventy (I was wearing my Bermuda shorts, slipped my hand inside the folds, fondled myself under my thick wooden table, which all the people at the good stands get set up for them, with their names written right on the wood; Peter suggested we use "Peter La Vine," which was always getting written "Peter Lavine," because he thought that "Peter Marcus" sounded too Jewish); once I waited on a couple with solid gold teeth and slanted eyes who turned out to be Kirghiz tourists (they wanted to buy Peter's television set with a hacked-up gold ring); rich West Berlin housewives, who get there at eight in the morning and walk around with empty wicker baskets and stiff, pulled-back ponytails and are shopping perhaps for Art Deco jewelry or *Jugendstil* picture frames and eventually give up and drink beer and eat sausages; European Community Europeans, from Italy or Greece or Portugal, working in Berlin and alone and desperately bored, and too friendly with me when they lingered in front of the television set pretending to understand the spoken German or spoken French or spoken English or English subtitles of the Ophuls films and complained about the weather; and of course other Germans (Germans and Germans!) who, increasingly, didn't seem like tourists to me, or like students or housewives or East Germans, who seemed one or two generations away from being peasants but were now factory workers, or teachers, or doctors or lawyers with bad taste, and who paraded through the colonnades, which are big enough to have made their fat strong bodies look normal-sized, until they bumped into each other, or into the columns, dripping their sausages—which often weren't *Currywurst* or bratwurst but some other kind of sausage that I didn't recognize, and which they held like ice-cream cones—onto, I imagined, their shined, leather shoes, and who were sexless, monumentally neuter, like the columns, which are too blank to suggest penises; fancy West German men, doctor-and-lawyer-looking doctors and lawyers who seem to be living in Berlin but also seem to be from somewhere else and who wear thin leather gloves which they would take off when they read the back of a video box, as though they were examining a piece of porcelain (when I think about them now, they remind me of the CEO from Koblenz who spied on his own computer company's research department for the Stasi and who looked elegant on Hans-Joachim's television—a couple of times I have had sex with Irmgard in Hans-Joachim's bed—claiming, on a talk show appearance, that he had done it for the money); my friends (though not Irmgard, who, as she would have it, has been busy sketching, though she did show up today, knowing it was my last day; she can seem a little crazy when she talks about her sketching, and seems to have stopped bathing altogether; the other night, in bed at Han-Joachim's, she actually smelled dirty—of body odor, of urine vaguely, and, at one point, of shit, but mostly of perfume; like someone had spilled perfume on the ground, I thought; I didn't bathe after that myself and for a while could smell her on me—the body odor and the shit, the perfume, the saliva, mixed, almost, with faint smells of Hans-Joachim's sheets, which he hasn't slept in for probably a month but which Irmgard hasn't changed and which still smell of his cologne, and of sweat, and, now, a little bit, of me; after she has finished talking about her sketches but is still seeming a little crazy, her voice becomes whiny, less detached; I have told her that I was leaving to go to Kalinin-grad and then going on to Milwaukee—though I haven't told Peter Marcus, whom I think I'll call from the train station Friday morn-ing on my way to Kaliningrad, saying I'm at the airport on my way to Milwaukee—but then after that I was coming back to Berlin and she has been asking me she if could stay in the new apartment until I get back; "why not?" I said once, having already composed the note telling that man and his mother that I wasn't coming back, that they could keep the futon and the bedsheets, and the blankets, which Sabine said I could keep): Kurt and Sabine came, without the children, and Kurt drank a beer, which I had never seen, while Sabine talked about the rained-on East German records that she had bought for fifty pfennigs apiece from someone in the parking lot; Hans-Joachim came, with two other AIDS patients and three male nurses, last Sunday when it was so hot (he had spent time under a sun lamp at the hospital's version of a health club and looked fine, like anyone else, except that he was wearing a turtleneck and a tweed sport coat, which, in addition to seeming inappropriate, seemed, because of the weight he has lost, over-sized, monumental; one of the other patients looked ill, and the other one, who was in a wheelchair, looked already dead, was, Hans-Joachim later told me on the phone, blind from shingles and deaf from something else that Hans-Joachim didn't know the English word for; the male nurses looked healthy and bored, and somehow tawdry, older than they actually might have been, like male prostitutes); Kerwin came, and I asked him if he wanted to fuck one of the security guards and he said, "I wash my fruit before I eat it"; he pointed at the TV screen—I was playing *Night and Fog* that day; "screwball comedies," I said. "What?" he said. "Jewball comedies?"; some of the landscape architecture students I used to know walked by, though they seemed to have forgotten who I was; Karen came with two of her West German students, and, by the time they got to me, they were all carrying armsful of sheets and pillowcases that they had bought from the Turks who also sometimes sell things in the parking lot and who supposedly get into knife fights with the Gypsies; the sheets, which are cheap and clean and soft, are rumored to be leftover hospital sheets from the Second World War; the cheap, strong coffee at the trailer *Currywurst* stand is rumored to be old East German coffee; I bought my new sheets, which are bright and geometric, Sante Fe–like, at the Kaufhof in Alexanderplatz and, at the market, drank Diet Coke after Diet Coke, which the Canadian man, who was always in the stand next to mine selling CDs he bought with the money he made selling pieces of the Berlin Wall—he has been in Berlin for years, earning his way by selling things at various flea markets—and who is gay and HIV-positive and broke and planning a trip to a beach in Croatia this summer to save money, bought for me, usually giving me back too much change; he was polite the first day and flirtatious the second day ("You're gay," he said. "Right?" "Sure," I said); and nervous the third day ("If you're positive, you know . . . well, not 'you' I mean . . . 'one' . . . you know . . ."); and very friendly yesterday and today, especially today, when he came over and stood behind the television to talk about his trip to Croatia, until Irmgard showed up, ducked under the wooden table and kissed me and stood with her ass in my crotch and I had

my hands on her waist; after she left, he still bought me the Diet
Cokes (he drinks special herbal teas, which he buys at a homeopathic pharmacy, was always running to the *Currywurst* stand for
cups of hot water), but then said nothing to me, until he asked if
I could change a thousand-mark note that a Russian man—who,
according to the Polish man, who today was on the other side of
me, was actually Georgian—had wanted to use to buy Beatles CDs;
I said I couldn't because I just assumed that it was counterfeit, then
changed my mind because I liked the idea of giving a counterfeit
thousand-mark note to Peter (I was surprised that the Canadian
man needed to ask; after paying his bribes, he must not make anything at all); Svetlana finally came; showed up yesterday with her
new, German, boyfriend, whom she speaks to in French, joking
about his Germanness with me in English after he went to get a
sausage and after she had given up pretending that she cared about
how everything was arranged; Kahula, who, independent of the
fact that I was there, always came, spends his weekends, he told
me, going from one flea market to another because "I love their
style, man" (he walked by the stand yesterday while Svetlana was
there though neither of them seemed to remember the other until
I reintroduced them, after which Svetlana said something like "Oh,
you're the one with the apartment. I have a friend, a nice American, who needs an apartment," meaning me, though she didn't
seem to realize that she had meant me; Kahula eventually
laughed—he had been contrite about the apartment the first time
he saw me at the market, which was the first time I had spoken to
him since our one brief conversation from the Krügers' apartment
on their reconnected telephone, while they stood next to me, like
policemen, when he hadn't seemed contrite—though he seemed
to have forgotten all about it, didn't really know at first what Svetlana was talking about), with his girlfriend and their child and his
legal wife and her boyfriend, who is also South African, and their
child (Germans call mulattoes *Mischlings*, which is what they call
mongrel dogs; once, after Kahula had walked by, one of the security guards asked, *"Wer waren denn diese Neger mit ihren Mischlings-*

kindern? Kennst du die? Dachte ich, Amerikaner—Weisse wie du—
hassen die Neger?"; he was the worst of the security guards, spending most of his time with the neo-Nazi coin dealers, who spent
most of their time harassing a Hungarian man who sells antique
cake pans, or just shouting insults at the Vietnamese cigarette sellers, or else pretending to be friends with them, trying to buy contraband cigarettes with zlotys, or with hundred-mark bills that
they would later claim were counterfeit); Burt Kaminsky didn't
come, though on that very first Sunday when I had gotten up early
and was on the S-Bahn by six-thirty, I actually saw him through
the train window (it was one of the old new East Berlin S-Bahn
trains, which are red and have large windows, unlike the old new
West Berlin S-Bahn trains, which are many-colored but also have
large windows; at first I had thought that the old new East Berlin
S-Bahn trains were the new West Berlin ones, or what could probably be called the new Berlin ones, which have only begun to re-
place the old West Berlin ones; the old East and old West Berlin
S-Bahn trains are really the old Berlin trains, with, often, the same,
or same type of, wooden seats from before the war but with dis-
tinguishing pre-1989 transit maps; I am not sure which ones I prefer, or if what I really prefer is the fact that every train is different,
that the city arguably looks different from inside the different
trains), at the Tiergarten S-Bahn station, going through garbage,
but that was two weeks ago, and I haven't seen him since, even
though the new apartment is right in the heart of Prenzlauer Berg,
midway between the Krügers' apartment and Herr Huberman's
apartment (I use the Laundromat I used to use when I lived at the
Krügers' and sometimes take the streetcar line I could take to Herr
Huberman's), a couple streets away from the Water Tower and all
the new restaurants and cafés; every time I would go to one of the
new restaurants or cafés I would run into Burt, though in the past
few weeks I haven't seen him once, even though I have been there
almost every night; Karen, rather coolly, said that he has disappeared; disappeared, I thought, thinking of the friend of the
German President who left his table at the casino in Wiesbaden

last week because, he said, he wanted to go to the bathroom and has been missing ever since, or would seem to be missing, letting everyone believe the stories that he had been working for the Stasi after all; in contrast to the CEO from Koblenz, the friend of the President didn't look at all elegant when I saw him on television at Hans-Joachim's: he looked almost Bavarian, like a large pig). Compared to the piles of things on sale, people at the market disappeared, like a landscape under a covering of snow. The kinds of things (officially) on sale at the market (besides videos and posters and CDs and Polish posters and stamps and cake pans and "pieces of the wall," now usually rendered into other things, like paperweights or earrings): new broken-looking fax machines, tea services with missing cups and saucers, apparently intact tea services, old photographs of strangers, old typewriters, old trays, comic books, leather jackets, *Lederhosen,* collected works minus a certain number of volumes of German philosophers, parts of cars, Bohemian glass, alarm clocks, ashtrays, beads, batik place mat–looking things, New Age crystal earrings, dried waterlogged boots, chess sets, old irons, Belle Epoque pornographic postcards, old UFA movie magazines (which don't count as Nazi propaganda), old Mitropa (the German, and then East German, chain of railroad restaurants) things, telephone cards (the little plastic things you need to have on you when you want to make a phone call, which have advertisements on the back and are collected like stamps; the neo-Nazis have begun to branch out into telephone cards), old shoes, wooden egg cups, books and books, riding crops, sunglasses, nineteenth-century French encyclopedia covers framed like paintings, widgets, nylon lace, real lace, speed skates, teddy bears, clocks, old money (expensive old money, kept between sheets of plastic, like stamps), radios, toasterlike space heaters, electric radiators, hats, suitcases, metal pillboxes, glass pitchers, an accordion with the inscription ERRINERUNG AN NÜRNBERG 1940, military telephones, paintings of castles, toasters, tumblers, nineteenth-century (or else just old) laboratory equipment, restored *Wiener Werkstätte* coffee tables, sewing machines, decades-old toothbrushes, field cameras and binoculars, puppets, brandy snifters, antique lace, old new (used) tooth-brushes, daguerreotypes, seersucker suits, pressure cookers, lamps, Zippo lighters, bed pans, camouflage gear, neo-baroque ebony pic-ture frames, Russian icons (sold in adjoining stands by Russian women with Jewish-sounding names—it could take them a long time to unpack, and I read their names off their wooden tables; they have the two best stands, right next to the main entrance, got their photographs on the cover of *Zitty*), mirrors, dolls, dolls in baby carriages, sheet music, wheelbarrows full of cheap old money (of billions and billions of Reichsmarks), Art Deco fans, Marlene Dietrich and Zarah Leander and Hildegard Knef—and even Ute Lemper—memorabilia, maps, newish telephones, old rec-ords that feel as hard as ebony, old record players, uniforms (Wehr-macht and Reichswehr and Bundeswehr uniforms; German and East German sailor uniforms; Soviet uniforms, which look old-fashioned enough to be old Imperial Russian uniforms; various American uniforms; East German streetcar conductor uniforms, and subway driver uniforms, and *Volkspolizei* and *Volksarmee* uni-forms, often complete, down to the wristwatches and identifica-tion cards and draped on mannequins that—like Peter's television and VCRs, and like the wooden tables themselves—aren't sup-posed to be for sale), beer mugs and menorahs, guns, water bottles, gun holsters, silverware; and, arguably, people: girls—prostitutes—from Slovakia, who, it turns out, are who I thought were the Czech girls just over the border from Dresden; they have been moving up from the Czech Republic and into Germany, and are now in Berlin, or at least at the Tempelhof flea market, lingering in thigh-high leather boots and skimpy raincoats near the place where the Gypsies sell their garbage or just whine at passersby for money, pretending to be Bosnians; I heard the Slovak girls are no-torious for getting pregnant, preferring to give birth to their half-German babies in the Czech Republic before going back home to Slovakia with their Deutschmarks (unofficially you can buy Nazi everything: party membership cards and back issues of *Der Stürmer* and the *Völkischer Beobachter* and well-worn copies of *Mein Kampf* and new copies of *Mein Kampf* published in English translation and sometimes actually called *My Struggle* and swastikas and medals from the Second World War and party congress things and parts of SS and Gestapo uniforms, as well as new, semi-automatic-looking guns and keys to stolen cars parked in some other part of town and—according to the neo-Nazis, who seemed, the days I was there, to be buying more Nazi memorabilia than they were selling—plutonium, which they always accused Russians of selling: they would come back from a stroll around the parking lot and say that it reeked of plutonium and garlic). At the market, especially today, I sensed a sort of mutability, that things were transforming: glasses were becoming cameras; West German students were becoming East German students or pillars or piles of clothes; the pillars were joining up, becoming solid, like walls; wet sheets had become fields of snow; I had a sense of things being terribly minute and light, static, of layers of things, of the Canadian man actually visible underneath his layers of CDs, of doctors and lawyers suddenly in East German subway driver or Gestapo uniforms, of a blank, planeless sky, of a landscape as gray and green as the racks of uniforms, of things becoming armies, of people becoming animals: I would think of that weird, famous Altdorfer painting I saw with Irmgard at the Alte Pinakothek in Munich, of its oceans of armies, of a painting looking as endless and finite as a human body, as though it had been painted underneath a microscope, by a surgeon rather than a painter; and I would think of the ocean, of piles of matter arriving like waves, of arranging waves into eras, like a city arranged into boroughs (or sectors), and then of those eras disappearing, like the border between Prenzlauer Berg and Weissensee—or, for that matter, like the present border between Prenzlauer Berg and Wedding—on a photograph of the earth taken from outer space, which must be like trying to identify a wave while looking up from the ocean floor, or a single face in an enormous crowd. At first the piles of shoes and eyeglasses and clothes reminded me of concentration camps, the Slovak prostitutes made me think of the Lebensborn program; then I didn't think those things, or I did, but not only; I thought about everything at once. The only thing I actually bought at the market (I bought it yesterday, while the Canadian man watched my stand for me) was a large piece of amber, many colored (or mostly brown, but complicated, like dirt), with small drilled holes; I thought of it, almost immediately, as a model of Creation—filled with clouds and waves and shapes and air bubbles and old insect legs and, I read last week while reading about Kaliningrad, actually originally pine tree resin—though it is in fact a button, useless, really, until it is connected to something else. It cost me three marks and ninety-five pfennigs, reduced from five marks, which the Russian in the parking lot (or whatever he was) was originally asking.

The Talk Show Guest and the Talk Show Host

Johannes didn't have his notebook, which had all his notes and thoughts and appointments written in it, which was like a model version of himself: he had set it down on a small table behind a row of television cameras and then suddenly it was missing, gone; now he was sitting on a small leather sofa, silently, with his new black socks slipping down, waiting for the taping to begin, feeling like a madman (Johannes losing his notebook makes me think of the hero of the famous Gogol story "The Overcoat" who goes mad after losing his overcoat). He noticed something out of the corner of his eye, not realizing at first that it was Vogt, the talk show's host, sitting next to him: suddenly, though only for a moment, Vogt's presence was overwhelming: Johannes smelled Vogt's breath on his face, could smell his body odor and his stage makeup—or was it, Johannes thought, actually his own?—and could feel his confusion becoming something else: a rage (running through Johannes' mind: a "How could I?" being drowned out by a "How could they?"); his teeth were clenching, he couldn't hear Vogt's voice. Vogt was famous, though Johannes, who didn't own a television set and didn't bother to watch Vogt's show on his girlfriend's television when he had gone back to Hamburg for the weekend (instead of going to Lemberg, which his new neighbor in Berlin, who was a doctor, warned him not to do until he gets a shot for typhoid fever), had only read about him in the newspaper; he knew that Vogt had spied for the Stasi and that he was a homosexual and a Jew, that Vogt, even when he had been a guest on other people's talk shows, where he made his reputation confessing and accusing while everyone else was merely chatting, was always getting hate mail, even death threats, that his talk show, which had just started in January, was important and that Johannes couldn't really turn down a chance to appear on it just because Vogt had worked for the Stasi (in the past few months, Vogt had become the most famous of the what now seemed like innumerable celebrity informers); after all, he thought, that hadn't stopped anyone else (Johannes read the TV listings in the newspaper, read TV reviews the next day, felt saved from something; Johannes's girlfriend, who did watch television and had seen Vogt many times, thought that Johannes shouldn't go on because Vogt had worked for the Stasi: she thought of Vogt as "the devil," while favorable newspaper and magazine articles liked to describe him as a "sibyl," which, in an early interview, had been Vogt's description of himself). "Herr Professor Doctor Gramm?" (Johannes, in fact, was not a professor, should have heard this as a warning.) "Are you listening to me?" "They . . . they've stolen my notebook," said Johannes, again (he had been saying it all afternoon to the crowds of stagehands and assistants); he wanted to cry, reached down to pull up his socks. "Yes, 'they' have." said Vogt. "Well, as soon as we find 'them,' we'll have to hang 'them' up by their necks." He stood. "You'll be fine, my dear. Next to the other guests, you'll be the vision of German manhood, a real Knight of the Teutonic Order." Johannes felt Vogt's hand reach for his knee (Vogt was short and ugly, which seemed to go against his claims that he had been working as a prostitute-informer for the Stasi), which he somehow found comforting, but then repellent; he pulled his empty hand, as though there were a notebook in it, up to his chest (the way Johannes pulled his hand to his chest and then mouthed something, as though he were reciting the contents of his notebook from memory, reminds me of the way Orthodox Jews repent on Yom Kippur, beating their breasts and muttering). "Just don't smile too much," said Vogt. "It doesn't suit you." Vogt of course was right about Johannes's Germanness: that week he had also invited a fat American Jewish woman in her forties who toured Germany performing old Joan Rivers monologues in heavily accented German, two black men from Detroit who were cooks at a U.S. Army officers' club near Frankfurt before becoming star DJs at a dance club in Berlin, an East German woman who had written a book about being a member of the Bund der deutschen Mädels—or BDM, the Hitler Youth for Girls—in the thirties and forties and then a high-ranking informer for the Stasi in the fifties and sixties before more or less becoming a dissident in the seventies, two gay men from Berlin who wanted to get married before the one who had AIDS died, and of course Vogt himself, who, even his most loyal fans charged, often acted like own guest. Eventually Johannes was escorted by two men—like a cripple, he would later think—and brought to the table and chairs at the front of the set; he drank mineral water out of a wineglass, looked around at the other guests, back and forth until one became the other; he looked out at the audience and thought that their heads seemed separate from their bodies (like—he might have thought—the baroque engravings of skeletons carrying their own skulls that, along with his other prints and paintings, he had still not unpacked from their large, wall-like crates). "I really feel as if I want to vomit," he thought. "I feel like I am going to have diarrhea." After the title music (it was the first movement of Mahler's Sixth, also known as the "Tragic," Symphony: the Allegro energico, ma non troppo—relentless, marchlike, grandly sad, and ridiculous for something like a talk show theme, which was why Vogt had chosen it: to be ironic), Vogt began with a piece of signed hate mail (he never introduced his guests all at once like the other talk show hosts on German television; he introduced himself, reminding the studio audience, whom he liked to have picked up off the street and taken to the studio in minivans, in what he liked to call "the Razzia," who he was): "Well, here we have a letter from one Gustavus Altbeiser,

Kohlmarktgasse 25, Freudendorf, which, as those of you who have atlases in your laps know, is in the wilds of Lower Bavaria. Herr Altbeiser writes: 'Why don't all you ape-fucking yids go back to Israel? We Germans have had it up to here with you Jews!' etc., etc., etc. Well, Signor Altbeiser, you know, I almost feel sorry for you. Your time is up—I assume you must be over seventy because you have the same handwriting as my 'yid' grandfather. I am sitting in your capital, talking to you on a public television station: you pay my salary. The big city has won! This is the nineties—the decade of cities and outsiders. You've had it your way in this country for sixty years; now it's our turn. So why don't you go back to your yodeling or play with your cows. Your turn will come again—if you live to see it. Until then, *shalom.* Now our first guest tonight is from Hamburg, which is almost a real city. It's raining today in Berlin, so he must feel right at home . . . oh, I see here that he has recently *moved* to Berlin, so perhaps he feels homesick." (Vogt looked through his notes as though he had forgotten Johannes's name.) "Herr Gramm? . . . Herr Gramm, I'd like you to meet Frau Kilo." Vogt pointed at the fat Jewish woman. "I'm only joking," he said to his silenced audience. Then he said to the Jewish woman, sotto voce, "These Germans! They don't like jokes." He turned to Johannes. "Herr Gramm is a young journalist with a rather peculiar interest, something that must make him a bit of an outsider with his liberal friends in Hamburg. Herr Gramm, tell us all about your love affair with Albert Speer."

It is not raining anymore, at least not really raining, but I am the only one sitting outside; Harald, the Canadian waiter, came out to bring me another drink and tell me that people inside think that I'm crazy (I seem to be surrounded by Canadians, who can seem to be English people in drag as Americans, or Europeans in drag as Americans, or the other way{s} around; Harold, who is a waiter at a restaurant in West Berlin as well as at the café in East Berlin and is a sometime heroin addict and, when he is not being a waiter, an assistant to a famous German stage director with a Canadian ex-wife, seems to have one ambition: he wants to go to Budapest to have his teeth fixed, because, he says, "they do beautiful work . . . and *sooo* cheap!"; we talk about dentists and America—he's about thirty, I think, and from Toronto and, except for his teeth, seems American to me—and he gives me free drinks). I felt crazy talking to my parents today from the video store (Peter has let me call America collect from his fax machine phone, though one day I only pretended to call collect, talked to my parents, and then Annette, and then someone I knew in Chicago, for a couple of hours), yelling at my mother when she told me that she hadn't made an appointment for me at the dentist yet; my father asked about what he had seen on the news, about all the attacks in Berlin, which people around here think has something to do with Hitler's birthday next Friday, or with a judge letting off two skinheads who beat up an Angolan in the Schönhauser Allee S-Bahn station last fall. I would seem to be leaving just in time (the train for Kaliningrad leaves Friday morning, stays there through Sunday, which is actually Kant's birthday, and gets back to Berlin Monday morning at seven a.m., and my plane for Chicago, with a change in London, takes off at ten): first there was the Orthodox rabbi from Israel who got spat on at Alexanderplatz as he waited for the U-Bahn (there was a strange article about that in a national tabloid, suggesting that the rabbi, who had been born in the Scheunenviertel and was on his way to Rosa-Luxemburg-Platz, which is only one stop away from Alexanderplatz, was too cheap —he was already a few hours over his twenty-four-hour transit pass—or too lazy to walk; then there were articles about that article, though somehow not about the attack itself); then a car stopped in front of the restored synagogue on the Oranienburger Strasse—to negotiate with a prostitute, it seemed—but, while the policemen weren't looking, someone threw a bloody pig's head out the window; the graves of Marlene Dietrich and of Bertolt Brecht were, again, desecrated with anti-Semitic graffiti (though not the grave of Brecht's wife, Helene Weigel, who actually was Jewish); a carload of people threw buckets of manure at the gates of the syn-

agogue on the Rykestrasse; and of course there's that asylum seekers' home in Marzahn that burnt down, though that happened
before the skinheads from the Schönhauser Allee were let off; all
the asylum seekers got out in time, except a little boy hiding under
some bunk beds who was taken to the hospital with smoke inha-
lation, and who, I read, was "about six" and, even according to
the tabloids, a "Romany," which is the politically correct way to
say—or to avoid saying—Gypsy. People (German people, and
German journalists, unlike, apparently, foreign journalists) haven't
really been taking these attacks *in toto*—because of Hitler's birthday and because of some recent statistics claiming that the number
of attacks this year compared to the number of attacks at this time
last year has decreased (although some people say that this has
more to do with the rain than anything else)—except around here,
where it's hard not to notice that the policemen at the synagogue
on the Rykestrasse, which is right next to the health food store,
have begun to wear bulletproof vests, which is actually what the
policemen guarding the synagogues in Vienna do, I think, as a
matter of course, though in Vienna the policemen carry machine
guns and here they just carry what look like pistols. My father had
heard about the little boy (though didn't make a connection between Marzahn as being both the place where skinheads start fires
and where I had been teaching English; actually I didn't either—
the burnt-down asylum seekers' home was on the very edge of
Marzahn, where there aren't even sidewalks, where it's still the
country, really; empty rather than emptied out) and about the
rabbi, said he was glad that I was coming home, until I told him
how much money I was earning working for Peter Marcus, and he
said, half kiddingly, that I should think about staying. My father,
I imagined, thought that Peter Marcus was a relative of Ben Marcus, who must be the richest Jew, if not the richest person, in
Wisconsin (he owns the Marc Plaza Hotel and all the Marc's Big
Boy restaurants and the Marcus movie theaters, and other things
that I don't know about; or "owned": he may in fact be dead, but,
unlike famous movie stars or writers who aren't yet dead but are

somehow absent, he is somehow still around; Elias Canetti, as I sit here, is not dead, though is sometimes talked about as if he were, and is bound to be less absent, at least for a while, after he does die), though I like to think that he must be related to Jack Marcus, who some people think is Ben Marcus's son, but is in fact someone who grew up in foster homes with my father and never "made it" and whom we used to see at Karl Ratzsch's with his family on Thanksgiving, sitting at one of the best tables. My mother is too worried about herself to worry that I might get attacked by skin-heads: in the past couple of weeks when I have called from the video store, I have only talked to my mother, or to my sister, who apparently now stops by often, because my father has been busy with the tax season, running errands or seeing his Pakistanis (he calls them his "Pakis," although I can't imagine that he knows what kind of English people say that). My mother says things like: "I hate Daddy" (they fight about groceries: she wants him to drive to the other side of town and buy fresh ground round at the PDQ in Fox Point because she says the meat there is fresher and he wants to buy meat at a discount warehouse on the South Side because the meat there is cheaper; they fight about my father hav-ing his prostate out, which my mother wants him to have done at the Mayo Clinic, with a private room and private nurses, and which my father doesn't want to have done, or wants to have done "next week" in a hospital in Brookfield that my mother said she's never even heard of; or they fight about everything at once and watch their televisions in separate rooms, on separate floors, won't sit in the same room even when my sister is there) "When are you coming home?" "Oh! my legs!" (my sister said that my mother's doctors in Milwaukee have put her on codeine) or just "Oh!" when I called there at about nine o'clock in the morning their time and she must have just fallen asleep; she didn't sound at all girlish or babyish, which is how she has usually been sounding ("Daddy won't have surgery at the Mayo Clinic!"), but low-voiced—like death: it's death, I thought (I knew), sounding like my mother. Today she got on the phone after I talked to my father and she sounded much better, like her old self, after she had become a hypochondriac but before she became an invalid. "How are you?" I said. "Practically dead," she announced, sounding cheerful and stubborn, then like a little girl when she asked me again when I was coming home. "Soon," I said. "Soon." Then I asked her if she had made the dentist appointment. When I called Annette, she told me that she was getting married, sounding happy and sad, and older, made a joke about the judge who would be marrying her and the judge, didn't ask how I was. I could see her eighteen-year-old face and her twenty-three-year-old face, and her twenty-five- and twenty-nine-year-old faces though not her thirty-year-old, Parisian, face, and tried to imagine her thirty-two-year-old face on the wedding photo she said she would send to my parents' house; a laughing, beautiful face, assured that everything is surrounding it. (I can't see Professor Whitlaw's face, though a few Germans at the market really did look like him; now, sitting here, I see their faces before his, as if his face were actually one of theirs; as if I were going to Kaliningrad—taking a train journey through all those old German provinces, on German-built Polish train tracks; a journey that takes as long as the trip home, including the stopover in London and the bus to Milwaukee—because of them: for them.) There is no phone in the new apartment (though, downstairs, there is a new phone store next to the new bordello and the new optometrist and the newly managed newsagents—which is the English word and which I must have picked up from the BBC or from reading English newspapers, and which, in any case, comes naturally—who get neo-Nazi papers from their West Berlin distributors one day but then West German liberal broadsheets the next day and West German conservative broadsheets after that, but always East and West Berlin tabloids and the new, national tabloids and the revamped Communist newspapers) and no central heating (it has been warm enough not to heat, or heat just by leaving the oven on; one night it was really cold, and I had to move my futon into the kitchen and sleep next to the oven, reminding me of when I lived in Chicago the summer before I came here and all the apartments in my building were studios with ceiling fans and the woman who lived below me had a broken ceiling fan that rotated irregularly just under my futon and I could never fall asleep, not that I could have anyway because of the heat, against which the ceiling fans were really just useless; I would often push my futon into the kitchen, try to fall asleep there), but the bathroom and the kitchen are large and there are two bedrooms as well as a living room; except for the futon and two old ornate tiled coal ovens (and my books and clothes, which, until yesterday, I had left in the hallway and which looked like garbage from a party the night before, but which today, because I had wanted to find a quote when I woke up at seven as if there were construction noises, are all over the floor), the apartment has been absolutely empty, like a museum exhibit after the exhibit has been taken down, or is about to be put up; there are no blinds on the windows and the view and the spring light can cancel out the East Germanness of the floors and walls: there is no back house and there are no back houses behind any of the other houses on any of the other nearby streets—on Metzer Strasse, my street; on Strassburger Strasse, the cross street; on the Prenzlauer Allee, the other cross street; and on Belforter Strasse, the street parallel to mine—because of an air raid in 1943 (according to the eighty-year-old woman across the hall, who was born in the apartment she is now living in, and whose father's shoe repair service is still advertised on the peeling façade downstairs in fresh-looking Gothic type that looks as new as the graffiti that surrounds it, or stenciled on, movie-settish); from my back windows: a square of houses with edges of walls where other houses used to be: an accidental courtyard, with chestnut trees, just now in bloom, and other kinds of trees, and a tree that looks like a poplar tree that hasn't yet bloomed, or looks almost dead, as if it will never bloom, and is topped with a large empty bird's nest; the "courtyard," which I have to walk through when I take my garbage out because the back door locks behind me and I only have a key to the front door, is like a labyrinth without walls, or with walls you can walk over, a model of complexity: there are the children's playground and the garbage dumps, the views of empty derelict houses and the lights and smells of lived-in houses; the green of the new leaves and the brownish gray of the four "walls" and the brown of the stony bits that cover the courtyard's "floor" and that may be rubble or loosened paving stones or fallen bits of houses, and that look like flashes of brown, like last year's leaves: a bounded world of life and death.

The Quarter-Jew and the Half-Jew

Vogt was drunk. "Outsiders," he said. "It's time for us outsiders." He had already told the story of how he had defected in West Berlin in 1986 on the arm of the Bulgarian diplomat whom he was supposed to be spying on; now it was time to tell the story of the old peasant woman who had hid his grandfather in a larder: "She hid Jews because she was too stingy to give them up. Too cheap. Like an unpaid tax. And don't think that she liked them. No, no. She hated them! She would go down into that larder with rancid sausages, which is all she fed them, and say 'It stinks of Jew down here.' At the end of the war she said to my grandfather, 'Now go back to where you came from, you.' " The other guests at the dinner had already heard both stories—in these exact words (if only on television)—except for Annette Green, whom a curator had brought along. Annette was in Germany for the first time, couldn't speak German, and had been bored over dinner, but now she was finding something intriguing about Vogt, and of course repellent: he chain-smoked, he had begun to drink vodka out of his wineglass; suddenly he stopped speaking his German, started speaking English and a little French, and only, it seemed, to Annette (Annette's father was a Jew from New York, and her mother was Parisian): "And you like Berlin?" he said. "I don't know," she said. "I just got here, actually." "And why, may I ask, are you *ici, dans la ville du moment?*" (His French made her cringe.) "Well, you know, I'm writing something—my thesis, actually—on Virginia Woolf. She visited Berlin in the 1920s, which most people

don't know. She went to Sans Souci, everything." "Woolf,"
he said. "She was Jewish, wasn't she?" "Well, no. Her husband, Leonard, was. I suppose you could call him Jewish."
"And their children, then, were half-Jews." (To the Germans,
in German: "I am just a quarter-Jew, not always enough to
have been gassed—but enough to have been kept off the
guest lists of all those Nazi *nouveau riche* dinner parties!") Annette wanted to laugh. "They didn't have children," she said,
actually laughing. "You're so cultured," he said. "So *gebildet*,
we say in German. And so beautiful. This must be because of
your mother, whom, I am told, is a Frenchwoman." He continued, but Annette had stopped listening, was thinking:
Vogt is just like Loerke! A favorite novel of Annette's was
Women in Love (she had once thought of herself as Ursula
Brangwen waiting to be made whole by a Rupert Birkin), and
here was Loerke—the German artist from Dresden whom the
Brangwen sisters and Rupert Birkin and Gerald Crich meet
during their vacation in the Alps—just as Lawrence had described him: the black hair and brown eyes, the puniness.
(Annette had her mother's blonde hair, her father's brown
eyes; she was tall and looked slightly older than twenty-
three—looked almost English, she had often been told; she
hadn't thought about being Jewish, not a whit, except once,
when she was sixteen and taken to a costume party at a
ruined medieval monastery outside Paris where everyone was
supposed to dress up in medieval costumes and people made
horrible jokes about the noses of the boys who had dressed
up as monks, though her cousin had to tell her later that the
remark a boy had made to her about her father being a
furrier—he was the director of an investment bank—had
been an anti-Semitic one; afterward she had felt confused,
vaguely irritated; why do people have to be like *that*, she had
thought; at Oxford, she would look at the obvious Jews, from
Golders Green and Manchester, and think, I'm not at all like
they are, which is what she thought about Parisians in Paris,
and Americans in New York—and especially about the English at Oxford, where at the end of every evening all the boys
she had known would leave their drafty rooms to vomit up
gin and wine and beer onto the frosty lawns or, now that

many of them were in graduate school as she was, sat like dons—or like monks!—in their rooms, stammering, heads disconnected from their white, bloodless bodies.) She thought of Ursula's sister, Gudrun, and Loerke at the end of the novel on the snowy alpine peak, of Gudrun not wanting to go back to England, utterly confused about where to go, and Loerke pursing his lips and saying that the wind blows toward Germany. There had been something unnecessary about her trip here (her thesis, which was really only partly on Virginia Woolf, meant nothing to her; before deciding to return to Oxford for graduate school, she had spent a year in Los Angeles working for a film production company, but that too had meant nothing). She remembered the book's last mention of Gudrun: "Gudrun went to Dresden. She wrote no particulars of herself." Yes, considered Annette, to disappear, and the idea made her heady, as though it were some exotic odor. She watched Vogt drink and drink; he was staring at her from behind the rim of his glass; suddenly he was talking about Los Angeles. "You too have lived there, in this city of devils." (How had he known? Had someone told him? How could they have? Karl-Phillip, or whatever his name was, didn't know. She cringed again.) And so the two talked about Los Angeles. Vogt, who had visited, and sometimes pretended to have lived there, talked about the car wash on La Brea and Fountain, about the Orthodox Jews and the male prostitutes at the bus stops in the Fairfax district; Annette talked about huge empty houses and aging neighbors of German émigrés with their anecdotes about Thomas Mann and Arnold Schoenberg and aging neighbors of English émigrés with their anecdotes about Christopher Isherwood and Aldous Huxley, and about restaurants on Melrose Avenue with white waiters and Chinese cooks and Mexican busboys talking to one another with calculators, in numbers. "Yes," said Vogt, finally. "Yes! You see it too. And I see it. We see it because we're Europeans." He looked around the table at the other guests—as though he were looking *through* them, Annette thought nervously—then spoke *sotto voce*: "And because we're Jeeewwss." His voice dwindled to a whistle. As for the others (the curator, the TV executive, his girlfriend, the host, the host's two friends—the crowd of them), they listened to the stories about the Jews and the Stasi (heard before, familiar, but unbearable; obliterating) and the other Jews, and the gas stations and the prostitutes and the drive-by shootings and the German émigrés (they—the others— had been in West Berlin for years, had once thought of themselves as émigrés, even refugees, from West Germany's obliterating affluence, which had, as if suddenly, caught up with them; that night they all dressed in elegant clothes, in the sort of clothes that they could actually afford but had been avoiding for years; in drag as one another) and they felt trapped, on a vanishing ledge. "Jeeeeewwwwssssss," said Vogt again, but only Annette could hear, because the others were already gone; the night had come to get them.*

From where I'm sitting, I can see the outside of the labyrinth—the line of houses on the Strassburger Strasse—leading away from the roof of the Water Tower, which, with its narrow chimney and flat, round roof, looks like the hat of the Tin Man in *The Wizard of Oz*; I can see the crowds of people inside the other cafés: I can see a

---

* All this talk of Virginia Woolf and novels and Berlin makes me think of something: If I were going to write a novel "about" Berlin and only incidentally "about" Joel La Vine, I would want to get a certain sound lurking behind the words, as Virginia Woolf had once wanted to do with *The Waves*: "Could one get the sound of the waves to be heard all through?" she wrote in her diary, as if a certain number of words could sound like something infinite; "all through" my book, I would want to get a specific sound that Joel can hear from his apartment, or rather from the apartment that he is staying in, but that he tends to treat as vague, as "construction noises": I would want the sound of cobblestone pavement being pounded back into place, one stone after another, pounded into place over the new or replaced telephone wires and gas lines and other cables, pounded into a bed of

sand, fitted together into a sort of horizontal wall (the replacing of cobblestones is something of an art—or actually a craft; in East Berlin, one sees old men, old enough to have learned their craft before the war, teaching young boys almost too young to remember the GDR; together they hover and pound and spit accumulated sand out of their mouths; but mostly pound); I would want that endlessly irritating noise to suggest a specific period of time—an era. I would want to describe something Joel had once seen in West Berlin in front of a building that was having all its windows replaced: the windows—as tall as, or taller than!, a person—were lined up on what looked like a cattle car, then a worker pounded his way through the windows, from the beginning to the end, breaking all the glass, climbing through as he broke (though Joel left after the worker was few people lingering near the memorial plaque in front of the Water Tower (I hadn't really noticed the plaque, which looks like an orderly pile of bricks, until I read the Water Tower issue of *Zitty*: there had been a concentration camp of sorts in the shadow of the Water Tower for a few months in the summer of 1933, and the Communists and Socialists in the neighborhood were rounded up and imprisoned there and either murdered or sent on to other camps; the place where the concentration camp had been is now a childrens' playground; the memorial plaque, on the other side of the playground, is always, now that the weather is warm, covered with people who can't find places to sit at the cafés and restaurants, or who like a little distance, who want to be outside, in

---

about halfway done, just assuming he was going on to the end). And I would set the novel on a single day, on one of those Christian holidays that people who grow up in America and end up in Germany always forget about, like Assumption Day, or Pentecost (or *Bus- und Bettag*, "Repentence and Prayer Day," which is actually only a Protestant holiday, though celebrated all over Germany, and my favorite, because its name, when played with by a nonnative German speaker, can sound like *Bumsentag*, which would mean "Fucking Day"), when absolutely everything is closed, including newsstands, and the few grocery stores that are supposed to stay open on Sundays; or, if Joel were a major character in the novel and trying to pick up money that his parents had sent him at the post office, I would set it on a Catholic holiday, like All Saint's Day, meaning that absolutely everything in southern Germany, like the post office in Saarbrücken, which all the American money transferred to the German postal service has to go through, would be closed, though everything in northern Germany would spitefully still be open. I don't know what I would call the novel, but if I were going to write a nonfiction book about Germany I would call it *Squaring the Square: Germans and Their Totalitarianisms*. If I were going to write a travel article about Berlin, I would write a travel article about Central Europe—about someone visiting Berlin and then going to Prague to get away, about returning to Berlin, about journeys within journeys—called "Meals in Prague," starting with a description of Prague's toilets, which have their own little rooms, are enormous, like sewers inside closets, then describe Prague's new Tex-Mex restaurant—Annette, Joel's Annette, would describe it as a Czech-Mex restaurant—which, in fact, used to be a Slovak restaurant where a now dead Hungarian-speaking Slovakian Jew who had survived the camps and became a minor party functionary until 1968, after which he became a janitor, would regularly roll up his sleeves after his spicy, fatty lunch and reach for a toothpick, rolling up his sleeves unconsciously perhaps, but showing his tattooed number—to my readers, at least— just the same; I would talk about the Brecht poem about Prague called "The Song of the Moldau" (though the politically correct among my readers might deluge me with letters, insisting I translate the title as "The Song of the Vltava"; though even politically incorrect readers who had been to Prague might prefer "Vltava," not really knowing, or believing, or understanding, that Prague had once been a German city, and then a

spite of the wetness and the sudden cold, as I do tonight); I can't see, but can imagine, the back of the house I am living in, the blindless windows of my apartment, can see the brand-new Foron stove on the other side of the kitchen window, and the toilet, which is almost up against the bathroom window; I can imagine the apartment of the eighty-year-old woman who was born in the house, who asked me what I am doing on Easter, and I said I didn't celebrate Easter, though in fact I am sort of celebrating it, though as Kant's birthday, which is on Easter Sunday this year; most of the people going to Kaliningrad are going because it is Easter, I was told at the strange travel agency—I suppose you could call it an irredentist travel agency, or even a time travel agency—that specializes in trips to former German provinces, which in Germany is treated as a phenomenon, called *Heimwehtourismus*, or "home-

---

German and German-speaking Czech city, and then a German and/or Czech city, and then a German or Czech city, let alone that "Bohemian" had once meant "Czech" and then "German" and then "Czech and German" and then "Czech or German, but mostly German" and now "Czech," except to the expelled Germans, and to many other Germans and virtually all present-day Austrians, for whom it means "German"; it never meant "Jew," although the ancestors of many Jews in places like Galicia—Loerke, whom Rupert Birkin in *Women in Love* describes, almost spitting out the words, as "a Jew—or part Jewish," claims to come from "Polish Austria," which would have had to mean "Galicia," which, except in Poland, but even there, invariably meant, and still means, even though there aren't any left, "Jew"—had actually at one time lived in Bohemia, which, before Poland, was a homeland of exiled Jewry):

Deep down in the Moldau the pebbles are
*   shifting*
In Prague three dead emperors moulder
*   away.*
The top won't stay top

The bottom is lifting.
The night has twelve hours and then comes
*   the day.*

(This is, of course, to some extent, and rather coincidentally, Vogt's philosophy—that it's his turn.) And I would talk about Paul Celan's poem about Prague called "In Prague," which ends with the following stanza:

bone-Hebrew
ground into sperm
ran through the hourglass
through which we swam, two dreams now,
*   chiming*
against time, in the squares.

This is the sort of thing Joel, in effect, thinks when he looks out the window, into the "courtyard": he thinks that things can become other things, but somewhere (I want to say "unconsciously") fears not entirely. (When Joel heard about the Jew who got spat on at Alexanderplatz, he recalled a strange metal plaque on the wall of Alexanderplatz's underground station — which has "works of art" on its walls instead of advertisements—onto which a quotation from Goethe had sickness tourism" (I once heard what I thought of as a politically correct *Heimwehtourismus* radio call-in show; people who had been expelled from East Prussia, Silesia, and so on, and then had visited their old towns and villages and often the houses they had been born in, could call in and talk about their experiences with a psychologist and a historian, both of whom tended to scold people who complained that their cars had been stolen or that their childhood bedrooms had been converted into pigsties, and to praise people who claimed to have mastered expressions in the appropriate Slavic language and who said they didn't want to move back but just wanted to visit several times a year). When I was waiting in line, though, I noticed a sign that read, "Experience Königsberg on the birthday of Immanuel Kant, Germany's greatest philosopher" (I thought of the sign advertising the Auschwitz tours at the hotel in Warsaw, and I thought of Professor Whitlaw waiting in

---

been written in braille, but which Joel at first thought looked like engraved Hebrew before realizing that it was braille and now thinks looks like both engraved Hebrew and German rendered into braille; he thinks of the Orthodox Jew covered in spittle as a real person and as a ghost, as real and/or imagined.) And I would talk about restaurants in Berlin, irredentist restaurants serving dishes from Böhmen and Schlesien and Pommern and Ostpreussen and catering to all those West German tourists coming to Berlin to take a look at their new *Hauptstadt*. And I would talk about Paul Celan's aforementioned poem about Berlin ("the menorah poem from Berlin"), which ends

feelings, frost-
mandrelled,

cold start—
with haemoglobin.

(Anyone, by the way, can claim to be a Berliner, like the fat Jewish woman on Vogt's talk show, who, when she brings her monologues into town, goes on about being a *"Berlinerin"* when she is

interviewed on locally produced TV talk shows and radio programs; she is invariably asked about "the new Jewish life in Berlin"—except by Vogt, who preferred to ask her questions about the old Jewish life, about Canetti and Alfred Döblin, about Weimar-era Jewish jazz musicians like the Weintraub Syncopators, about whom she knew absolutely nothing though pretended to know something, making her seem like a fool—and then she will talk about how wonderful it is, how wonderfully her audiences respond to her, but she misses bagels, which she always defines—teetering back and forth between German and English, which she likes to call "Engleutsch"—as "a Jewish *Pfannkuchen*.") And about Brecht's poem "Germany 1945" (which Joel has read in a highly anglicized translation):

Indoors is death by plague
Outdoors is death by cold.
So where are we to be?
The sow has shat in her bed
The sow's my mum. I said:
O mother mine, O mother mine
What have you done to me?

line, as I was, but with a book in his hands, bumping into people). Easter here is celebrated on Monday as well as Sunday, and the woman who finally waited on me said that the train that weekend was fully booked, but that I would be number one on the waiting list and that in the year and a half that she has been running these special trips to Königsberg (she seemed to be Russian, said "Königsberg" to the crowds of old Germans booking places on trains, only said "Kaliningrad" to the other travel agents, who were young and East German–seeming), the first few people on the waiting list have always gotten places; I paid the 2,340 marks and got a voucher on what looked like old East German scrap paper. (I always forget about holidays here—which are always "Christian"—except the main ones like Christmas, and of course Easter, which we also more or less celebrated in Milwaukee: we would go out for dinner with my uncle and aunt and cousins on Easter Sunday and everybody else in the restaurant would be non-Jewish and "dutchy," and my mother and my aunt would laugh at all the non-Jewish women, with their white stockings and Easter wrist

---

And I would mention the shit stains on the sidewalk outside the synagogue on the Rykestrasse (the *y* is pronounced like a double *e*). I would mention German toilets, which are built with ledges above sudden deep holes, catching the shit in a nice neat pile, like a sample of something, before it disappears. It would be the opposite of a travel article—an attempt to make people stay at home. I want people to stay at home, to be where they belong; I want them to see where they are differently, as a new place, rather than a new place the way they already see where they are. ("Don't adjourn yourself, you," writes Celan in a late poem, sounding a bit like Brecht in one of his early poems.) I would want "here" to be different from "there," and then for them both to become impossible, or at least unlikely: no more origins; no destinations. (Vogt's Annette has discovered—or just recognized—her need for "there," and now it woos her, like a distant smell, like an edge; Joel's

Annette, in her new romance novel, has her heroine meet a Jewish English teacher from Chicago just back from Prague, though by the middle of the book it is already clear that she will want to end up with the middle-aged carpenter building her new bookshelves.) I would give the travel article the subtitle "Where We Are to Be" (which, somewhat coincidentally, would echo Lenin's "Where to Begin" and "What Is to Be Done," in which he makes his famous call for the dictatorship of a vanguard), by which I would mean, rhetorically, "nowhere," or perhaps, really, "never," which has to do with what the listener, for lack of a better word, thinks when he or she begins to notice that noise outside the window of cobblestones being replaced, of metal hitting stone, of a city clenching and unclenching its teeth (and clenching and unclenching, as if forever); I want to drive people out of their fucking minds.

corsages; in the weeks leading up to Easter, my mother would buy cookies shaped like chicks and bunnies, and sometimes chocolate rabbits, at the German bakery in the Mayfair shopping center, when it was still a shopping center and not yet a mall; I have tended to forget about the other Christian holidays, when everything is closed and which I merely think of, after I have no other choice, as extra Sundays, and about the Jewish ones: I think today might have been the first—or third, or last—day of Passover.) When the old woman in the house promptly asked why I don't celebrate Easter, I said, "because I'm Jewish," feeling excited and a little terrified—my mother had actually told me not to tell people in Germany that I was Jewish, which I thought was nonsense, until these attacks around the corner, and until talking to some Jewish teenagers from West Berlin who, after buying videos from me at the market (I gave them a discount), told me that they don't know of any Jewish family in West Berlin that hasn't gotten hate mail and strange phone calls in the middle of the night—like when I would smoke pot in my college dormitory, cleaning out the seeds with one of my sister's old record covers. "Half or whole," she said, leaning away from me (or so I imagined). I wanted to laugh; "whole," I said, later thinking, in German mixed with English, of a "half *Jude*," which sounded like *Hofjude*, or court Jew, which, before emancipation, is what protected Jews who were allowed to live in places like Vienna and Berlin (usually because they were so rich) were once called, and what I imagined I could call myself, that I was "the *Hofjude*" of my courtyard (later *Hofjude* also made me think of *Hofspitzel*, which is what an adviser to the Chancellor who had been working for the Stasi got called, though I can't remember if it was an adviser to this chancellor or another one; all I remember is the man's face, which I once saw in a magazine: his nose and glasses, which looked fake, and his hand reaching out to cover up the camera). Sometimes the old woman waits for me to walk out the door, and then asks if I will go to the grocery store on the corner and buy her a sack of potatoes, which I always do, though after I told her that I was Jewish I gave her back too much change; on Friday, she opened up her door as I was walking out and said, "Shabbat Shalom," which sounded like both a password and a taunt. The trip to Kaliningrad, where of course I have never been and which I almost can't even imagine, is practically a return: one of the first places I went after I arrived here was Danzig, which is just across the Gulf of Danzig from Kaliningrad; it was a warm fall weekend and I thought it would be nice to swim in the Baltic, but in Danzig the man at my hotel told me that the water was so polluted that it was unhealthy even to walk on the sand (I thought about swimming in the water anyway—it was as gray and flat as the sky, would have been like swimming in the sky, and it reeked pleasantly, or familiarly, like Lake Michigan—and now wish that I had; it will be too cold to swim in the Baltic while I am in Kaliningrad); in addition to all the *Heimwehtouristen*, there seemed to be "World War II tourists," like the British man and his German wife, who told me that they met after the war when he was on occupation duty in Hamburg, looking at all the places of military interest fifty-odd years later; they, like I, went to the spot outside town where the Second World War officially began when German gunboats fired on the free city of Danzig's token Polish garrison (some people talk about turning Kaliningrad—which, separated from Russia by Lithuania and Byelorussia, looks on maps like a piece of fallen masonry—into a free city, about it becoming the "Hong Kong of the Baltic"); actually I spent most of my time getting lost, trying to find discos and gay bars and restaurants that I had copied into a notebook from the various guidebooks I had bought in America and didn't want to bring along from Berlin, finally giving up and eating most of my meals at the McDonald's in the redbrick, really Hanseatic, though decidedly Polish, except for the McDonald's, train station; eating that food, which tastes— and especially smells—exactly the same wherever you find it, like at the McDonald's in Wenceslas Square in Prague, or at the Mc-Donald's across from the Marienkirche—and the television tower, and the Rotes Rathaus—in East Berlin, can send you tumbling back to other McDonald's elsewhere, back and back, like Proust's mad-

eleine, or even forward to, for instance, the McDonald's in Budapest (if there is one, and there must be), where I have never
been, though I sometimes think that I have been to Budapest, have
to remember that I haven't (once I was going to go but gave up
on the fifteen-hour train ride and got off after five hours in Prague;
another time, when I thought I was going to visit Auschwitz, I was
going to start in Budapest—according to Primo Levi, Hungarian,
after German, was the language most commonly spoken at Auschwitz, where Hungarian Jews died by the hundreds of thousands—
but changed my mind about visiting Auschwitz, though not about
visiting Cracow, which I did, as if instead): I can't imagine that
there is a McDonald's in Kaliningrad. When I think about Danzig
now (I can never bring myself to say "Gdansk," which sounds like
pig Latin for "Danzig"), I can summon up some sympathy for the
Germans, who go there and find all the rebuilt German buildings
covered with Russian and English and Polish inscriptions; afterward, the train to Warsaw went through the East Prussian coun-
tryside, which, I have recently learned, wasn't always German, but
had been Polish—it was the landscape of Nicolaus Copernicus—
which made me feel sympathetic toward the official history you
find in old Communist guidebooks to Poland as well as in the new
guidebooks, which only have to change the history of Communist
Poland because the Communists already polonized the rest of history for them; Copernicus, I think, is on the thousand zloty bill,
which, the last time I was there, was worth about 3 cents. (My idea
of a trip to Poland: start with the small town between Danzig and
Kaliningrad where Copernicus discovered—I almost want to say,
decided—that it was the earth that revolved around the sun, ush-
ering in the Age of Science, and then go on to Auschwitz, where
that age ended; in Kaliningrad, the age of Copernicus and Auschwitz has, at least in photographs, vanished without a trace and—
except for the ruins of the cathedral where Kant is buried and
which was on all the posters for "Königsberg" at the irredentist
travel agency—there are probably not yet traces of any other: there
is only betweenness, like in Milwaukee, where so little of my child-

hood is still around—the Melody Top is gone; Karl Ratzsch's descendant, Karl Ratzsch, shot himself on a bluff overlooking Lake Michigan; my old school district has expanded, and my high school is now a junior high school; my bedroom has become my father's bedroom—except for my parents, who are dying, one before the other.) Since deciding to leave, I have been going back to places I went when I first arrived: I walked by the pension off the Kurfürstendamm that I stayed at on my first few nights here and saw that it had become a hotel; I went for a walk down one of the narrow, hard-to-find streets in the Scheunenviertel, past the dubious rental agency that had sent me to live at the Krügers', and I saw that it had changed utterly—metamorphosed, I thought—into what looked like a wine store or perhaps a wine bar; I walked past the Krügers' building, through the front house, through the first courtyard—but not to the second courtyard, not through to the back house, not to the apartment—and saw a notice just inside the front door from the man who had recently bought the building and who ended his too friendly, computer-printed note with the bold-faced number of his cellular telephone, telling the tenants to call him "even if you"—in the informal, second-person plural that Germans use most often with a group of children—"just want to say '*Hallo*' " (I thought the note was too friendly, though East Germans take West Germans' too friendliness quite seriously, as a threat). Apparently this era, which is perhaps really an era of betweenness, is ending (this era, which also seems eraless, merely one end after another, or a variation on an end, like a satyr play), or has already ended, like in a travel article I read that profiled the cafés and restaurants around the Water Tower, all of which had actually been other things under the Communists, like a police station or a butcher shop or a laundry (the café where Harald works had been a flower shop before and during the war, and then was nothing until it became a squat a year or so before the wall fell, and then after the wall fell, a bar for squatters and *Autonomen*, and then began to become a regular café last summer after one of the former squatters persuaded the building's temporary owner to

lease him the space), and look indisputably like cafés and restaurants, until after you find out what they had been and they start
to look like what they were as well as what they are (this era: the
era of everything looking destroyed and rebuilt, of destruction at
the center and newness on the outside, of death that looks lifelike,
of a lively image of death, like, perhaps, what happens after your
parents die and you have finished mourning, have rebuilt yourself
but carry their absence around inside you); the writer (the article
was from an American newspaper, though I can't remember which
one, and for a while last week everyone near the Water Tower
seemed to be an American tourist with a photocopy of the article
in his hand) didn't mention the concentration camp or the playground (I would have mentioned both, might even have mentioned the windmill that had been there before the Water Tower
was built); he mentioned complicated-sounding desserts made
with kiwi fruit and the satellite dishes on all the houses and people
eating borscht while talking on cellular telephones, and he mentioned the store for fetishists; he interviewed an owner of one of
the many new wine stores who had a pocket-sized encyclopedia
that he had bought in Hong Kong with a small video screen that
flashed up a map of Germany whenever anyone entered "Germany"; he talked about what he called "after 'after the wall,' "
which was an expression that I thought I had coined and by which
I meant something more sinister than hopeful, a willful forgetfulness, and by which I might now mean just as sinister as hopeful,
mere forgetfulness, but which for him was merely hopeful, like an
all-clear siren (perhaps I had really been meaning "before 'after
"after the wall" ' "); there are lots of articles and stories like that
now, taking as their theme the "newest"—or just "newer"—
" 'New Europe,' " like the one about the two business students
from Brooklyn opening up a chain of bagel bakeries in Hungary,
where Jews—the murdered ones, and the surprisingly large number of Jews still there—had never eaten, "didn't know from," bagels; the business students had only vaguely Jewish-sounding
names, and the Hungarians interviewed—it was on "Europe To-

day," I think, which lately is hosted by an Australian—thought of bagels as American, as a kind of donut; about successful advertising campaigns on Russian television (in a poll I read about in a West German business magazine—which is the sort of magazine they have at the health club, where most of the members are, or at least seem to be, unemployed—a majority of Russians, after viewing commercials for Uncle Ben's rice and sauce products, said that they would prefer Uncle Ben for president over Boris Yeltsin and Vladimir Zhironovsky): articles and stories which seem to have exhausted the irony of the situation, or which take the irony for granted, like a local custom, are more descriptive than anything else, describing success, like the list of top ten U.S. box office draws (which I have heard broadcast, or seen printed, in English, German, and French whatevers), as though communism, let alone fascism, were as remote, and as quaint, as vaudeville; or articles and stories describing the present in terms of the future, like the way they all call the European Community the European Union as though it had always been called the European Union (I call it the European Community, as though no one were calling it the European Union and had never called it the Common Market); sometimes I play along, like to imagine, say, a European press roundup including that Latin radio station in Finland. Of course these articles and stories, if only accidentally, are also right: something has ended, is moving on: the Friedrichstadt Arcade has gone, without my noticing, from being a hole in the ground to being the skeleton of a very long building; the Potsdamer Platz is a series of holes in the ground (making the wilderness at its edges seem even more wild, about to fill in the holes, as if the holes had to be redug every night); statistically—except around here—the skinheads are perhaps breaking up (or just finding peaceful ways of staying out of the rain); the radicchio in the grocery store where I have been buying Diet Coke comes from Bulgaria; today Irmgard told me that she has decided to get her Ph.D. in art history, and she seemed happier than I have ever seen her, happier than I could ever have imagined her (but then sounded unsure, said her parents didn't want her to go back to school, were threatening not to pay for it, that she didn't want to do the degree here in Berlin, didn't want to have to go back to Munich, asked me again about staying in the apartment), and I am leaving. (Yes! I really feel, as I am sitting here, that I am leaving! can smell the departure lounge at Tegel Airport, can feel the weight of the presents I will buy my parents and sister, and perhaps, even, my brother-in-law.) At the market, everything is supposed to be "used": there are special flea market policemen (actually "trade policemen," though everyone calls them the *Flohmarktpolizei*) who show up in plainclothes and can fine people who are trying to sell "new" things; the videos I was selling of course couldn't have been "used"—or could have been, in a sense, if they had all been pirated, but I am not sure if the flea market policemen could have fined me for copyright infringement; in any case it didn't come up, (and it won't come up, because today was my last day at the market, and is actually my last Sunday in Germany, because [Joel sticks his hand in the pocket of his jean jacket, fingers his plane ticket, his travel voucher] I am almost gone). I don't know the *Flohmarktpolizei's* legal definition of "used," though "belonging to the past" sounds right to me, with "the past," perhaps, beginning any time before the market does; though as it happens, the past, for lack of a better word, seemed to overtake the market, flooded it, reclaimed it, pushed the present out to the edges; or perhaps just the opposite: the fact of the market, of everything immediately up for sale, of all those onetime intimate things reduced to a series of negotiated prices, pushed the past out to the edges, like an empty canvas pushing out its frame (similarly, sitting here, I feel as if am already gone, as if I have just left, and as if I am still sitting here).

The CEO's Daughter and the German Baron

Annette was leaving tomorrow; she was packing, was a little tearful—she had done nothing, she thought, she had wasted her trip. It was raining and everything smelled like cold steam, like metal; time, she thought, had simply disappeared, like boiled water. The most wasteful event—when she thought about it now, it seemed like a black hole, simply missing—was an evening spent on a blind date with the friend of a boy who had been with her at Oxford. He had looked like a bird (the date, not the friend, though the friend, who was also German, and aristocratic, also looked like a bird: when she thought about it now, all the possible details came back at once), had talked and talked, didn't ask her anything, said dumb things about America (about how America had no history, no culture, which was the exact declension of a butcher Joel had once met in Dresden, who talked about Dresden as the "city of art"—Joel, of course thinks of it as the city of parking lots—and about Saxon culture, and about how America, where he, like Annette's date, had never been, had *"keine Geschichte, keine Kultur"*; he talked through his thick accent {*"keine Geschichte, keine Kultur"* pronounced in a thick Saxon accent can sound like one word}, about the opera house in Dresden, and about Mozart, who was his favorite composer, while Joel looked at the palms of his hands, which were enormous, monumental, as big as two faces; he had hacked-up fingers that looked as thick and white and hard as bones) and talked about England as though it were 1910. He talked about the island of Rügen, off Germany's Baltic coast ("Germany's largest island," he told her, sounding offended when she eventually asked him what Rügen was; she couldn't really imagine Germany had islands; she tried to picture the map of Germany in her head; she pictured mountains in the south and strange dirty cities in the north, picturing the water itself as a kind of outer space, and the earth as flat and endless), about how the Communists hadn't entirely ruined it; he talked about a house on Rügen that had been in his family until the end of the last century (she thought of her Parisian cousin, how she would be impressed) and how his family was now trying to buy it back from some West German property developers. (Here's what Vogt has to say about Rügen: he says that the seaweed that has been washing up on shore at the end of every summer since the fall of the wall, giving Germans rashes and ruining their vacations, is the hair of the gassed Jews at Auschwitz.) There had been one nice day spent at Sans Souci, walking to the palaces in the spring heat through the thick, wild-looking park, listening to music on her little sister's Walkman; the trees were already deeply green, so different from the pale, wet English green that she had come to know well, and from that other green she knew from springs in Paris: this was like green wool, she thought; she walked past a felled tree and saw a thick branch cut off just where it split into two more branches and she thought that it looked as perfect as a Greek torso; she looked beyond the moss-covered trunks, and could see only more trees, and more, while the music played and played; it was Beethoven's Ninth Symphony, and Schiller's German was like foliage on the tree of Beethoven's music (which is how Annette's date, the young baron, might have described it; he loved German forests and German rivers and German music and German lakes; he tended to think of the Baltic as a kind of German lake, remembering the Hanseatic League, of a time when Germans and their Germanness spread from Bergen to Riga; he thought of Germany as a vast greenness). And it wasn't just Beethoven's Ninth: it was Herbert von Karajan conducting the Berlin Philharmonic—the baron loved von Karajan—in a recording from the early 1960s (actually Annette hadn't paid much attention, had simply grabbed a few of her sister's cassettes during her recent week in New York, ending up with rap music and a couple of Beethoven symphonies); von Karajan, of course, had been a member of the Nazi Party, a fact which had helped him get his first conducting job at Aachen (known in French as Aix-la-Chapelle, which Charlemagne, whom the Germans call Karl der Grosse, made the capital of his Holy Roman Empire, which was, most important, a union between what makes up present-day Germany and France and is sometimes talked about as a forerunner of the European Union, which uses Beethoven's Ninth Symphony as its anthem, and is what the Germans mean when they say "the first *Reich*"), when his predecessor there, Professor Peter Raabe, took over the presidency of the Reichsmusikkammer from Richard Strauss in 1936 and further "purified" German music. Von Karajan, to my mind, can make Beethoven sound like Richard Wagner, his many versions of the "Ode to Joy" might as well be so many choruses from *Die Meistersinger von Nürnberg,* and I prefer an original-instrument version of the Ninth Symphony, a purifying of the purifiers; Joel, who, after watching, or partly watching, all those Holocaust documentaries hour after hour, has imagined other versions of Holocaust documentaries, of those familiar pictures of skeletal people with their pleading dead faces, of the dead bodies in piles and the Germans of the nearby towns retching as they are forced to walk by and view the piles, with, say, Beethoven's Ninth Symphony playing in the background (in recent weeks Joel has given up on Elvis Costello and the Beatles, on Crosby, Stills, Nash and Young and Neil Young, on Joni Mitchell—the tapes lie in piles with his winter coat and his sweater and his books, all over the floor, though sitting at the café he wishes he had his sweater, has fantasies of going back to the apartment to get it—and has started listening to classical music, and mostly to German classical music, tuning in to Berlin's many excellent classical radio stations and going to Berlin's largest record store, in the Europa Center, to buy classical music on cassette; Beethoven's Ninth—he bought a von Karajan recording from the early 1980s—is his favorite Beethoven Symphony, and Gustav Mahler is his favorite composer); he has come to believe that things can become other things, that things are one another, as though life were a musician's right hand and death were his left, which makes me think of that now dead Hungarian-speaking Slovakian Jew who had cancer of the mouth, recovering in the hospital from having much of his tongue cut off (he eventually died of another, unrelated, cancer, of the lung): his son asked him what he was thinking and he wrote back, in Czech, "I won't be able to lick any more pussy." Annette kept walking; she had started at Sans Souci Palace itself, looking forward to the grotto, with its shell-embedded walls, which had so impressed Virginia Woolf during her visit in 1929, only to find out that the grotto was actually at the other side of the park, in the New Palace, that Virginia Woolf had made a mistake (Joel makes mistakes; he doesn't know that the Canaletto who painted the views of Dresden and Warsaw was actually the nephew of the Canaletto who had painted the views of Venice, one of which hangs in the country house of the grandmother of a "boy" Annette had had sex with during her first year at Oxford; on Joel's parent's walls: a twenty-eight-year-old still-life bought on sale at Gimbel's; on the tables, pictures of children, lined up with the older pictures in front, looking newer, as if the children were getting younger and younger); she walked to the New Palace, catching along the way a view of the whimsical eighteenth-century Ruinenberg, or "mountain of ruins" (a hill with three worn-looking pillars hovering colonnadelike over piles of things, and a durable example of the fake ruins so popular in the baroque imagination, a style which to some extent anticipated the love of real medieval ruins so important a part of the Romantic imagination, and which, I imagine, was bombed during the Second World War, had to be rebuilt), through the park, which she could only think of as a forest and which, at one point, when the Chinese teahouse came into view, looked as vast and magical and separate as an underwater city, to the New Palace, through its marble rooms with the walls covered with copies of Italian masters, until she reached the grotto, which amazed her: it was covered with hunks of precious stones—amber, even—that shimmered in the darkened room; behind: a view of the green trees and the green lawn; it was like standing in an aquarium, like being surrounded by ocean. She had begun to tell the baron about Sans Souci, but he interrupted her, complained about what the Communists had done to Potsdam, about a cluster of high-rise cement blocks intruding on some vista or other; she noticed that his eyes were glassy blue, that he looked like a stuffed bird, and she simply stopped listening, turned her head to look at the crowd in the restaurant, although the baron just went on and on; he wasn't paying much attention to Annette: he was thinking—while talking about something else—about the springtime, about the snows melting, about a trip he was planning to the mountains, to the rocky blank summit (above the green trees) away from the dirt and crowds of Berlin.

The Jews in *Badenheim 1939*, I remember, begin to fancy their deportation to Poland as a return, though actually many of them might be said to have come from Bohemia, or Germany, or godknows-where: the geography of wandering, of a diaspora, is interchangeable, arbitrary, with "heres and theres" seeming to repeat themselves, and time is specific, but long, seemingly endless [evidence of Joel's "diaspora": the parking lots in Los Angeles and Dresden: the "real" parking lot in Los Angeles and its imitation in Dresden, and the "fake" parking lot in Dresden and its anticipation in Los Angeles, all seem now, as he sits, forever ago]. I suppose the Jews in Badenheim in 1939, like Jews anywhere, at any time, could be said to have originally come from Israel, though Israel can sound like a putative, or just a mythological, beginning, and a provisional ending, a never-was and never-will-be [*From Jerusalem to Jerusalem*: a Palestinian's polemic]; I'm not sure I believe in political zionism: I think I believe in a zionism of the soul, or of the personality; I believe that people are heading backward even as they seem to be moving forward. Peter Marcus's favorite movie is *La Ronde*, the movie version of the Schnitzler play, the basic premise of which (that A sleeps with B and B with C until Z sleeps with A) had something to do with syphilis when Schnitzler wrote it and now, in its updated versions, could be said to have something to do with AIDS, but when Max Ophuls made the movie, just after the war in recently occupied France (I have sometimes confused Max Ophuls with his son Marcel Ophuls, which Germans shopping at the market did all the time, even after I explained that they were two different people; Germans know that Max Ophuls— actually, in German, Ophüls—was a Jewish film director who fled Germany and that Marcel Ophuls now, in some sense, makes movies "about" Germany; the idea of that same Ophuls returning to Germany—surviving—seems to comfort them; in all of the German made-for-TV movies about the Holocaust that I have ever seen, the exiled Jews always come back and the Nazis always get killed in action during the last days of the war; in the German documentaries about the Holocaust or about Jewish life in Germany, no one ever comes back, and interviews with German Jews have to be filmed in New York, or London, or Israel), the movie was "about" collaboration, that characters played by actresses who were collaborators have sex with characters played by actors who had been in the resistance or had been émigrés (this is all according to Peter Marcus, who gets things wrong, who didn't realize himself that Max Ophuls and Marcel Ophuls weren't the same person). I have always liked *La Ronde*, or *Reigen*, or whatever you're supposed to call it (there doesn't seem to be a way to translate that title into English, out of European): I like the story, because it ends with the duke, or prince, or whatever he is (Peter hasn't let me sell it at the market, runs it over and over again for himself, and I haven't really seen it, except for bits and pieces in the store, in years: once in a film class and once in New York, at the Thalia on the Upper West Side, where the seats all smelled like piss, and I have read it of course, in German, have held on to it in bookstores; and he won't let me sell *Shoah*, which he won't even carry because he once met Claude Lanzmann at a party in Paris and then ran into him the next day and Lanzmann didn't remember who he was), meeting up with the prostitute from the beginning, ending exactly where it began. [Vogt says that the twentieth century is like *Reigen*, ending in Sarajevo, where it began: Joel might think that the war in Yugoslavia, which keeps getting ignored just after it happens, disappearing as it accumulates, is like Grenada, that his youth is ending near where it began.] Something—for me, of course, and for what I suppose would have to be called history—began in Königsberg: I feel as if I learned how to think—if not exactly about political philosophy—in Professor Whitlaw's classes; and Professor Whitlaw thought that Kant was the destination, then the origin, of Western—perhaps even of human—thought: the perfect species of philosopher [Kant thought of himself—as Professor Whitlaw would begin every semester—as a kind of Copernicus: as moving away from the center, so that the center could be analyzed], though I like the idea of a direct flight from Kaliningrad to Milwaukee, in being able to imagine that I am actually going in one direction from here. [Joel's secret fear, that something has begun in Germany, that he will have to come back, although to come back, he might think, to comfort himself, he will have to leave first.] And as for time, or history for that matter, I feel that time has saved me [the Jews of Badenheim, being loaded onto freight cars at the end of the book, are said to be "sucked in as easily as grains of wheat poured into a funnel," which must make at least some people think of sand in an hourglass], that this period of my life is about to end (this era within an era, within the span of my life, and within the spanlessness of history, history, which feels endless inside its particular shape, like a memory, as vague as a dream inside a lifetime). Once I called my father when my mother was in the hospital having her medication regulated, and I confused my sister with a woman I thought my father might be having an affair with; it was seven-thirty a.m. his time, and he said he couldn't talk, that an IRS agent was coming to talk about a client's audit, and seven-thirty seemed awfully early for that, and then I heard a woman's voice in the background, which turned out to be my sister's voice (she was there helping my father prepare): she got on the phone and said something like, "Oh, I was watching *Cabaret* last night and I was thinking of you." My sister has the tastes of a gay man, listens over and over to my mother's old Broadway musicals (my mother listens to Julio Iglesias and Placido Domingo, who sometimes sing songs from Broadway musicals; my father listens to radio call-in shows; when they drive up to the Mayo Clinic, they fight about what they should listen to; sometimes they fight about my mother's funeral: she doesn't want to have a funeral, to spite my uncle and his wives and my cousins, it would seem, who, she thinks, won't come to visit her until she's dead, but my father won't want to talk at all about my mother's funeral), and watches and rewatches *The Wizard of Oz* and *Cabaret* on her VCR. Harald is probably my idea of Sally Bowles: he always has outrageous, somewhat apocryphal, stories to tell; and the Canadian man at the market is my idea of the Christopher Isherwood stand-in, with a highly contemporary version of the Isherwood stand-in's famous detachment, by which I mean a sort of static hysteria; perhaps their Canadianness helps: Sally Bowles, in the book and then the play and its movie and then the musical and its movie, was English or American, and the Christopher Isherwood stand-in was also English or American; anyway: another reason to be able to leave, something else to cross off a list—"Have you met Sally Bowles?" my sister has asked, more than once, and included a "Say Hello to Sally Bowles!" on last year's birthday card (sometimes I yell at her when she asks about Sally Bowles)—errandlike. At the hospital, Hans-Joachim and I watched a Marlene Dietrich revue on television, which East and West German actors staged together and supposedly imperceptibly, though the East Germans tended to sing the German songs and the West Germans tended to sing the American and French songs, with everyone coming on at the end to hold hands and sing "Puff the Magic Dragon" in German (a hit here for Dietrich in the 1960s), as some display, it seemed, of a peaceful, united Germany, even though the song itself, of course, is about growing up, about longing for a lost past. A favorite show tune of my mother's is "Time Heals Everything," which I remember Bernadette Peters singing on the Tony Awards, which we used to watch every year to decide what shows we would see when we went to New York (though I asked my mother about it the other day and she didn't seem to know what I was talking about, hasn't listened to those records in years, usually just watches regular TV shows the few times I have seen her over at my sister's); my mother thought that Melissa, my girlfriend in New York, looked like Bernadette Peters. I remember when Melissa and I were still living together and my parents came to New York and we met them at the Palm Court for lunch: instead of a sandwich, my father ordered cheesecake with extra whipped cream and some of the whipped cream fell onto the floor and he scooped it up off the carpeting with his thumb and then stuck his thumb in his mouth; my mother ordered a roast beef sandwich and sent it back after chewing and then spitting out all the roast beef; my father said to me that the obvious out-of-town Jews at the next table, screaming and eating, were *"landsmen* of yours"; my mother said to Melissa, who is also Jewish, that she liked New York because it was so "Jewishy," by which she might have meant, at least in part, wealth. A few weeks before Melissa and I had gone to Sammy's Famous Roumanian Restaurant on the Lower East Side with her parents, who were visiting from Cleveland, and who wanted to go to a real Jewish restaurant; the mashed potatoes were made at the table by the waiter, who mashed them in a big bowl using, instead of butter, chicken schmaltz, bottles of which were on all the tables; by the time the boiled potatoes to make the mashed potatoes had come, though, we had already moved twice because Melissa's father said there was "a draft," each time taking our chicken schmaltz, like our glasses, with us; he had a video camera and filmed the waiter making the mashed potatoes because, he said, the chicken schmaltz reminded him of his childhood; her mother and father kept asking me questions at exactly the same time about what my "plans" were. Melissa and I talked about it later and it was all actually funny, and comforting (we were both hating living in New York, living in our apartment as though we were living in two separate apartments, merely occasionally bumping into each other), like, perhaps, a Quarter-Pounder with Cheese in the Tower of Babel; it will be strange to be around that kind of Jewishness again, which, like the "German" cathedral in Kaliningrad, is a sort of remnant, a ruin (I think about the children my sister never had, and about the children that I don't like thinking about probably never having, about their Jewishness, which would have been as vague as a rumor), but know that once again being around that kind of Jewishness as unconsciously as possible will be evidence of something—that I have survived. I feel like I am about to survive, that time, as it were, has saved me. (Time: history as well as memory, mixed, distinguishable but inseparable, like the voices in the clothes chute in my parents' house, which can carry in different ways, with the voice coming from the basement sounding louder than the voice coming from the den, with my voice, coming from my room, sounding softer than the voice coming from the basement and the voice coming from the den, as though the voices were inside my head; like the courtyard, with its derelict walls partly, though not entirely, obscured by the chestnut tree blossoms inside, or by leaves or bare branches from trees towering over it; like an outer life seeping inward and an inner life moving outward; like the picture windows in Brookfield, concealing, from a distance, the love and sorrow inside, but from another distance, revealing that love and sorrow, or both revealing and concealing, irritating and confounding, and comforting, like a constellation coming and going out of view; from where I am sitting, the line of houses on the Strassburger Strasse reminds me of a family lined up in front of its picture window.) I am tempted to leave the books by Jews here in Berlin, not to mention the books by Germans in English translation, which I have also been reading, though a little covertly, like pornography; they seem to belong entirely to this world, am tempted to bring home only the Mahler symphonies that I have been buying, which seem to be part of this world and of any other, which seem entire, models of everything.

The Opera-Lover and a Stranger

The baron's favorite composer was Richard Wagner, and his favorite Wagner opera was *Tristan und Isolde*; he also liked *Parsifal*, though wouldn't be able to see it in Berlin next week on *Karsamstag* or *Ostermontag* because he was going home to Bavaria for Easter (his father: the surviving son of a Junker who, along with his brothers and uncles and older sons, had all been a part of the plot to murder Hitler and were executed accordingly; his mother: the daughter of a Franconian count who had been an officer in the SS; sometimes, though not often, the two families—or, rather, his mother's family and what had survived of his father's family—got together, sat around a single enormous table). The baron had been brought up Catholic, had spent a lot of time with his mother's father (his father, who was a banker in Munich and of course had been brought up Protestant, was often away; his mother, who owned a boutique in Munich, had also often been away), had gone to an Upper Bavarian boarding school run by monks (he could still remember his Latin grammar). The third act, which was his favorite act of *Tristan und Isolde*, was about to begin, and he could barely wait because of the *Liebestod* at the end; the *Liebestod*, in fact, was his favorite piece of music, as it had been Thomas Mann's (the baron's favorite writers were Goethe and Thomas Mann; his mother's father, who lived with his parents, used to read Goethe out loud until his father stormed out of the room in boredom); he asked the stranger what time it was; it was only 9:20: good, he thought, I have ten, maybe even twelve, minutes (the wet night air was refreshing). Did you like the singing? he asked the stranger, and the conducting? His favorite conductor of Wagner was Furtwängler, though his favorite Ring—he had just bought the set on CD—was Karl Böhm's. Have you been to Bayreuth? asked the stranger (holding back his laughter). Mmm, said the baron, but not last year; last year I did a language course in the south of France (the baron was studying business in Berlin this year, would study business in Geneva next year, needed to improve his French). The stranger thought that the baron—he just knew he was a baron, or thereabouts—had the face of an eagle: a beautiful face, whole and delectable, also doglike, ugly; the stranger believed that this was an era of ugliness (he sat through hours of Wagner —which he thought of as sounding like the nineteenth century, or else as the sound of time itself passing, like an aural equivalent to a ruined neo-gothic church—disgusted at the way all the late-twentieth-century Germans were enjoying it; how they love it! he would think, fascinated and disgusted, as though the music itself were something vague, merely in the background {Vogt, who didn't mind mixing his metaphors, also described the twentieth century as "a butcher shop with jazz playing in the background"}), of shards and fragments, of fragments of fragments; the face, he decided, looking again, was stony, barely there at all. Do you like music? asked the baron (the baron was too tall, like a giant, but youthful, too youthful; his face was as smooth as a girl's). He decided to think about the question (this reminded him of an East German he knew who had recently been to the United States for the first time and had gone into a McDonald's and the cashier had asked him how he was and he stood there thinking, How *am* I? until another man in line told him to give his fucking order). Well, he said, I don't think I do. Then what are you doing here? asked the baron. Well I guess I sort of have to be here. Oh, are you a music critic? Well, no, not exactly. I love music, do you know Schopenhauer? he's a great German philosopher, he thought that music is to ideas what ideas are to things. (The stranger cringed, was charmed and irritated). And I suppose you think that Wagner is to music what music is to ideas. Oh, Wagner is the greatest German composer, I would see *Parsifal* twice next week, but I have to go home for Easter. (They were standing quite close; the stranger could see the peach fuzz on the baron's face, the rings under his eyes; they were bluish green eyes, jewellike, upsetting.) *Parsifal* in time for Easter! he thought, and *Lohengrin* on Good Friday!; Germans at opera houses instead of in church, aesthetics dressed up as theology. And Germans are to Europe what Wagner is to music? he asked. Oh, I don't know, said the baron, laughing, almost blushing. I do, thought the stranger. I do.

About shit: once I called my parents from the Krügers' apartment and my father answered and I said, "How are you?" and he said "Fine—now. Your mother crapped all over herself again last night and guess who had to clean it up?"; the closest I have ever felt to Annette was a night in Los Angeles, where she had come on a job interview, and we went to see some terrible Hollywood movie at a shopping center and she began to fart (I thought) and I didn't mind the smell at all, then actually began to move closer to it, but just after the movie, as I moved closer and closer, could feel her hair catching on my stubble, I heard the old man in the row in front of us complain about how "gassy" he had been all night (I never mentioned anything about it to Annette, who is horrified, or just disgusted, by such things, whose worst memories, she once told me, have to do with the single bathroom in her parents' house and the lingering reek of her father's shit, which she politely called "his smell"); Harald told me a story the other night about gay men who pretend they're babies and walk around in, and piss and shit in, diapers, said he was recently in a gay bar in Amsterdam and there was a diaper full of shit under the pinball machine; I was one of a few people chatting with the policemen outside the synagogue on the Rykestrasse the night after the *Täter* (what criminals get called in German; literally, I believe, "doers") had thrown their buckets of manure, though it turns out that the buckets hadn't been filled with just pig manure, as the papers had reported (only the Berlin papers seemed to cover that story; I did see an article about it in an English newspaper, though the journalist had gotten the street wrong and described the neighborhood as "elegant"; I thought of my East German linoleum and of the eighty-year-old woman, who, when I don't go to the store for her, walks there in bloomer-looking shorts and support hose); it had been, it turned out, only partly pig manure, had also been human shit, and piss (the two policemen had opposing, but also somewhat similar, styles: the first spoke clinically, scientifically, didn't use the words *Scheisse* and *Piss*, and the other, who had a heavier Berlin accent, was more crude, would only use *Scheisse* and *Piss*, but still managed to sound clinical, detached; no one asked them how they knew); as for me, I have come to think of shit as part of everything; I think of the definition of evil in the *Zohar*, in which the origins of all sin are said to come from Adam separating the Tree of Life and the Tree of Knowledge (I don't know how he separated them; by naming them perhaps), separating what should have been together. I worry about separating what actually *is* united, connected; take the Strassburger Strasse, named after the French and/ or German city, the place where Goethe went to university, and the site of the Jewish Skeleton Museum, which some SS officers set up during the war with the bones of Jewish "Communists" who had been murdered for the purpose, and the headquarters of ARTE, which is the new joint German and French cable TV channel and sometimes talked about as a symbol of a peaceful, united Europe, and the city where the European Parliament meets, with Jean-Marie le Pen and Franz Schönhuber as sitting members of the "conservative" minority (or of the "fascist" minority within a conservative one), next to the members of what is usually thought of as a socialist majority, and of course practically the street I live on, but it's indisputably one place, one—at least in some sense—idea. [What might also appeal to Joel, although he doesn't see the word every day: Weimar, which is much smaller than Strassburg and only goes by one name, where Goethe and Schiller lived and are buried side by side in the ducal sarcophagus; where the first German republic was founded; where the Bauhaus was founded; where Buchenwald was built, around, as it happens, the famous tree that Goethe loved to sit under, reminding visitors of Goethe and/or of the camp itself (Buchenwald means birch forest, though Goethe's tree was an oak, an anomaly), where, after the war, East German political prisoners were put and murdered in the still intact camp, where, for years, the official commemoration plaque only mentioned the Communists killed by the Nazis, where, after the fall of the wall and the erection of a new memorial mentioning Jews, skinheads attacked the memorial, burnt it to the ground, where new security forces, armed with guns and German shepherds, patrol the grounds, apparently to prevent any further attacks, with most people assuming that the guards had been guards of some kind under the Communists and/or are sympathetic to skinheads; one place.] As I have come to think of the past as a sort of confusion, I have come to think of Creation as something distinct, of a solar system rather than a universe, of an absent god, but of a world united in God's absence, united because of his absence. I should go to a concentration camp before I leave [going to a concentration camp for Joel, at this point: a pilgrimage and an errand; theological, if really logistical: a contemplation to be fit in], although, after watching all those movies, I feel as if I have already been to one, as if actually going, say, to Sachsenhausen would be like having been there and now watching it on TV (the last time I saw present-day Auschwitz on TV, I was changing the channels at Hans-Joachim's and saw Belgian schoolchildren on a field trip, wandering around near the ruined gas chambers at Birkenau, a few of them smiling for the camera). The playground at the Water Tower, where the Konzentrationslager Wasserturm had stood [officially, on Kolmarer—Colmar—Strasse], is popular with parents in the neighborhood, though the playground itself is unusually dusty, with nothing growing in it [as though salt had been plowed into the soil]; now, though, that the trees are in bloom, it seems altogether less barren, and the children, not to mention the parents, seem altogether happier; I have to walk by the playground to get to the gym, and when I walk by I try to hold all of it in my head: the children and the trees (the chestnut tree blossoms are cone-shaped, look like trees themselves, like trees within trees; I don't think we have that kind of chestnut tree in America, but am sure they have it in France); the concentration camp, the windmill, the Water Tower (which, I read in *Zitty*, was built in the middle of the nineteenth century with English and German money, which the magazine referred to as a collaboration), and the playground in the summer, after I am gone, then in the fall, after I am long gone; like different channels playing all at once, like a crowd of images. Here, outside the café, I feel outside the crowd inside, and outside the crowd of images of the playground, and of the courtyard, but not beyond them; above them perhaps, as if I were on a mountain.

[Karl Marx and Sigmund Freud, etc . . .]

Karl Marx, a baptized Jew like Gustav Mahler, was, unlike Mahler, baptized at his father's behest. (It could be argued that Joel's coming "to know" Germany, his tacit belief that to be a Jew you have to know Germany, which was the starting point of one kind of Jewishness—Joel's kind—and the starting point of the end of most other kinds, has been a baptism by fire; perhaps Joel and his stay in Germany has been in some way like Alfred Döblin [a Jew, who, like Aleksander Wat, became a Catholic late in life] and his trip through Poland in the 1920s after which Döblin wrote: "What an impressive nation Jews are. I didn't know this nation; I believed what I saw in Germany, I believed that the Jews are industrious people, the shopkeepers, who stew in their sense of family and slowly go to fat, the agile intellectuals, the countless insecure, unhappy refined people. Now I see that those are isolated examples, degenerating, remote from the core of the nation that lives here and maintains itself," with one tempting to change "that lives here and maintains itself" to "that died there, disappeared." Perhaps in some way Joel feels a variation of that about all the dead Jews, that their deaths were "different," but he's all mixed up, feels that the direction he is moving in is both forward and backward.) Everyone knows about Kafka's "Letter to His Father," but what about Marx's letter to his father? (An eerie moment, by our standards, in Kafka's letter: where Kafka refers to his father's irritation with Ottla, Kafka's sister, who had "a taste for associating with poor people, sitting together with maids," and who was later gassed—along with maids and professors and businessmen and peddlers and . . . —at Auschwitz.) Marx wrote his letter from Berlin, in 1837, at the age of eighteen, having recently recovered from what we would now call a nervous breakdown: "I was advised by a doctor to go to the country," he writes, "and so it was that for the first time I traversed the whole length [of Berlin] and went to Stralow." In Stralow (wherever that is; I haven't been able to find it in my atlas; perhaps it's in Poland now), as he recounts in his letter, he recovered by reading all of Hegel— by traversing its length, as it were—which changed his life, not to mention everyone else's. (A little less than a century later, Virginia Woolf came to Berlin with her husband Leonard Woolf, and her sister, Vanessa Bell, and *her* "husband," Duncan Grant, to visit Vita Sackville-West and her husband, Harold Nicolson, who was First Consul at the British embassy; they saw Pudovkin's *Storm over Asia*, afterward debating its anti-British overtones; Harold Nicolson apparently went with Duncan Grant and Vita's cousin, Edward Sackville-West, who was also in town, to gay bars; Virginia and Vanessa made the trip to Potsdam; none of them much cared for Germany or the Germans: Virginia—like Vanessa—found the people "unattractive" and upon her return had to spend three weeks "in bed" with a near breakdown.) It is of course interesting, if not exactly fruitful, to compare Marx's letter with Kafka's: in Kafka's letter, which is to some extent a series of accusations, Kafka eventually assumes the voice of his father and accuses himself; in Marx's letter, Marx, to some extent, is accusing art, and lyric poetry in particular, which distracted him from studying law, especially just prior to his "going to the country," and which at one point he refers to as "the dances of the Muses and the music of the satrys": he doesn't accuse his father of anything, though does ask him not to show the letter to his mother, unlike Kafka, who showed the letter to his father to his mother, who, in turn, never showed it to his father. Exactly one hundred years later, Sigmund Freud wrote a letter to the French Nobel Prize–winning "leftist," now often forgotten (except in East Berlin, where there is still a street named after him) writer Romain Rolland, as a sort of birthday present, it would seem, which ends with an insight into Freud's own father: the letter has to do with what Freud calls "a disturbance of memory," which he experienced on a trip to Athens in 1904, when he thought of himself, years before that, as somehow doubting the existence of Athens, though later deciding that he had never doubted it at all: "It is not true," he writes, "that in my school-days I ever doubted the real existence of Athens. I only doubted whether I should ever see Athens." It is a letter about travel, which Freud understands to be a kind of running away, and he understands the "theme," as he calls it, of Athens and the Acropolis as having something to do with the guilt the son feels toward the father. "Our father had been in business, he had no secondary education, and Athens could not have meant much to him." (What could the deleterious effects of lyric poetry, let alone the animating features of German idealistic philosophy, have meant to Marx's father, Heinrich, who, according to the *Jewish Encyclopedia*, was a "successful lawyer"? What did the Nazis, in Berlin in 1929, mean to Virginia Woolf, let alone Harold Nicolson, who, upon returning to England a few years later, promptly become a supporter of Oswald Mosley's British Union of Fascists? What might Kafka's letter to his father have meant to his sister Ottla? What would a trip to a concentration camp mean to Joel's father? to Joel's mother? "So those things really did happen," they might say to themselves, "those things we have heard about all these years." Joel's suspicion that the pictures of concentration camps are somehow more real than the camps themselves makes me think of a form of impiety—actually, piety in the name of impiety—found among Christian, and I believe, Jewish, gnostics, which had to do with changing sacred numbers, talking about eleven commandments, say, or thirteen apostles, makes me think of someone bringing a mirror into Plato's cave, of an image of an image replacing an idea. (It is interesting to consider the decade from 1822 to 1832, in which Beethoven finished composing his Ninth Symphony and died and Goethe finished the second part of *Faust* and died and compare that to the same decade a century later, in which Hitler finished writing *Mein Kampf* and Goebbels started complaining about "un-German" music getting played on the radio; Joel thinks that you can't separate—or that he can't separate—Beethoven from Goebbels, that things are next to each other, confusable, as though separating them would almost be a form of neurosurgery, that time is merely a form of distance.) Marx's famous remark about history repeating itself ("Hegel observes somewhere that all great incidents and individuals of world history occur, as it were, twice. He forgot to add: the first time as tragedy, the second as farce") would seem to be traceable to Hegel's *Lectures on the Philosophy of History*, which was published in 1837. (German history: a series of satyr plays; or one satyr play that won't end.) As for Walter Benjamin and the Germans: in the section of *One-Way Street* that deals with the German inflation, he writes: "The people cooped up in this country [he means Germans in Germany during the inflation] no longer discern the contours of human personality. Every free man appears to them as an eccentric. Let us imagine the peaks of the High Alps silhouetted not against the sky but against folds of dark drapery. The mighty forms would show up only dimly. In just this way a heavy curtain shuts off Germany's sky, and we no longer see the profiles of even the greatest men," having written just before that: "People in the national communities of Central Europe live like the inhabitants of an encircled town whose provisions and gunpowder are running out and for whom deliverance is, by human reasoning, scarcely to be expected." (Gershom Scholem read an early version, which Benjamin was then calling "A Descriptive Analysis of the German Decline," and wrote years later of his reading, "It was hard for me to understand what could keep a man who had written this in Germany.") As for Brecht, whom Benjamin considered, because of the way they both used the German language, as a non-Jewish Kafka (and whom skinheads think of as merely a Jew), here's what he had to say about the Germans to Benjamin, in 1938, in exile in Denmark: "The Germans are a dreadful people. It is not true that you cannot draw conclusions about the Germans from Hitler. In me, too, everything is bad that is German. What makes the Germans unbearable is their narrow-minded self-sufficiency. Nothing like the free imperial cities, such as the detestable town of Augsburg [Brecht's birthplace in Bavaria], ever existed elsewhere. Lyons was never a free city; the independent cities of the Renaissance were city-states" (which reminds me of Joel in the gay bookstore: after having bought Hans-Joachim his presents, he walked past the nonfiction section and noticed a book called *Queering the Renaissance*, though at first he had read it too fast, had thought it was called *Queering the Holocaust*). (Canetti thought of Kafka as untouched by Friedrich Nietzsche, whose refusal to distinguish between good and evil—merely good and bad, as in good or bad music—came to suggest to him a refusal to distinguish between life and death; Canetti on Nietzsche can sound like Nietzsche on Wagner, whose music Canetti once complained about to the non-Jew Alban Berg, who said, "You're not a musician or you wouldn't say such things.") As for Scholem and the Germans: one need only consider the name of Scholem's essay, which was more or less an open letter to a German reader, called, when published, "Against the Myth of a German-Jewish Dialogue" (Scholem as Karl Kraus, as Kafka might have had it: "What German-Jewish dialogue?), which seems, in the language of the law, to "speak for itself." As for Scholem on Hannah Arendt and the Jews: upon reading *Eichmann in Jerusalem*, Scholem wrote an open letter to Hannah Arendt, whom he had known years before (he ends a letter to Benjamin, written in December of 1939, with "Give my regards to Hannah Arendt!" who was in exile in Paris with Benjamin): "In the Jewish tradition there is a concept, hard to define and yet concrete enough, which we know as *Ahavat Yisrael*: 'Love of the Jewish People . . .' In you, dear Hannah, as in so many intellectuals who came from the German left, I find little trace of this." Scholem accuses Arendt, who referred to Rabbi Leo Baeck—or rather referred to people referring to him—as "a Jewish *Führer*," of what he claims is "well expressed by the English word, flippancy." (If you think that's bad, you should hear what Scholem, in a letter written to Benjamin in 1940, had to say about a Max Horkheimer essay on the Jews—and, through that, what he had to say about Marx's "On the Jewish Question"!) As for Joel and the Jews: he experiences a relief at saying, or thinking, unkind things about Jews, but then feels remorseful, guilty but technically innocent, as though he were libeling the dead. (I almost forgot: in that section about the German inflation, Benjamin worries about "ambiguity replacing authenticity"; it is interesting to think of Kafka's work as unambiguous, as being on either side of ambiguity—ontologically flippant; it is interesting to think of Joel's father at the Palm Court, with his thumb in his mouth; in the Kabbalah, devils are sometimes said to be four-fingered, thumbless; Joel's father: a Jewish devil; and of course, a baby.) Hannah Arendt, in her essay on Brecht, writing about Ezra Pound quotes Goethe: " '*Dichter sündgen nicht schwer,*' " by which she thinks he meant something sexual, perhaps: "light" sins, not political ones like Brecht's (or Pound's), whose sins, about which she is unambiguous, have to do with using his poetry to praise Stalin, which, as if necessarily, made it bad poetry, the writing of which is perhaps the poet's greatest sin. (Joel's sins: Joel thinks that time—whatever that means—has saved him; he thinks that his sins will become memories, fading out of, and then into, view, like constellations, as though remembering could take the shape of repenting. At this point I am tempted to refer to Oscar Wilde, to *The Importance of Being Earnest*, in which the following conversation occurs: "CECILY: I keep a diary in order to enter the wonderful secrets of my life. If I didn't write them down I should probably forget all about them. MISS PRISM: Memory, my dear Cecily, is the diary that we carry about with us. CECILY: Yes, but it usually chronicles the things that have never happened, and couldn't possibly have happened." In Kaliningrad, Joel might feel as if he had never been in Berlin; in Berlin, on his way back from Kaliningrad and on his way to the airport, he may feel that he never went to Kaliningrad, that Kaliningrad doesn't even exist; in Milwaukee, the whole European continent will have slipped away, as it started to do when he was changing planes in London; Joel, in Milwaukee, or actually in Brookfield, where Milwaukee is something of a durable rumor, will, like Alice at the very end of *Alice's Adventures in Wonderland*, be in "the after-time," with nothing left of his youth but a story to tell, unless he is like Moishe after he has stopped humming the cossack's melody, without even that.) As for Joel and poets, or artists, for that matter: when he and Irmgard were together in Munich at the Alte Pinakothek, something about a self-portrait of Dürer, which was next to Altdorfer's *The Battle of Alexander and Darius on the Issus* (Germans use the word *Schlacht* to mean both "battle" and "slaughter"; when Joel bought his sheets at the Kaufhof and ate lunch in the cafeteria, eating what has been the closest that he has come in the past few week to real German food, he ordered the *Schlachtteller*, which usually includes liverwurst and blood sausage and sauerkraut and boiled potatoes, conjuring up images, perhaps, of a battle between man and animals, and of the animals losing), made Joel cry. In Hannah Arendt's essay on Walter Benjamin, she mentions Benjamin's essay on Karl Kraus, in which Benjamin, in response to the question "Does Kraus stand at the threshold of a new age?" answers "Alas, by no means. He stands at the threshold of the Last Judgment"; she also reports what Benjamin said Brecht said about Karl Kraus: " 'When the age dies by its own hand, he was that hand.' "* It might seem that Joel's idea that he can go in two directions at once comes from Benjamin's idea that an origin (*Ursprung* in German, with *Sprung* actually meaning "jump" and *Ursprung* meaning something like "primordial jump") is more than just a beginning, but what Benjamin calls "a process of becoming and disappearing." (Actually, of course, Joel *is* going in two directions at once; he has, in effect, two tickets in his pocket, catching on each other, feeling, between his fingers, almost the same.) It could be argued that Benjamin's ideas about *Ursprung* came in part from Karl Kraus, whose poem, "My Ambivalence," has a second stanza that reads: "Where freedom became a meaningless phrase / I was a reactionary. / Where art they besmirched by their arty ways / I was a reactionary. / Backing up all the way to the origin." (In the first stanza, he had been a "revolutionary.") Or, as Kraus also put it (he wrote and wrote, tended to repeat himself): *"Das Ziel ist die Ursprung"*; the target is the origin. (Or perhaps it was the other way around, with the origin being the target; I can't remember.) There is an interesting pun in German having to to with the prefix *ur-: Urzeit* means prehistory and *Uhrzeit*, which is pronounced exactly the same, means time, as in time of day, which Germans, like other peoples, ask about in terms of possession (fun to imagine: Germans turning to each other all over Germany, asking each other if they have any prehistory; what I imagine Joel imagining in the gay bookstore: a book called *Queering Prehistory*). The prefix *ur* is quite often used with *wald*, or forest; Germans like to take vacations in the Bavarian Forest, which, unlike the replanted Black Forest, is an *Urwald*, monumen-

---

* Oh Jews! with their Torahs and Midrashes and Gemaras and their Arendts on Benjamins on Krauses: the flesh of their faith is this, commentaries upon commentaries (the spirit of their faith is a God without a name; or else an absent God), which reminds me of a line from the Gemara itself, a line which, among other things, is about the weariness of remoteness: "That which is about to be burned is like already burned." Or, in Isaac Bashevis Singer's paraphrase: "That which one is preparing to be abandoned is already abandoned." Which makes me think of Joel the other day walking down Unter den Linden, between the rows of park benches, on his way "home," and the buildings weren't there overshadowing the park benches, weren't there at all, had been forgotten in advance.

tally old. (Actually the Bavarian Forest is a forest-covered range of mountains that, in spite of the border, turns seamlessly into the Bohemian Forest; the columns at Tempelhof airport look like trees in a petrified forest, suggest something over with permanently, a perennial end.) Karl Kraus is himself something of an origin in Benjamin's sense of the word, as Brecht's remark demonstrates: Benjamin, let alone Kafka, or Scholem, or Canetti, or Arnold Schoenberg, or perhaps even Arendt, perhaps even Brecht, are not imaginable without him. Kraus himself often wrote about animals, often about dogs—"the heart of all hearts," says Kraus, in Benjamin's essay, "that of the dog"; (interestingly, on the subject of origins, this time of modern architecture: the aforementioned remark, or rather question, about Karl Kraus standing on the frontier of a new age was in fact a pronouncement of Kraus's friend, and *Landsmann* in both the Yiddish and German definition though more in the Yiddish one, Adolf Loos, who would seem to be the origin—again in Benjamin's sense of the word—of modern architecture; his ideas, expounded in his famous essay "Ornament and Crime," another title which speaks for itself, is like the First Commandment of modern architecture, one of the earliest examples of which would have to be Loos's own building across the street from the Imperial Palace in Vienna, which, because of its lack of ornamentation, the Viennese anthropomorphized—à la Joel—christening it "the building without eyebrows," which Joel, while recently reading his architectural guide, imagined defaced, with eyebrows scrawled on; I said "origin in Benjamin's sense of the word," though perhaps meant something else, with Lewis Carroll, or Ludwig Wittgenstein, who was Jewish and/or homosexual and/or not Jewish and/or not homosexual, in mind, because so many later buildings without any ornamentation were associated with [political] crimes: there is very little ornamentation, so to speak, on the buildings at Tempelhof, except for stone eagles above the doorways, which actually were built with their claws holding on to swastikas that were sandblasted off after the war, and there was even less ornamentation on Speer's Reich Chancellery; and there is certainly no orna-

mentation at all on the concrete housing blocks in East
Berlin's satellite cities, though there is a scheme under way
to paint them with intricately simple patterns that are meant
to suggest the kinds of patterns used in the 1920s on Berlin's
many socialist-inspired utopian housing projects); Karl Kraus:
the laundry that became the café. Which brings me to Zeno,
which will eventually bring me back to Kafka, who, of course,
also (to be crude about it) wrote about animals (one is
tempted to say that they both wrote about Creation), or
rather, to Zeno's paradox (Zeno's paradox: that an arrow that
has reached its target never reaches its target), which Kafka
mentions in his diary: "Zeno, pressed as to whether anything
is at rest, replied: Yes, the flying arrow rests." To expand, I'll
refer to the arrow as a moving object: the moving object,
which is in fact not moving at all, which is trapped between
its origin, in the conventional sense of the word, and its destination, which, in Zeno, is in fact its origin. There is something of Zeno's paradox in Lurianic Kabbalah's ideas about
creation, which have to do with what has been called "divine
contraction," or God's absence at the moment of creation, as
if it were nothing, rather than God, that had created the
world, thereby, according to one interpretation, bringing
forth creatures that were not perfect, that had nothing of
God in them, so they could perfect themselves by separating
the power of evil from the power of goodness: Creation: between nothingness and goodness. (In Berlin: Joel has learned
to separate and then not to separate, would seem to be moving away from nothingness. He should be mindful of the
other definition of evil in the *Zohar*, which has to do with
unifying that which should remain separate, which is, perhaps, the real moral of the story of Moishe and the cossacks
and one of the morals of the story of the city of Berlin, which
artificially became one city after having artificially become
two cities.) Canetti, like Kraus, often writes about animals, in
fact very much like Kraus; consider his remark, published in
1992, in which he imagines "a land in which every woman
has to spend time as a waitress and every man as a dog."
("Waitress" perhaps means prostitute: just as the dog was
Kraus's "emblematic beast," in Benjamin's phrase, so the

prostitute was for Kraus a sort of Everywoman; for Annette—
Joel's Annette, not the baron's—"prostitute" is a term of self-
abuse: the heroines of her novels, when they are wearing too
much makeup, denounce themselves in the mirror as prostitutes; Irmgard wears lots of makeup or none at all; lately
her pale blue eyes have begun to seem even paler, as pale as
her face; Joel's mother, who once wore lots of makeup, has
fought with Joel's sister, who often wears none; in restaurants, when her mother told her that she should think about
wearing darker lipstick, Joel's sister would grab her mother's
napkin and wipe off any lipstick she had on, once wiping so
violently—perhaps suggesting the religious police in certain
Arab countries who scrape off women's lipstick with razor
blades—that she dotted her lips with blood, bled into her
mother's napkin; Joel, arguably, thinks of women as waitresses, thinks of men as waiters, essential in their peripher-
alness but interchangeable.) Which brings us near to where
we began: to *Crowds and Power*, which begins: "There is nothing that man fears more than the touch of the unknown."
Canetti goes on to talk about "the unknown" almost as
though it were a forest, which, as you'll remember, was his
crowd symbol for the Germans, a sort of army; he ends his
book with an epilogue called "The End of the Survivor"
(Canetti—whose ancestors were expelled from Spain, and
who himself, after becoming, as it were, Germanized, fled
from Vienna—can seem to have survived, in the Jewish
sense, not just the century, but the millennium), with references to a forest, and to armies, and, indirectly (symbolically)
to literature (as represented by Stendhal); in a section called
"Crowd Symbols," which precedes the section on national
crowd symbols, he talks about the forest's "mutiple immov-
ability," which is why, at this point, a forest is most like an
army: it is like an army that has taken up a position—a fortress (names of German cities often end with the suffix *burg*,
which means "fortress"). In the same chapter, Canetti also
talks about sand, whose preeminent quality is its shifting
(wandering), as though it were something between a fluid
and a solid (who among you would begrudge the Jews their
betweenness? or begrudge me a description of the Jews as

"being between"?). I notice that he does not talk about mountains, which Germans can seem to treat as their crowd symbol (my crowd symbol for the Germans: slices of what get called *Kinderwurst*, which have a pink background and a brown foreground containing profiles of animals' heads, usually German shepherds, though sometimes pigs and, recently, dinosaurs), though, as Benjamin says in *One-Way Street*, deferring to what he calls "a witty Frenchman," " 'A German seldom understands himself. If he has once understood himself, he will not say. If he says so, he will not make himself understood.' " (Jews, of course, often seem to have "understood" Germany, with "Germany" in this sense usually meaning German culture; indeed, before they were driven out or murdered, just before, they had become its most recognizable custodians, with Kant and Goethe and Schiller becoming like holy books to be commented upon, attesting, perhaps, to the Jews' un-Germanness, to their almost-Germanness; mountains can only be climbed— "understood"—by a few; Jews, it would seem, tend to avoid mountains, except, of course, for Moses; the most famously anti-Semitic part of Europe has often been the Tyrol, where, for much of the millennium, there have often been practically no Jews whatsoever, Jews measured in tens; they never really came back after being expelled, except, I suppose, on vacation.) What especially fascinates Canetti about armies (and what can also fascinate other people about mountains, when they think of mountains as a kind of crowd) is their stubbornness, their staying put when (or, in the case of mountains, as if) commanded to do so. Canetti, at the end of the book, says of commands: "Their threat of death is the coin of power," with "coin of power" being a reference to his own discussion of the German inflation. (Zeno, in his way, commanded the arrow backward; a series—like a series of lovers, or a mathematical series, which Joel doodles at the market on his block of receipts while waiting to sell more and more—is commanded forward.) Another thing that probably horrifies Canetti about the forest is its cycle of life and death (a series of series; a moving forward and then back), of things living off of each other, which for him is the hallmark of being alive ("each of us has grown strong on the bodies of innumerable animals. Here each of us is a king in a field of corpses"). Death, in all its forms, is a kind of negative totem for Canetti; he refuses to accept it, connecting literature, which he would seem to place above everything else, to immortality; he talks about literature in the chapter called "Immortality" as an example, with Stendhal as an example of the example, of the living feeding off the dead but in such a way that, in Canetti's words, "the sting is taken out of survival." (The last remarks in *Crowds and Power* imply a distinction between power that is obeyed and power that is understood, "known," invoking the image of a command "deprived of its sting," of "sting," as it were, being killed; the final word in the German edition of *Crowds and Power*, of *Masse und Macht*, not including the footnotes, is *"beraubt,"* "deprived," though it can also mean "robbed.") At the end of Canetti's novel, *Auto-da-Fé*, the main character kills himself, was commanded, in some sense, by the writer, to die, though you really do have to make a distinction between the novel and his subsequent books. Canetti's dead hero (though of course he is really an antihero, negated, a hole burnt at the center of the book) was at one time called Kant and his book was called *Kant Catches Fire* (I can picture Joel first learning about this, but recently, after having decided to go to Kaliningrad, and not months before as he actually did; how his head swims as he reads! how the title *Kant Catches Fire* woos him!), though to avoid confusion between his hero and the famous philosopher, he changed Kant's name to Kien (on the advice of Hermann Broch, another Jew—yet more Jews! Jew upon Jew!—who wrote a novel set in the mountains, which he actually at one time was calling "the mountain novel," narrated by a doctor, who sounds like some sort of Jew himself, who is weary of the city and has gone to live in some Tyrolean-like village, which is about to succumb to a Hitler-like character, about to become a crowd), which means "pinewood." Kant—the philosopher—did in some sense actually catch fire a few years after Canetti sometime in the 1930s changed the name of his character; the cathedral where he was and is still buried, in the center of what had been Königsberg, but somewhat on the periphery of the center of Kaliningrad, was bombed of course, and its ruins—which is Kaliningrad's great concession to Königsberg and not at all like the ruined churches that dot, though I want to say "populate," German cities, but more like a trophy, like mounted stag antlers—look like a pile of charcoal. (Or so Joel thought, standing in the travel agency, looking up at the poster of the ruins {though he was also thinking about the Krügers' ruined living room, of "my" bedroom}: in fact, Königsberg's cathedral was being rebuilt—as Joel would later learn in the middle of the night while reading updated brochures that he found in the same East German envelope as his voucher—from the outside in, with German money, had become a perfect edifice {the inside, though, on the eve of Joel's *Sonderzug*, was still charred, or charred looking}; dwarfed, as the ruins recently were, by the ruins of Kaliningrad's Communist Party headquarters, a thirty-something-story concrete block with broken windows that birds like to fly into and out of {ruined because it was never finished, over with—as an interrupted dream is felt to be—before it had begun}; later Joel tended to forget about the rebuilding of the cathedral, he maintained it as ruined, though if I were going to write a book about the millennium as seen from this end, I, too, might try to keep the ruins {of the cathedral} in mind {remembering a thousand or so years, especially of Germans and their Germanness, I would dismiss Kaliningrad's ruined Communist Party headquarters as a speck, a brevity, as hermetic, as Kaliningrad's concession to itself}, would want to call the book *Kant Catches Fire*.) Joel's piece of amber, which is in the other pocket of his jean jacket and which the Germans call *Bernstein*, was originally (by which I mean millions of years ago) pine tree resin before becoming a jewellike fossil that washed up, possibly quite recently, on some Baltic shore; I like to think of Professor Whitlaw's shrug—or of Joel's grandfather's hands, for that matter—as preserved, as if in amber, as something left over from what feels like forever ago; I don't know how, if at all, Germans distinguish between *Bernstein*, meaning amber, which they seem to treat as a kind of gold, especially valuing the pale, gold-colored kind, and

"Bernstein," the Jewish name, so Jewish that it is almost synonymous with the word "Jew" (amber washes up in especially significant quantities near Kaliningrad, on what the Germans call "the *Bernstein* coast"; I tend to think of "Bernstein" as evocatively translated into English, as meaning "burnt stone"). (Kinds of distinctions: Kant's distinction between knowledge and thinking—his "greatest," according to Hannah Arendt, who was born in Königsberg, which at one time was associated with the Knights of the Teutonic Order, who had a monopoly in the Middle Ages on the trade in amber, before being associated with Prussia's kings, who were crowned in its cathedral, and which, as Kaliningrad, was associated with the Soviet Navy, who turned it into a fortress {or rather turned it, once again, into a fortress; actually East Prussia is synonymous with the word "fortress"—with Marienburg, with Frauenburg, etc., which were sometimes Polish between the time the Teutonic Order founded them and reconquered them, eventually laying the foundations for the state of Prussia, which, after coming up with the idea of a conscript army in the eighteenth century, became synonymous with the word "Sparta"; the Teutonic Order founded the fortress of Königsberg in the thirteenth century—the fortress itself, after Königsberg became more of a city and less of a fortress, housed the city's famous amber collection—and named it in honor of their ally, King—*König*—Otakar of Bohemia, with *berg*, which means "mountain," being, or at least sounding like, a corruption of *"burg"*}; the Kabbalistic distinction between the Tree of Knowledge and the Tree of Life; the distinction between the Königsberg of Immanuel Kant, which was a kind of Tree of Knowledge in the poetic sense, and Kaliningrad, which is a kind of Tree of Death {the Königsberg of the Knights of the Teutonic Order is distinct from Kaliningrad in many ways, though mostly in its scale; Kant's Königsberg was, for Kant, something of a fortress: he was famous, even notorious, for never leaving it}, but really I mean the distinction as contemplated by *Heimwehtouristen* who have already revisited, who are planning to return to Kaliningrad after having returned to Königsberg (the *Heimwehtouristen*'s "Königsberg" would be, architecturally, more or less Hannah Arendt's, not to mention Adolf Hitler's; Hitler, I imagine, often passed through on his way to or from his East Prussian, fortresslike, "Wolf's Lair," the ruins of which ended up in Poland, and which, since the fall of the wall, have become a German tourist attraction, easily reached from Germany by car), over, perhaps, the initial shock, between vacations; the distinction between the Jewish idea of redemption, which is communal and temporal, or anti-temporal, and logistical (where all Jews will be at the end of time), and the Christian one, which can be personal: Joel's idea about redemption would seem to be rather Christian; he "feels" saved, though his ideas about Christianity probably come from *Jesus Christ Superstar*, which his Reform Jewish summer camp staged the first summer he was there (he wasn't in the production, merely wrote up the program). Actually Canetti often writes about killing animals (which makes me think of the Tiergarten, where Joel first read *Crowds and Power*, and where Turks and Germans go on Sundays now that the weather is warm and grill without a permit, which is against the law in Germany and consequently thought of as typically Turkish and untypically German, and the cool green smell of the trees is interrupted by the smells of burning fat; here's what Vogt has to say about the Turks: "Turks and Germans have a lot in common. Just go ask some Armenians"); he can seem to be in mourning for them. Kafka was a vegetarian (somewhere, there is something about Kafka's father—whose own father was a butcher and who himself, like Freud's father, like Joel's father, could be said to have been "in business"—forcing him to eat meat), and so was Adolf Hitler (so is Joel, or has been in the last few weeks, except for his "slaughter plate"; walking down the Potsdamer Strasse, past a window of a Turkish restaurant featuring roasted sheeps' heads for the feast to end Ramadan, Joel thought that the charred heads, which were still covered with glands that looked black-and-white, charred and raw, were like birds' heads, and he also remembered his lunch breaks in New York, when people would flood out into the streets and eat shish kebab, the sight of which always turned his stomach; the meat smelled like burnt blood), and so

was Richard Wagner, who wrote pamphlets promoting veg-
etarianism but then went on eating meat with heavy French
sauces (at one point in his farce *A Capitulation*, which satirizes
Parisians starving to death during the Prussian siege of Paris,
a chorus appears and sings "rats with sauce! sauce with rats!";
Wagner—"wisely," according to one biography I read—
never showed *A Capitulation* to his then friend Friedrich
Nietzsche), who wrote anti-Semitic pamphlets and went on
using Jewish singers and Jewish conductors (Theodor
Adorno—father: Jew; mother: something else—compared
Wagner's treatment of Hermann Levi, who conducted the
premiere of *Parsifal*, to a cat playing with a mouse {cf.—I
would like to think—Kafka's "A Little Fable"}, whose final
opera, *Parsifal*, is a kind of ode to chastity, which he wrote
after a lifetime of infidelity; Nietzsche, who had broken with
Wagner by the time *Parsifal* was being composed, called it
Wagner's "satyr play." (To go back, before I finish, to where
I recently began: Marx and Freud and parents and children:
elderly parents at the mercy of their adult children makes me
think of a revolution, of aristocratlike, or factory-owner-like,
parents serving their peasantlike, or factory-worker-like, children; "parents and children" and their perennial conflicts
make me think of Germans and Russians, of a woman Joel
once saw in a television documentary: she was the woman
who served as the official caretaker of the ruined Königsberg
cathedral, a Russian woman who had been deported to Germany during the war as a slave laborer, where she learned
German, and who, after being liberated, had been sent to a
gulag, like many Russians who had been slave laborers in Germany, as a "collaborator"; now, in Kaliningrad, she likes her
job of sweeping out the ruins, she said, likes chatting with
the German tourists, doesn't hold grudges {the Hungarian-
speaking Jewish Slovak held grudges, spat, in spite of his
partly missing tongue, at the first waves of post-1989 German
tourists, but never stopped smoking, which was his passion,
and which he had learned to do at his labor camp, where he
was interned before being sent to his first concentration
camp and where cigarettes, like in West Germany after the
war, were like money; he never talked about the labor camp

and the concentration camps, would talk about cigarettes, about the cigarettes he got to smoke after the Americans had liberated him); Joel imagining the deaths of his parents, which he used to do as a child on Saturday nights, imagining his parents getting into a car accident on their way home from dancing somewhere, feels himself falling in all directions, and then landing, stinglessly, and grown-up, but then somehow "next," almost dead himself; or: he feels like a dog finally freed from its very long leash, but still dragging the leash around with him, pulling and pulling, waiting to be pulled back.)

It really is cold! (I feel drunk and cold.) The sidewalks are covered with chestnut tree blossoms that have fallen off just after blooming, the air, after days of being clear and warm, is once again filled with coal smoke; inside the café, of course, it's too hot, and the crowds make it hotter; I can't get something from Mahler's "The Song of the Earth" out of my head: the very end, with Christa Ludwig—in my recording ["Where am I going? I'm going, wandering in the mountains"]—singing, in what sounds like a murmur and a wail, about the spring (I went to the library to look up the words), and about eternity (the last word, repeated over and over, is *ewig*—"eternal"), about a spring that goes on forever; she has just said good-bye to her rather mysterious "friend," the friend whom she is waiting for at the beginning of the movement (called *Abschied*, "farewell," which, Kurt told me, is the most meaningful word in the German language; I told him that I was leaving, going to Kaliningrad and then to Milwaukee, leaving for good; he told me that I would have to come by for a real farewell, asked what I was going to do with my apartment, which he said he would like to use as a studio so he can get away from Sabine's children), who, even as she is saying good-bye to him, would seem never to have shown up, who may indeed be imagined. **Someone in the Park [the Writer]** Marcel Ophuls's movie *The Memory of Justice* begins where it ends: with Yehudi Menuhin—who lived in Berlin as a child prodigy in the 1920s, when Berlin was the undisputed capital [center] of the musical world, and who was the first well-known Jewish artist to return to Germany after the war, in the 1950s—back in Berlin again (at the beginning he is obviously rehearsing something that at the end he is obviously playing). The movie is "about" the Nuremberg Trials (when I went to the library to look up the words to "The Song of the Earth," I also read in the transcripts of the Nuremberg Trials), but it is also about other atrocities, about Algeria and Vietnam, and it's about Ophuls (Marcel) himself: along with the lawyers and the judges and Albert Speer and Daniel Ellsberg, he interviews his wife, who is a blonde German woman: he films her reminiscing about being in the Bund der deutschen Mädels and recalling neighborhood Jews disappearing, and eventually films her asking her husband to make musicals instead of documentaries like the one he is making. The phrase "the memory of justice" comes from Plato (I read on the back of the video box), refers to his idea that each of us carries around what sounded to me like a primordial memory of what is "just"; the movie's real themes, perhaps, are injustice and forgetfulness (in German, the word for "to think" {*denken*, with the past participle *gedacht*} and the word for "memory" {*Gedächtnis*}, both personal and communal, "political" {as in the Gedächtniskirche}, can sound, almost certainly are, related; I get them mixed up in my head, as if a memory were always something formal, political, as if something political, formal, were whimsical, imagined). Real life—as symbolized by Yehudi Menuhin, and by Ophuls himself—can seem to end where it begins, with Menuhin in Berlin and with Ophuls with Germans, as if what had happened in Europe had been a kind of bloody interlude (in spite of the fact it would seem to be repeating itself—creating interludes—elsewhere), though of course "real life," in this case, is also a symbol—for art, it would seem. One night last week, I had a real-life *La Ronde* experience: I was at the café, talking to one of the waitresses (she is East German, was telling me about wearing her dead mother's crucifix to school and the teacher told her to take it off and she refused and so she was expelled from high school and had to become a bricklayer—she had wanted to become a painter—and now at the age of twenty-nine is going to night school so she can graduate from high school so she can go to college and become a curator), then I talked to the owners of the café (who, I thought, as I think of the men I see at the gym, in other eras would have been peasants or soldiers—or, perhaps, in the 1920s, prostitutes—or would have certainly been factory workers and then soldiers, and who, now, after having been squatters, got money from a West German brewery and an Italian coffee distributor to improve their "café"), then to the new owner of the building (who is from Flensburg in northern Germany and has a father who bought the building for him, speaks his English with the same flat *a* that people use where I grew up, was wearing a Ralph Lauren shirt, is my age, or a little younger, and tolerates the café owners but plots behind their backs, seems to confide in me because of my Ralph Lauren shirts, which cost about three times more in Germany), then to his friend, who was a baron: the man who owned the building left after complaining about the food at the café, and the baron and I talked about the member of the Hohenzollern family who had been spying for the Stasi; he liked the photograph accompanying an article about him in an East Berlin tabloid that showed the Hohenzollern fortress in Swabia on a mountain overlooking the Danube River, with its punny caption (*Spitzel* means "informer" and *Spitze* means "peak"); he had studied philosophy and is now a banker and talked about Heidegger, who lived in a village not too far from the Hohenzollern's fortress (and came to confine himself in his village, I think, like Kant in Königsberg), and about East German laziness and West German philistinism and German laziness and East German philistinism; the night ended where it had begun, with the bricklayer-turned-waitress bringing him the bill, which I paid (or pretended to pay; I went in, paid Harald instead, didn't have to pay at all). I stayed on until closing, which I have regularly done (nights at the café, which last until two or three or four, end like nights at college did, elementally, in a sort of drunken collapse). I have to get up at five on Friday morning and I may just come here on Thursday night, when Harald will be working, and then stay up all night, drinking grappa and coffee (Harald's favorite drink) and listening to Joni Mitchell (Harald's favorite, because she's Canadian), though the owners have talked about closing early because of Hitler's birthday, which, presumably, like other German holidays, and, of course, like Jewish ones, begins the night before (because the café used to be a hangout for *Autonomen*, they sometimes get threats from skinheads, unlike the fancy-seeming tapas restaurant next door, which gets threats from *Autonomen*), though it's supposed to get much warmer this week (I'm not sure what I'll do this week, except come here at night and lazily shop for presents; no packing, which would be something between un-necessary and impossible, like cleaning up), might be too crowded to be attacked. I have spent the last few weeks in crowds—at the market, of course, and on the S-Bahn and U-Bahn, in the travel agencies, in record stores, in taxis, which I have been often taking, feeling that I have nothing else to spend money on (my pockets are filled with wads of Deutschmarks), and even at the video store, which is small enough to make the few people who come by in the afternoon seem like a crowd; I drink Diet Coke even when I am not at the market, and cups of coffee here at the café (they don't have Diet Coke; tonight I drank two grappas and coffee, and then just vodka), or elsewhere; sometimes after Irmgard has left my apartment, or after I have left her at Hans-Joachim's apart-ment, I go out to clubs: I have been to one of those East German nostalgia parties (which are sometimes called *"Ostalgie"* parties, though the one I went to was called *"1978: es war ein schönes Jahr"*), where everyone dresses up as Young Pioneers or *Volkspolizei* and smokes East German cigarettes and you can buy drinks with old East German money (I have been sometimes smoking a lot, buying cigarettes from the Vietnamese at the market, or from the Vietnamese husband and wife—or sister and brother, or whatever they are—who sell around the corner from me on the Prenzlauer Allee, across the street from the new asylum seekers' home; I often lose patience with the graciousness of the Vietnamese, which can seem so out of place in Germany, and wretched, like dusty palms under all those oak and chestnut and linden trees, all that loud high greenness; sometimes I think that they look like spiders, moving in and out between the columns at the market, and especially the other day on the Prenzlauer Allee, when the husband and wife were chasing some boys who really did look like Bosnians, screaming, it would seem, that the boys had stolen something or other, moving along like tufts of black hair); I have been to the famous Techno disco across the street from the Luftwaffe building, of which, especially when the sun is coming up, there is an unusual view, like the kind you get in New York when a skyscraper has been torn down and nearby skyscrapers suddenly look different, as new as if they had just been built; I went with Harald to a bar for gay East German squatters in an unrenovated bunker (there were gay skinheads the night I was there, which would seem to be, aside from everything else, oxymoronic, but is in fact, I was told, sincere, that they hate all the people the regular skinheads hate, except themselves); and, especially after the market, when I really can't think about anything but sex, I have gone to porno movies, which have been packed, as—according to Harald—they should be on rainy weekend afternoons; at the porno theater that I have been going to half of the movies are for homosexuals and half aren't, with each movie—or rather TV show, because all of the movies are shown on video screens—in its own little theater, like Hollywood movies at a shopping center, or you can go to a main room, where people sit on motorcycles, and watch all the movies at once on a row of video screens that looks like some sort of technically advanced comic strip; the movies for heterosexuals usually only initially have a premise: the man is a businessman and the woman (or women) is (are) his secretary (ies), or the man is a burglar and the woman is, I guess, the home owner, but then there's just a lot of fucking; the gay movies have a recurring, or more complicated, premise: one had men about to be shipped out to some war somewhere, fucking each other while repeatedly watching news about the war on TV (though the news of the war also looked like a porno movie); one—the one with the young boys—was filmed in Prague but was supposed to be taking place in a turn-of-the-century German schoolroom, with a picture of the Kaiser above the chalkboard that the boys were supposed to look at while the "teacher" took down their pants and spanked them (that was the European one; most of the gay movies seem to be set in Los Angeles, or at least seem to have been shot there; the actors all look like the kind of people you see in line at the discount gourmet grocery store on Santa Monica Boulevard, who are all assumed to be porno stars, or else actors); one was from the 1970s, with funny disco music and none of the men wearing condoms; one was very high tech, with a set that looked like a Japanese restaurant and a man, alone, masturbating while looking at a photograph of himself. One day at the market, I talked about the porno movies with a prostitute I know; he isn't always a prostitute; or rather, he wasn't the night we spent together last fall; he is a Viennese medical student working his way through school here in Berlin as a prostitute (he certainly seemed to have a lot of money that day at the market; he was wearing one of those very expensive horsehide leather jackets that some people wear here and that look as thick and shiny as a piece of granite), about which he was perfectly frank when we met at a café (I was reading a Joseph Roth novel, and we started talking); over dinner, which he paid for, he told me stories about his father's anti-Semitism and his mother's nervous breakdowns, about his Croatian grandfather's Nazism and about his half-Jewish grandmother's baptism the week after the Nazis marched into Vienna; actually, during the night we spent together, I felt like the prostitute: he kept fondling my chest, which feels hard and flat from all those sets of bench presses but which was flabby enough back then to be treated as women's breasts; in bed, we talked about Joseph Roth and Karl Kraus and he wanted me to fuck him, which I didn't really want to do, and couldn't have done in any case, with a black condom, which might have looked black when I had it on (I never got a hard-on; he did, masturbated himself right away while sucking on one of my nipples), like something from a porno movie—it occurs to me now—with a minstrel show as its premise, and which he had waiting in his book bag; afterward, he gave me money for cab fare (he lived in the far south of West Berlin, in a loft, which I didn't even know they had here); "this is my fantasy," he said, more than once after he came and I couldn't fuck him and we were just lying there with his head on my chest. He is tall and hairless, looks like a girl (the waitress at the café, whom I had a sort of romantic moment with once on the landing of the apartment building next door, though the building is now locked from the inside because it's next to the synagogue, looks like a boy, except for her breasts; she is as tough and impatient as an eighteen-year-old boy). I especially wanted to talk about the 1970s porno movies with the prostitute (the Canadian man told me later that the Viennese medical student was a prostitute, and I told him that he was a Viennese medical student) because of a connection I had made between UFA movies, especially the ones from the late 1930s, with all those soon-to-be Wehrmacht—or worse—extras, and the Yiddish movies from Poland that are always being shown at movie theaters in West Berlin, made in the 1930s with casts that presumably mostly died in the camps, and those '70s porno movies, with casts of people presumably partly, or mostly, dead of AIDS: I wanted to talk about kinds of doom, which the prostitute, that day at the market, didn't want to do, deferring to the fact that he was Viennese, that he couldn't take anything seriously; before walking away, he said he would check back sometime to see if I got in any pornography (we spoke, both times, in English, because I couldn't really understand his Viennese accent): he had noticed the boxes of videos and had been wondering if there was any pornography ("those wonderful little dirty movies you Americans are so good at"), hadn't noticed me at first; "So you're still here," he said, instead of "hello." The last time I visited Hans-Joachim, one of the nurses came in to ask him if he wanted to see "the movie," which Hans-Joachim said was a safe-sex porno movie starring people who are sick—some, he said, very sick—with AIDS, which occasionally gets shown in the library of the AIDS wing; he said he didn't want to see it again, though the nurse said he should because it would cheer him up. At the market, people hurrying past the TV set sometimes blushed at the Holocaust documentaries, as if, it occurred to me, they were walking by so fast that all they saw were the naked bodies, thought, for a second, that they were walking past porno movies, which is sort of what happened to me one day in the video store when Peter had been playing *Night and Fog* and I walked in and didn't pay much attention to the television set and out of the corner of my eye saw a man's penis and for a second really didn't realize what it was (it was a pile of dead bodies, with a spread-eagled corpse at the top), felt very peculiar after I did realize, ran out suddenly into the winter air (after leaving the porno theaters, which I do just after coming into my hand and rubbing the come into my thigh, I feel relieved and disgusted, like I do after eating at McDonald's). *Where are you from, the baron had asked him, eagerly, having heard something in his accent. (He is walking, has walked farther than he thinks, walks from the darkened street into the park, which is also dark, and green, as if the new leaves were pieces of darkness.) He had thought of the end of* Badenehim 1939, *when an old rabbi shows up in a wheelchair just in time to be deported. (" 'Where are you from, Jews?' asked the rabbi as people used to ask in the old days. An ancient grief glazed his eyes.") From elsewhere ("anderswo"), he had said. Tonight at the opera he had met no one. After the opera, walking and walking, he could feel sand from the construction sites between his teeth, inside his shoes, can smell it in the park; it is everywhere, he thinks, like a mist.* Today at the market, just as I was packing up, an English journalist came over to buy videos; we talked about Jews and movies and Germany, and he said that before the wall fell half of the Jews in West Berlin had been working for the Stasi and the other half had been working for the Mossad, and that nearly all of the few Jews left in East Berlin had been working for the Stasi (I thought of the teenage girls and their hate mail, then thought of extracurricular activities at a German high school, of an Informers

Club); "Really?" I said, as though I believed him. *Europe, he has thought, a continent without deserts, but with dust, with salty mud. "I shall call thee dust."* Today, just after watching porno movies, I went to the gym, which felt like a parody of a porno movie, with the men who seem to be unemployed repressed homosexuals eyeing the men who seem to be employed and contentedly homosexual, or else unconsciously dancing to the terrible music (German *Volksmusik*, the same Prince album played over and over again, Marilyn Monroe's greatest hits, *Sgt. Pepper's Lonely Hearts Club Band*, once *Carmina Burana*) and flaunting their outfits, which are invariably covered with logos from real American colleges, or made-up ones ("North American University," "Football College"); with their clothes off, or in their outfits, which always include a backward baseball cap covering up their shaved or mostly shaved heads, it is hard to tell the regular unemployed people from the ideologically unemployed ones, which is to say, the factory workers from the skinheads and the *Autonomen*, though of course even the factory workers, or whatever they are, or were, shave their heads; the other day some American students showed up, talking among themselves about Prague (they are students on an exchange program at Humboldt University, and "hang out," one of them told me, in Prague on the weekends, but I thought of them as versions of the Slovak prostitutes, moving up this way; at first I didn't talk to them, which felt silly, until I started talking to them, which felt sillier, like I was pretending to be one of them, or like I wasn't); they all had outsized, imbecilic faces, like Hapsburgs, seemed garishly young; also today, a famous *Stasi-Spitzel*, an ex-friend of Kurt's, showed up for his training session: he had been in America, Kurt had told me, and at the gym was wearing Top-Siders instead of tennis shoes (he was a famous painter before becoming a famous informer and is now supposed to be ghostlike; I met him a few times before everyone found out that he had been working for the Stasi, then he and Kurt had their falling out, though about something other than his informing, and I didn't really say hello to him anymore, didn't say hello to him at the gym; on my way out, I asked one of the girls at the juice bar if she could recognize that man in the funny shoes; she said that he was the new *"Sportgast,"* which is the gym's euphemism for member, and I told her that he was also the famous *Stasi-Spitzel*, Uwe Vogel, which didn't ring a bell until she asked one of the owners, who is from West Germany and who at first also didn't recognize the name until I told him that Uwe was a painter—"Right," he said, his face lighting up; he asked me if I knew Uwe personally and I said I didn't, really). I only have four more days at the gym—sixteen more sets of this and twenty-four more sets of that, three hundred and twenty more sit-ups: there's something consoling, or perhaps just habit-forming, about so much counting, like following along with some inner outer clock; when I study that piece of amber, I sometimes try to count—or at least try to keep track of—the shapes, or the kinds of shapes, inside it, like keeping track of the trees and windows in the courtyard. *The air is thick and warm, but cooler in the park. Yes, he thinks, the cold is finally past; at the opera, the air had been stifling, he could smell the pyorrhea of the man sitting next to him, the onions and cigarettes of someone else nearby, the dust on the seats, but he had made it through—six hours! And now the walk feels good, as if he were recovering from a sickness, as if a fever had just broken. ("To listen to Wagner," he remembers from* Nietzsche Contra Wagner, *"I need pastilles Gérandel.") The second act—that long famously doomed seduction scene (is it, he now wonders, supposed to go on for years? like Amfortas's death scene in the third act?; he couldn't spend the day before refreshing himself, couldn't, as was his habit, read the program just before; he couldn't fix his eyes on one more German word)—had been the best, with all those television sets, and pictures of Kundry and then of other women dressed as Kundry, and then of those women dressed as something else, all flickering back and forth while Kundry sang offstage, (images of images, he thinks [of images]), until Parsifal finally "resists" and the TV sets are smashed. But now he doesn't really want to think about it; he is tired. Wie sind wir wandermüde, he remembers from the Eichendorff poem that Richard Strauss had set to music:* Wandermüde, *"tired of traveling." Germans! he thinks (he is sick to death of them) Why not the French instead?; he played, thought of the end of* Un Amour de Swann: *to think that I have wasted years of my life on a people who, really, after all, aren't my type. (The word "German" and the word "dead" are practically interchangeable, he had once told somebody, a Germanophile—even the word itself sounds antique, dead—is merely a necrophile.) [Joel has sometimes imagined not running into Professor Whitlaw in Madison, but into, perhaps somewhere in Chicago, an old counselor from his Jewish summer camp who would have been, perhaps, a rabbi, who would have arranged for him to teach English in Israel to Russian immigrants, that he would have spent the last few months—though it seemed like years, like decades—not leaving Israel.] He thinks of Richard Strauss's* Jugendstil *villa in Garmisch built with the money Strauss had earned from* Salome, *which he had once driven past: he thinks of it as a tombstone on the grave of German music (or of Germanness, or of German Romanticism, or of Germany itself; he knew it was a conceit, but he couldn't be bothered to distinguish between them), built in advance, of German music as its own elegy; again, he thinks of Nietzsche: all true, all original music, is a swan song. (He thinks of Nietzsche what Karl Kraus thought of Freud {Kraus on Freud: "Psychoanalysis is the disease of which it claims to be the cure"} or thereabouts, thinks of Nietzsche as both a disease and its cure.) He thinks of an Alpine cemetery he once saw built on a slope, of wooden crosses spreading and dipping, like a field of something. Germans and their mountains: he thinks of Kafka's "The Bucket Rider," of the ignored, dejected "I" in a vain search for coal, giving up at the end, riding off forever into something called "the Ice Mountains"; a Jewish Hell, he thinks, but a German Heaven. (Jews. He thinks of something Professor Whitlaw used to say about Thomas Aquinas, that Thomas Aquinas had made Aristotle safe for Catholics; he thinks of Gustav Mahler's adagios and Wagner's* Liebestod—*Mahler makes Wagner safe for Jews, he decided. Jews. He thinks of Kafka's aphorism—or quip, or commandment—about getting tied up by robbers near a captain's fire; robbers and captains, he thinks, Germans and Jews, or Jews and Germans; he thinks of absent, stolen, Jewishness and*

of incomplete—stolen, too—Germanness, of days of judgment, of traces
of days of judgment, like a calendar from a distant year that some-
one has printed in advance. He thinks of Zeno's arrow in its target never
having left its bow, like a German-speaking Jew in a German city,
German in every way, but still reeking of the ghetto; like the Jewish-
German finding his way back, though really forward, to the ghetto.
"Here" in drag as "over there," he thinks; and also finished off, over
with, now in drag as then; over with, pieces among other pieces; a desert
that was once a jungle; he thinks of the Liebestod *and of Strauss's "Four*
Last Songs," which he loves, and especially of the last of the "Four Last
Songs," with the lyrics by Eichendorff, which he loves most of all: after
the end, he thinks, like before it: an image of the end). Germans and
Jews, he thinks: stuff for archaeologists (though the archaeologists of
this period, he considers, would also have to be something else—musi-
cologists, perhaps.) As if I were counting faces: these are my mother
and those are my father and that one and that one too are you
and those small ones are he and that big fan of a one is
. . . and that other one, which isn't really a shape, but light bounc-
ing off another shape, could be, perhaps; leaves and windowsills
and ashes and shoelaces; rings and clouds and antennae and
specks and the holes, like doorways [doors, bridges, courtyards];
the courtyard is like the amber and the amber is as big as a small
fist, like a child's heart [buttons]. *(Joel would think of the robbers'*
ropes and the captain's fire as each other, simultaneous, as if the fire
were burning off the ropes, as if he were about to be freed.) Wagner's
music (or rather the pleasure it gives) and Wagner's Jew-hating have to
be separate, he thinks, if the music is to give pleasure. He thinks of other
things, related but actually separate: of a scene at a flea market, when
a wheelbarrow full of old Reichsmarks was knocked over in a spring gust
and the "money" blew across over a parking lot full of Gypsies, of the
Gypsies scattering, knocking each other over to get at the money; of a
poem by T. S. Eliot—whom he thinks of as English rather than Amer-
ican, and as a certain kind of English rather than another, as
European—that reads, "The worlds revolve like ancient women gather-
ing fuel in vacant lots"; he thinks of himself, picking up books and

newspapers off a floor; he thinks of something he read in a newspaper about a mass grave in the Ukraine filled with Jews shot by a Sonderkommando *[he also thought:* Sonderkommando, Sonderzug, *and* Sonderkonzert, *which is how a concert given in Berlin by Kurt Masur and the New York Philharmonic was advertised], opening up after the wettest spring in half a century, of Ukrainians, with bags of "coupons" like wheelbarrows of Reichsmarks, rummaging through corpses, looking for gold fillings, of corpses littered with coupons. What do they have in common? he thinks, except that they are filling up my head; he thinks again of Eliot, thinks that America is to Europe what Europe already is to itself—a contradiction, a devolution; he thinks of a burnt-out sun and of clouds of dust, orbitless.* My heart is full! I feel, really, that I have made it through, or that I am about to make it through, to have survived! I feel like I am doomed to survive—like an American who doesn't know any better, or perhaps like the Jews, who, in spite of everything, are still around, know too much; I feel that knowing too much and knowing nothing at all belong together, as if knowledge were a fuel and the absence of knowledge a spark. *Kinds of Jews: "Jews are different from other people but, in reality, they are most different from each other" (according to Canetti, who got to be both kinds of Jew, as well as the third, fallen, kind). (Americans aren't like other people, though other people are becoming more and more like them.) (Homosexuals are just like other people, but more like themselves than anyone else; heterosexuals are merely everyone else—praiseless, in this one respect, and, as they themselves would have it, blameless.) (Germans, in their way, aren't like one another, though they used to be more or less like other people; now they are not at all like other people and, by other people's standards, very much like one another: it is Auschwitz that has unified the Germans.) (Germans and Jews, especially German Jews, are sometimes talked about as being like each other because of what would seem to be their flair at making money and their love of— hoarding of—books, as though the Holocaust were the story of a twin killing his brother, as though it were a farce, or a fairy tale; Joel thinks of himself as somewhat German, doesn't know what else to call the time he has spent in Germany.)* I felt this the other day at the library on

Under den Linden: between reading about the Nuremberg Trials (I read about the doctor, Frau Doktor Oberheussen, mentioned in *The Memory of Justice*, who had volunteered to be a camp doctor at Ravensbrück, where she amputated women's limbs as part of a series of bone-regeneration experiments, and who after the war became a pediatrician in Schleswig-Holstein) in the reading room on the first floor (also reading about Königsberg in old guidebooks found in pre-1945 card catalogues, which are actually large books with vertical lines, like accounting ledgers) and reading about Gustav Mahler (and about German music in general, browsing through the bound volumes of German music journals that stop in 1941 or -2 or -3 and start up again with slightly different titles and different typography in 1949 or 1950) in the reading room on the second floor (the concrete walls on the first and second floors were covered with painted-on grout, like at Alexanderplatz's U-Bahn station, and with strange dots that I supposed were meant to suggest the "roughness" of the stone—looking dappled, I thought; there was the same kind of strange linoleum in both reading rooms, thick, carpetlike, vaguely resembling the indoor-outdoor carpet my parents have on their screen porch, though of course very East German, half-Soviet and half-German; two kinds of *Mischling*), I went to the bathroom on the first floor, just to go to the bathroom, but then lingered, waited for a stall to open, then I went in and closed my eyes; the man undid my shirt (he smelled of food and sweat and soap), moved his hands over my chest, then sucked my cock until I came in his mouth, then he kissed me on the mouth and I tried to leave but noticed that he had locked the stall; he opened it for me, and I left, with my pants pulled up around my thighs and kept in place with my elbows; my pants slipped down as I washed my hands and cock, then I pulled my pants up and rinsed out my mouth, ran my hands over my hair, thought, among other things, that my hair had lost its bristly feeling and that I should get it cut before I leave, then went up to the second floor, to the books about music: everything, I was thinking, on my way past the dappled bricks, *all* things (I was shaking; my head was throbbing with things, rattling); later, too, walking up Unter den Linden, between the rows of park benches, I thought of everything in the more specific, German, sense, of Kant and Hitler being born on practically the same day, separated, this year, by a Holy Saturday, between the day Christ was crucified and the day he was resurrected, by what I guess you could call his absence: I walked and walked, until I reached the empty apartment. *Pieces of pieces, clouds of dust, with each piece unto itself, a kingdom of ends. Nietzsche, he remembers, like Kant, thought of himself as a Copernicus, as forcing people to get rid of what they had always taken for granted; what Nietzsche proved: that the earth revolves around a burnt-out sun, that the world is ablaze with unnatural light.* It had rained that morning but then the sun had come out, and the apartment was filled with light filtering through the trees; it looked whitish green, like moonlight. *He can't—or won't—get something out of his head:* "O alter Duft aus Märchenzeit, berauchest wieder meine Sinne," *"O, old odor out of fairy tale times, intoxicate my senses once more": so awkward—ridiculous in fact—in English; it's worth learning German just for that, he has thought, knows. [The line comes from Schoenberg's* Pierrot Lunaire, *a song cycle written for soloist and chamber ensemble with a text taken from a book of short poems written in French by the Belgian Albert Giraud, translated into German by a man with the rather comical name of Hartleben—"hard life"; the character Pierrot is taken from Italian commedia dell'arte, and in the recording indirectly referred to above, played by an English ensemble, bought on cassette in Prague, with new Czech, as opposed to Czechoslovak, or Czecho-Slovak, crowns; the soloist is not meant to sing, but half-speak, half-sing, in what Schoenberg called a* Sprechstimme, *which on musical scores appears with notes to indicate the direction the voice should be moving in, but which could almost be written with vectors, as a kind of drum score; it was composed in Berlin, in 1912, just before the Scheunenviertel began filling up with Jews, though Schoenberg—who was a baptized Viennese Jew with Hungarian citizenship before 1918 and with Czechoslovak citizenship after, and who reconverted to Judaism in 1933 after fleeing Berlin for Paris, but before fleeing Europe for America—lived on the other side of town, in*

*Steglitz, where Kafka later briefly lived; after reading about Schoenberg,
he thought of Dr. Ludwik Zamenhof, the inventor of Esperanto, who
was a Polish Jew (What else* could *he have been?* he thought, laughing;
he thought of Zamenhof's house, or the place where his house had stood,
in what later became the Warsaw ghetto and under what is now a block
of Stalinist housing blocks, tenementlike, but monumental, like an opera
set of a tenement).] There are noises in the park, a human rustling, screaming and laughing. *He walks past the splashing Märchenbrunnen [a Berlin landmark, built in 1913, in the Volkspark Fredrichshain (which actually seems, on maps and in real life, to be in Prenzlauer Berg, while
the Volkspark Prenzlauer Berg seems to be in Weissensee), with a neo-
baroque colonnade behind; the fountain and the colonnade are topped
with carved figures from Grimm's fairy tales. Also in the park: a World
War I cemetery, two landscaped rubble hills from the Second World
War, and a memorial erected after the Second World War to the German
Communists who died fighting in the Spanish Civil War] and toward
the colonnade, with its stone figures—boys with lambs, shepherd girls,
pigs, and cows (he can't connect the statues with the stories, as any
German child could)—obscured by trees; he can smell the mild reek of
the fountain; everything is dark but visible, the fountain smells of wet
night, the stone children and their animals look, together, like mythical
beasts; the colonnade looks like a tombstone. Germans. He remembers
a feature on a German tabloid TV show about the German surrender
just outside Berlin in 1945; the TV show had been shamelessly cynical,
had played the last strains of the Siegfried idyll from Götterdämmer-
ung, which, he thinks, he must have been able to separate from the
images because the music had moved him. He thinks of Walter Benjamin's image of the Angel of History as inspired by Paul Klee's painting,*
Angelus Novus, *of an angel being flung into the future backward while
staring at the accumulating ruins that are the past; he thinks of a
pleased giant with its eyes on a rebuilt ruin, of an idyllic past (the
colonnade, he knows, had been bombed, rebuilt; he thinks of Joel fretting
over the memories of his "youth" like a mother fretting over her stillborn
child), but then he remembers that he is tired of thinking these things,
though his fatigue makes him edgy—German* Wandermüdigkeit, *he*

thinks, and Jewish nervousness, diaspora-weariness. The smell of the trees reminds him of a trip he made last fall up into the mountains. I have different dreams every night now, sleep four or five hours straight through until the construction noises wake me up, and then go back to sleep for three or four more hours, promptly forget my dreams. *He thinks, again,* "O alter Duft aus Märchenzeit . . . " *(a musing and a lament; an ode, a* Yizkor*)* though I do remember one in which I am in bed and I can't move and someone is in bed with me, holding on to me, someone shorter than I am, then I am let go: It was like death, I thought, like being held on to, and then being let go of, by death. I thought the dream was about leaving Germany. *At the top of the tallest mountain, the rocky blank summit was like a pile of something (at first, he didn't have words for it); unexpectedly empty, a hard gray-brown, horrible (from above, the valley looked like a green hole). The cable car to the top had been packed, mostly with short dark Bavarians (he could imagine Vogt, shorter and even darker, in the cable car, his eyes level with the Bavarians' necks; he imagined Vogt thinking that the crowded cable car—there was no room, no air, only a small vent above everyone's heads; how wonderful it is to be tall, he had thought, as he maneuvered his way toward the vent, and the thin stream of air began to blow over his lips—should remind the Germans of Jews on their way to Auschwitz); the inside of the car reeked—of sour breath, of babies, of sweat, of sausage and beer, of socks (some north German had taken off his hiking boots); across his lips he could taste—could smell—the trees, and for a moment, as they passed over a mountain hut, a wood fire, while the breath and the socks and the diapers lingered behind him, like a noise; the moment had smelled of everything, he considers, of cruelty and refinement, of kinds of life, and of death; it was like the half-sung words, he thinks, the voice—trying to sing but really almost screaming, as if screaming came just before singing—and the music, which Schoenberg had meant to be "light and ironical" (when he read Schoenberg's words, he was reminded of Heine praising Goethe at the expense of the German Romantics), but which sounded contradictory, with itself and with the voice, like two armies, he thinks, mutinous and at war with each other, together, ne-*

gating and complementing, until they disappear. I wonder what I will be like after I have left; I think of the Kafka line: " 'And he went back to work the next day as if nothing had happened' is a line which appears in many old fairy tales, though perhaps its occurs in none," which makes me think of Moishe the tailor long after he has stopped humming, of his healed-over burns and of his forgotten melody, of a refugee in flight from his own imagination; I have thought about buying a camera, taking pictures of things, of looking at them years from now, as though they were a souvenir I will have bought myself. (I have also thought that I may not leave, have premonitions of a satyr play to my own tragedy, which is more like a farce, of a satyr play that would be a tragedy: getting blown up in the café, say, with the story getting on the Latin news broadcast, with them getting my name wrong, and the story sounding like a requiem for a Joel Levine; or not getting a place on the *Sonderzug*, losing my patience at the train station with some Vietnamese I was trying to buy cigarettes from, slapping one of them, ending up in a German tabloid—NOW THE FOREIGNERS ARE BEATING EACH OTHER!—as "Joe L.") Brecht's definition of a refugee, I read at some point, in a book, or on a wall, where homilies of that sort are often put up and defaced: a bearer of ill tidings. I have been thinking about the Canadian man on his way to Croatia (I almost thought of him as "the Croatian man"): I think of him on a beach, with his homeopathic cures, as a kind of refugee. (When I begin to think of myself as a refugee, I also begin to think of myself as a tourist, fleeing from boredom.) I think of all the refugees now actually in Berlin, of the Serbians, the Croats, the Bosnians, the Rumanians, the Russians, the Ukrainians, the Belorussians, the Albanians, the Bulgarians, and of the Gypsies, who no matter where they are from, seem to have come from nowhere, from anywhere, all crowding into derelict warehouses that have been converted into temporary dormitory housing, like the one around the corner, with gray concrete walls that look like vertical sidewalks (in the daytime, they sit on the sidewalks, spread their horrible-looking blankets over the cobblestones, take off their exotic-looking slippers, or the shoes that seem to be made out of Naugahyde, and sit with their legs straight out—or, if they're Gypsies, have to sit away from everyone else, underneath the newly planted linden trees, where, because the trees are so little, the accrued dog shit looks outsized, as big as bricks, and which the Gypsies just brush off when they stand up, like dust—screaming, above the construction noises, at their children, or crowd around a disemboweled car and seem to scream about that; many of them have what I think could be called swarthy faces, faces that could pop up on the video screen of an electronic encyclopedia if someone entered "swarthy," or perhaps "refugee"); I think of them as blurry, about to be sent back to where they just came from, or on their way to somewhere else (I think: "Will you, won't you, will you, won't you, will you join the dance?"), as recurring refugees. In Germany, the new refugees, in addition to being bearers of ill tidings, are déjà vus, seem to be coming from the past into the present as well as from the east into the west: the way Germans treat the refugees on the street—the way they look through them—reminds some people of the way Germans treated slave laborers during the war (the asylum seekers' home doesn't have any police protection like a synagogue, though it is camouflaged with a new sign above the door, reading MÖBEL, which means "furniture"; when I have to walk past, I often cross the street and walk past from there, as though that would be a safe enough distance during an explosion); it has occurred to me that I will be bringing ill tidings with me to Kaliningrad (irredentist guidebooks, the German language itself) and ill tidings of a sort to Milwaukee, with stories of burnt synagogues (the synagogue in Lübeck, which is where Thomas Mann and marzipan come from, was set on fire, which was the first time something like that has happened since Kristallnacht, though most people just assumed that something similar had happened last month or last year), or defiled synagogues, or defaced cemeteries, though as if they were souvenirs—facts weighted down into things, like the stuff on sale at the flea market. And I have thought about the little Gypsy boy (after a tabloid ran a picture of him in his hospital bed, underneath his oxygen mask, there was a *Lichterkette* on Unter den Linden, but it rained, and not very many people showed up [I showed up accidentally, couldn't find a cab, was walking down Unter den Linden to get to one of the already rebuilt S-Bahn lines]; in any case, since the number of attacks has started decreasing, people seem to have started worrying less, or have just accepted it all, which, perhaps, is what I have done, turned it into background noise, as something less than other things); I have thought of him as being like the little Gypsy boys I once saw in the park eating grass, whom I thought of as being like myself: after watching them, I remembered finding something on the sidewalk on my way to school that I thought was a piece of a candy bar but must have been some kind of animal dropping, though I ate it before I smelled it—it had no taste, was chalky—and I didn't realize what I had eaten until I smelled my fingers. About "everything": recently I saw the word "Auschwitz" scrawled somewhere, but then I looked again and thought that it read "Arschwitz," which would mean a joke about asses, but I was in a hurry and didn't check it a third time, now I think about them both having to be there, imagine myself adding the one that wasn't there, or just writing "[*sic*]" next to the one that was; "yes," I have considered, "both." The coal smell is vague but powerful; it reminds me of soon after I first got here and the nights started getting cold and I first smelled it: I thought then that it smelled awful, ominous, and now I think that it smells familiar, almost luxuriant, like a bakery, and also that it still smells awful, which reminds of what I was thinking before I started thinking about Peter Marcus and the flea market (which are fading, like a dream recalled just as it disappears, like so much that has faded before): I was thinking about the word "passion," about two of its meanings (in German the two meanings have their own words: the sexual kind of passion is *Leidenschaft*, which comes from *Leiden*, which means suffering; the religious kind of passion must come from Latin, is called *Passion*) as meaning the same thing (I think of the sexual kind of passion as meaning something short-lived, practically over with just as it is beginning, perhaps before it even starts, and the religious kind as meaning something endured, a kind of eternity): both, euphemisms for "the end." Though perhaps I was really thinking about the airline flight home, of the sustained minor torment that will register first in my stomach, then drop, and drop, until it fixes my feet onto what has to pass for the floor.

Permissions Acknowledgments

Grateful acknowledgment is made to the following for
permission to reprint previously published material:
Persea Books and *Michael Hamburger:* Excerpts from
"Death Fugue," "In Prague," and "Leap-centuries" from
Poems of Paul Celan, translated by Michael Hamburger,
copyright © 1972, 1980, 1988 by Michael Hamburger.
Published in the British Commonwealth by Anvil Press
Poetry Ltd., London, 1995, in an enlarged and corrected
edition. Reprinted by permission of Persea Books
and Michael Hamburger.

Plangent Visions Music Limited: Excerpt from "Beyond
Belief" by Elvis Costello, copyright © 1982 by
Plangent Visions Music Limited. Reprinted by permission
of Plangent Visions Music Limited.

Methuen: Excerpt from "Germany 1945" from *Bertolt Brecht
Poems 1912–1956*, translated by John Willett. Rights
outside the United States reprinted by permission of
Methuen London, an imprint of Reed Consumer Books Ltd.

A Note on the Type

This book was set in ITC Stone, a typeface designed
by Sumner Stone for the International Typeface
Corporation in 1988. Stone is really three typefaces:
Serif, Sans, and Informal; each stands on its own
but is also part of an integrated family, planned to
be compatible when mixed on a page.

Composed by PennSet, Bloomsburg, Pennsylvania
Printed and bound by Quebecor Printing
Martinsburg, Martinsburg, West Virginia